Praise for *Cruel Care*

'Silverstein lays bare what is at stake in policymakers' claims to care, concern and compassion in their treatment of children. She shows in this brilliant account that the language of humanitarianism, and the brutal treatment of children and adults meted out in its name, are part of the long and violent history of white settler governance. Through its entrée into the worldview and emotional registers of the policymakers themselves, Silverstein invites us to rethink the flattering stories Australians tell themselves and others about who they are and what they stand for. *Cruel Care* reveals the deep harm that the quest to control national borders and colonised land inflicts on the vulnerable refugee.' **Frank Bongiorno AM, Professor of History, Australian National University**

'*Cruel Care* charts the way so-called "Australia" metes out violence in the name of care to the most vulnerable among us, children seeking asylum. Blackfullas are all too familiar with this violence and its perverse justification from politicians, policymakers and the general public. This book represents a most vital truth-telling of "history", with an anger that does not compromise the discipline. I strongly recommend this text, which is demonstrative of the type of intellectual work needed in this time, in this place.' **Chelsea Watego, Professor of Indigenous Health, QUT, and author of** *Another Day in the Colony*

'*Cruel Care* is a reminder that political strategies built on the innocence of some assume the guilt and disposability of others, and reinscribe the authority of the colonial state to decide between the two. It is a tender but exacting call to think, dream, write and organise based on justice that far exceeds settler benevolence.' **Sanmati Verma, managing lawyer, Human Rights Law Centre**

'The aptly named *Cruel Care* is a groundbreaking book – confronting, deeply disturbing and revelatory.' **Arnold Zable, writer and human rights advocate**

'A powerful and damning account of the way Australian government policy, policymakers and the media have conspired to create the current conditions for the treatment of refugees and their children. In this meticulously researched book, Silverstein weaves interviews with policymakers, archival research and media accounts to tell a new critical history. Taking sharp aim at the Australian state and its policymakers, and the discourses they create and perpetuate to govern and control refugee children, Silverstein's analysis reveals the links between Australia's treatment of refugees and First Nations peoples, along with related racist discourses. Drawing these connections is crucial for fighting these brutal systems, and so this book will be vital for those who seek to create a new world where people are treated with humanity and dignity. Closely evidenced and told with incredible skill, *Cruel Care* will push you to challenge ideas you may hold about state benevolence and good intentions. Each eloquent page delivers analysis that strikes blows at the cruelty of the policy and practices of the government towards refugee families. This book is an urgent call to action for us all, to demand better from the government and to overhaul a brutal system.' **Crystal McKinnon, Associate Professor in History, Law and Justice, University of Melbourne**

Cruel Care

Cruel Care

A History of Children at Our Borders

Jordana Silverstein

Published by Monash University Publishing
Matheson Library Annexe
40 Exhibition Walk
Monash University
Clayton, Victoria 3800, Australia
publishing.monash.edu/

Monash University Publishing: the discussion starts here

Jordana Silverstein © Copyright 2023
Jordana Silverstein asserts her right to be known as the author of this work.

All rights reserved. Apart from any uses permitted by Australia's *Copyright Act 1968*, no part of this book may be reproduced by any process without prior written permission from the copyright owners. Enquiries should be directed to the publisher.

ISBN: 9781922633873 (paperback)
ISBN: 9781922633897 (epub)

A catalogue record for this book is available from the National Library of Australia

Cover design by Leslie Thomas
Author photograph by Leah Jing McIntosh

Printed in Australia by Griffin Press

Contents

A Note on Language	ix
Prologue	1
Introduction	7
Chapter 1: Starting Points	21
Chapter 2: Best Interests of the Child?	43
Chapter 3: Crisis	79
Chapter 4: Legislation	103
Chapter 5: The Immigration Minister	143
Chapter 6: Politicians and Political Parties	197
Chapter 7: Public Servants	231
Conclusion	261
Acknowledgements	267
Notes	275
Bibliography	297

A Note on Language

While legally 'asylum seeker' and 'refugee' are two separate categories, with the first someone who is claiming refugee status and the second someone whose refugee status has been recognised through a legal process, in this book I avoid making such a clear distinction. I do so in order to try to deprioritise the role of law in determining someone's status and reaffirm that there are multiple ways in which people can identify and be identified; the way a person sees themselves is the higher-order priority. Governments and policymakers tend to use the legal terminology, as well as terminology such as 'unaccompanied minor' rather than 'child', yet this can be a form of minimisation and attempted dehumanisation.

Throughout this book I have retained the original language that appears in documents, judgements and interviews, in order to reveal the ways that words, narratives and discourses work to produce ideas and stories about refugees, children, law, politics and Australia.

Prologue

In 2017 I was talking with a friend from overseas, explaining to him that when asylum seekers take boats to Australia, Australia sends them back. Our border stretches 24 nautical miles into the oceans. The navy and coast guard turn small boats found in these waters around, returning the passengers to the harms they were fleeing, I told him. I explained that when we do this the government tells the public it is to save the children, to stop them from drowning. The idea that we turn boats back because *we care too much about the children* has become widely accepted. It has become normal in Australian political discourse. My friend was taken aback.

I did not have a good explanation to offer him as to why this policy exists and where the story around it had come from. So I turned to history to try to understand it. To ask why – and how – these rationales and practices of what we can term 'cruel care' came to be so powerful in shaping government and public responses to those seeking to come to Australia by sea. Where did the focus on children come from? Why has it come to play such a large part in how refugee journeys are talked about in Australia? And what does it reveal of the role that emotion plays in the life of this nation?

This book is the result of that questioning. What I found was that there is a certain highly emotive politics around children and childhood, based on how both are configured in the national imagination. This politics draws on the sentimentality around children to create political responses that are often violent and appear vindictive. This is 'cruel care': a form of care where policymakers claim they are being compassionate as they act in deeply harmful ways. Where systemic violence is perversely justified as acts of necessary kindness.

Once I began to think about this form of care, I saw it everywhere. I saw so many examples of people describing themselves as 'doing good' even when – if we think of the effects on the children themselves – it seems they were causing harm. They typically used emotive language to justify their approaches. I saw how strongly Australia's attitude towards asylum-seeker and refugee children has been shaped by this rhetoric.

I also saw more clearly that Australia's settler colonialism has a deep impact on child refugee policy. Settler colonialism is a project of genocidal dispossession: the primary object is the land itself, and so the aim is to displace Indigenous people from Country and replace them with an enduring settler nation. Colonialism in Australia has always necessitated control over the stories told about the occupation of this land. In one of these tales, before refugee children 'needed' to be detained for their own good, First Nations children 'needed' to be torn away from their parents, community and culture. The ways that Australian policymakers – a category that includes politicians, public servants, political party operatives and more – think about their task of controlling and governing is shaped by our nation's colonial mindset. Their approach to policy begins from the belief that Australia's key national imperatives are to control the land and the population. This control is created and reinforced every day by individuals in positions of power. The past continues to be (re)enacted in the present.

Prologue

Our familial and personal histories also shape the stories we tell about identity, belonging and nationhood. My maternal grandparents, Zosia and Wolf Stawski, came to Australia in July 1949 on the SS *Sagittaire* – a boat that was not turned around. They were Jewish Holocaust survivors from Poland, who had endured the ghettos and camps of eastern Europe and spent their first post-war years in a Displaced Persons camp in Germany. They came to Australia as stateless refugees, describing themselves on their landing documents as 'ex Polish' and 'formerly Polish'.

Growing up, the Holocaust loomed large in my life. My family knew themselves as descendants of that hell. And this past continues to shape so much of the way we live. We see possibilities of harm everywhere, store more food than we could ever eat, cling closely to people. We don't know our family's history beyond a couple of generations back. We are moulded by trauma, endurance, resistance, luck and survival that is carried across generations in ways that we often cannot fully understand. The border crossing is not the end of the story.

It is in the gaps and the not-knowing, in the urge to grasp history, that so much of my thinking rests. There is great loss, beyond what can be imagined: I can't conceptualise what my grandparents and their relatives – most of whom were murdered – went through. I have few reference points for what their family and community life was like before the war. But alongside this loss there is also continuing exuberant life. Our histories and futures contain both.

My grandparents came here as survivors of genocide, and became citizens and in some way joined the Australian project, so now I am a settler and a coloniser. There is no escaping that truth. The question is, what next? How can those of us who are not Indigenous understand ourselves as colonisers and work against the many harms of colonisation?

Looking to the past, understanding what has come before, can change the way we think about the present and the future. Understanding that life in Australia, and Australia's political stories, and Australia itself, are constantly being made and remade can open new possibilities. These are the impulses behind this book. I want us, communally, to understand the stories that we tell ourselves and one another. To grapple with their difficulties, their effects and their implications.

Millions of words have been written in newspapers and academic journals about child refugees and how Australia treats them. But there remains an untold story at the heart of it: a difficult tale that reveals much about who Australians are and how our governments function. That reveals why successive governments keep producing strikingly similar immigration policies. That shows why Australian governments of all persuasions end up acting brutally against children, their families and their communities.

To write this book, I spent years grappling with the policies that have led to distress for many. I met some of the key figures who devised and enacted these policies, and I scoured archives whose roots extend deep into the colonial structures of Australian history and society. I did so in order to piece together the story of how immigration policymaking operates, and why. What I heard in interviews often surprised and unsettled me. Reading about what I learnt may be discomfiting for some. But we need to hear about, and talk about, child refugee policy and why it is failing children. Doing so can help us to see the systemic changes that we need to make.

How do Australian policymakers involved in refugee and asylum-seeker policy understand themselves and their tasks? What stories do they tell themselves, and others, about the government's approach? These are, it seems to me, essential questions to answer if we are to change fundamentally how we understand and enact child refugee policy.

Australia currently treats refugees and asylum seekers with cruel care. This book details the history of this treatment, opening up a discussion, so that we can find our way to a more just future.

Introduction

At 5.00 am on Monday 5 March 2018, members of Australian Border Force, police and guards from the private security firm Serco raided a Tamil family's home in the regional Queensland town of Biloela, on the unceded sovereign Country of the Gangulu people. Kokilapathmapriya 'Priya' Nadesalingam's bridging visa had expired the day before, but she had been in regular contact with the Department of Home Affairs and was waiting for a new visa to arrive by mail. Instead, in the early hours Priya and her husband, Nadesalingam 'Nades' Murugappan, were given ten minutes to collect their belongings and gather up their daughters, two-year-old Kopika and nine-month-old Tharnicaa.

The family was separated, with Nades in one van and the rest of the family in another, and driven 116 kilometres to Gladstone Airport. While Tharnicaa and Kopika travelled with Priya, the guards did not allow them to sit beside her, despite their repeated pleas. All four were flown to Melbourne and placed in immigration detention. Priya and Nades were reportedly pressured to sign documents stating that their removal had been 'voluntary'. They were told that if they refused to sign these documents, they would be separated from each other, denied access to phones and forcibly deported.[1]

The parents and their children remained in MITA (Melbourne Immigration Transit Accommodation, an immigration prison in

Broadmeadows), for eighteen months. One evening in August 2019, they were once again bundled onto a plane, and this time told that they were being sent to Sri Lanka. After an emergency injunction prevented the plane from lawfully leaving Australian airspace, it landed in Darwin. The next day the family were taken to the immigration prison on Christmas Island. For most of the next two years they were imprisoned in a house behind barbed wire, sharing a room with few facilities. Each day Kopika, and later Tharnicaa, was taken by armed guards to and from the local school.

Nades and Priya are Tamil refugees from Sri Lanka who came separately to Australia in 2012 and 2013 respectively, seeking asylum. They met in Australia, where both Tharnicaa and Kopika were born. In a flawed process, which has been described by legal experts as being 'geared towards fast-tracking refugee claims and punishing asylum seekers who arrive by boat', the asylum claims of both Priya and Nades were dismissed.[2] Kopika was also listed on the application for protection and was rejected. However, because Tharnicaa was not yet born when the paperwork was lodged, her claim for protection remained separate. Because of this, the family could temporarily rely on the right to stay in Australia while Tharnicaa's application was assessed, with the hope that the Immigration minister would decide to grant her, and her family, a visa.[3] Immigration ministers have extreme discretionary powers. These are popularly called the 'God powers', for they hold sway over individual lives and generally sit above judicial review.

Over the next few years, campaigns reverberated around Australia, calling for the family to be released. Rallies were held, songs were sung. 'Biloela' means 'cockatoo', and while accounts differ of whether biloela is a black or a white cockatoo, an image of a white cockatoo with the children's names written on its wing was widely shared and reproduced. The family became synonymous with the town of Biloela – 'the Biloela family', they came to be called.[4] The campaigns focused on the children: Kopika and Tharnicaa were soon known around Australia.

Medical care for refugees and asylum seekers on Christmas Island is inadequate. In June 2021, three-year-old Tharnicaa developed sepsis and pneumonia and was airlifted to Perth Children's Hospital with her mother. A few days later Nades and Kopika were flown to Perth too, where the family sat in community detention, trapped in Perth, while Tharnicaa received medical treatment. Alex Hawke, the Minister for Immigration, Citizenship, Migrant Services and Multicultural Affairs in the Coalition government, granted Priya, Nades and Kopika bridging visas, but not Tharnicaa, thereby trapping the family in Perth.[5] It was not until the new Labor government was elected in May 2022 that Tharnicaa was granted a bridging visa. This allowed the family to 'return to Bilo' – which they did in June, to great celebration.[6]

But in June 2021, before anyone knew if proper medical care would be provided or when the family would be reunited, people around Australia mobilised. A photo of Tharnicaa crying in a hospital bed while Kopika leaned over and kissed her cheek went viral. The image led to an outpouring of emotion. Many expressed bewilderment, wondering how such cute children could be treated in this way. What, people asked with grief, has Australia become?

The problem is this: we hadn't 'become' anything. This is what Australia and its governments have long done to child refugees. Some Australians have hurt refugee children, and some of us have cried about what is being done. And some of the most powerful among us, who bear significant responsibility for cases like this, do both of those things at the same time. This process is repeated over and over, as we forget the last time we hurt, the last time we cried.

How many children have been treated like Kopika and Tharnicaa? We do not quite know. We very rarely see, much less remember, the children who have been in immigration detention. This collective amnesia has been facilitated by a procession of federal governments that have little interest in letting the public know how many child refugees and asylum seekers are under their control. Sometimes, it seems, they themselves have not really been sure how many there are. As we will see in Chapter 4, social workers engaged with unaccompanied child refugees in the 1970s and 1980s complained that they were not sure how many children should be under their care: how many were in their state, or precisely where they lived. Today, information is not readily available. After all, the federal government can simply classify one building within a detention centre as no longer part of the complex and then, suddenly, they can claim that there are no longer any children in detention, as then Immigration minister Peter Dutton was reported to have done in 2016.[7] Such forms of disingenuous obfuscation have been undertaken multiple times over decades.

This book charts the stories that have been told by (overwhelmingly white) Australian policymakers about child refugees and asylum seekers. I sketch the current state of Australian child refugee policy, drawing on historical background to help us understand the present. By gathering up and examining the words and actions of politicians, public servants and government workers, in documents available in the National Archives of Australia, the National Library of Australia, Hansard and the media, and in oral history interviews I conducted between 2017 and 2019, I examine how immigration policies directed towards asylum seekers and refugee children function. I ask: what work do they do? What stories and ideas are they enabled by, and what do they enable and produce? What ideas of refuge and of childhood,

Introduction

of race, immigration, nation, family, bureaucracy, neoliberalism and government, do they instil? How are children seeking asylum leveraged by governments and public servants for political ends, and why does the public allow this to happen?

Discussions of both children and refugees are saturated with feeling, and emotion has come to play a significant role in how policies are developed and implemented. Emotion has become the lens through which governments, bureaucracies, public servants and human-rights advocates see and articulate a vision of themselves, of child refugees and asylum seekers, and of the Australian nation. This book explores those sentiments that swirl around child refugees, refugees in general, the Australian population and the management of the Australian border, and how they are adopted or co-opted by governing bodies and institutions. This is not to argue against emotional responses to an unarguably emotive subject, but to examine how emotions function, what work they do. It is not that there is no place for emotion – for grief, rage or love – in our discussions of the treatment of child refugees. Indeed, on the contrary: we will feel, and we must respond. But the sentiments with which we engage need to lead us towards justice and self-determination for refugees, rather than towards pity or control, or into a humanitarianism that generates white saviours and perpetuates the myth of a benevolent nation. They need to help us see the long histories in which we are living and acting.

For, of course, if we are to consider the way that Australia views refugee children, we need to acknowledge that *not all children* are seen through the same lens of emotion. Within mainstream white Australia, white citizen children are often granted more freedom to make mistakes than others. It is not that non-white children are any more likely to undertake 'criminal' behaviour, but that as a result of ongoing systemic racism, they are more likely to be thought of as criminals and to be punished by the state and its infrastructure.[8] For instance, in April 2022 *The Guardian* reported that 'young Indigenous people are only 5.8% of all young people aged 10–17 in Australia but make up 49% of all young people in detention'.[9] Only four months later, in August 2022, *ABC News* reported that in the much-criticised youth prison in the Northern Territory, Don Dale, which was subject to a royal commission in 2016, '[s]ome of the children … are as young as 10 years old, almost all are Indigenous, and the majority are on remand awaiting court verdicts'.[10] This is the result of a colonial system that is designed to stop certain children from flourishing. We will return to this point in Chapter 1.

Refugee and asylum-seeking children are understood, imagined and represented by governments and the public in various ways. More readily seen as innocent and needing rescue – including from their parents, who are often depicted as pernicious lawbreakers – they are also understood to be incapable of helping themselves, and less capable in general than citizen children. But 'refugee children' is not a stable category: it is used and made visible in different ways and at different times. When we look closely at government policy discourses around child refugees, including the terms that are used, and the histories, hidden meanings and agendas at play, we see the ways that governments use language to control and confine, and the at-times insidious stories their representatives tell both in the service of that work and in order to rationalise it. We see how governments have practised cruelty while claiming they are acting out of compassion and care. We see the ways they move to limit the ideas, imaginations and possibilities of how Australia responds to those seeking asylum. And we can come to understand that the history of children at our borders is fundamentally

Introduction

interlinked with Australia's colonial history. We cannot grapple with the implications of border protection and its effects without first grappling with Australia's treatment of First Nations peoples on this continent and recognising the force of Indigenous presence 'as one of insistence and persistence', as Munanjahli and South Sea Islander public health researcher Chelsea Watego has written. We need to reiterate, following Watego and others, that the problem is the colony and how it governs.[11]

Of course, there are crucial differences in the ways that First Nations peoples and refugees are governed and treated, and their relationships to (being on) this land. First Nations peoples are sovereign with this land. The rest of us are colonisers, whether we like it or not. Because of Australia's foundational settler colonialism, the formative attempt to create colonial sovereignty, every non-Indigenous act of governance in this country is settler-colonial in intent and content. That is why there can never be true justice at the border while Australia remains a settler colony.

This book looks primarily at how child refugee policy has worked from the 1970s to the present, the period of modern policymaking for refugees. It was not until 1945 that Australia had an Immigration minister, and only in 1958 that we passed a Migration Act. And it was not until the early 1970s that Australia dismantled the official White Australia policy and its explicit racial bar on migration. So while the text dips back further in order to situate this modern period, the focus is the 1970s onwards. In particular, the first years of the twenty-first century, which saw the Howard government focus on controlling asylum seekers and exploiting the sentimentality around child refugees through the *Tampa* affair and Children Overboard, were a turning point in the history of Australia's governing of child refugees, so this period is examined in some detail. I tell this history of children at our borders primarily thematically, rather than simply chronologically, in order to help us grapple with the continuities, repetitions and resonances across time.

I wanted to place the focus of this book squarely on policymakers because we in Australia have not focused our attention on them properly or sufficiently. We have not held them to account for what they have done: for the words spoken, the policies created and implemented, the violence perpetrated. I want this book to be useful in laying bare the acts of successive governments so that we can reflect on where we have gone wrong. I see this political moment as one of change – where there is an appetite to understand how government works and to create space for it to work differently – and I want us to seize it.

By choosing to interview those in government, my intention is not to say that these are the only stories that matter, but rather to say that it is helpful to pay attention to the words and work of policymakers more than we do. There is much that we can learn from the people subjected to these policies, but those who enact them bring a different and important perspective to the story.

There are vital accounts about what it is like to live under these policies, but those are not the stories this book contains. This is a book about policymaking and policymakers, not about refugees' experiences, although of course policymakers and the work they produce always comes as a result of the presence and action of refugees. We will see how this dance works throughout the book.

In these pages I access the expertise, insights and ideas of child refugees through written sources aimed at intervening in policy and governmental processes, such as submissions to inquiries, statements on Facebook and other social media, and public representations in traditional media. I have prioritised this over oral history interviews with child refugees and former child refugees for three reasons. Firstly, child refugees face oppressive state surveillance and documentation at the hands of state and non-government organisation bureaucracy. They are also regularly called upon to contribute to research undertaken by white researchers in extractive ways. I did not want to replicate that pattern, even inadvertently. Secondly, it is difficult to do justice to the vastly different stories and experiences of the many child refugees who have come to Australia across the long period this book examines. A project needs to know its limits. Thirdly, I am not the person to tell their stories. I am the granddaughter of refugees, but I am not a refugee myself. It is important that these stories are gathered and told by those who have experienced life as a refugee and can speak with the knowledge and expertise which come through that experience.

A significant part of my research was these oral history interviews I conducted with people involved in policymaking. This includes approximately thirty-five interviews with former Immigration ministers, former secretaries of the Immigration department, politicians, public servants, ministerial advisers, members of the United Nations International Children's Emergency Fund (UNICEF) and the Australian Human Rights Commission, and others. The interviews took place in people's homes, in cafés, in offices. One occurred in a private men's club. Most of the people I interviewed were white men, and thus they offered an opportunity to encounter slightly different forms of the limited range of white Australian governmental masculinity. Through these interviews we can come to grips with some of the behind-the-scenes thinking, political machinations and feelings within this field of policy and governance.

Oral history interviews are generally long – mine lasted anywhere from half an hour to five hours, in which I spoke to someone about their life, their work and their ideas. They were fairly free-flowing. Together we opened up a space for a conversation, for ideas and histories to be shared. Some of the interviews were fraught. Regardless, my role was to ensure my interviewees were comfortable and to encourage them to share something new – a story, a sentiment, an idea. The goal was to create a space for intimacy and reflection. After each interview, I had it transcribed and the transcription was sent to the interviewee for approval – because of the obvious political sensitivities around the topic and the ethical considerations in conducting oral history interviews.

These were conversations with people with significant social and political power. Unlike more common forms of oral history projects, which seek to gather the voices of people who are rarely heard, in this case most of my interviewees hold significantly greater cultural and material capital than me and most of my readers. Some have already recorded their oral histories as part of other projects and these recordings are held in national institutions, such as the National Library of Australia. But I tried not to let this stymie me. I aim to be open to hearing others' views, to work to understand where they are coming from – what their personal and collective histories and memories are, and how and why they voice the stories and philosophies they do. Nevertheless, my depiction of the interviews in this book shows how I saw my interviewees understanding themselves and their circumstances – it is my own reading. I explore faithfully the ideas that I felt the interviewees highlighted, but I might see the interviewees' words differently to how they do. I am not quoting from these interviewees in order to endorse their work or to ask my reader to empathise with them.[12]

Along with interviews, I drew heavily on archival material. Such material can illuminate the structuring role of government – the way

Introduction

that a government produces knowledge about a population – and sometimes they provide spaces for people's voices to be recorded. The archives I examined show how those within governments and bureaucracies think about child refugees and asylum seekers. In many of the archives I examined, these children are not present. It's remarkable, for instance, how little children were talked about – let alone to – during the Children Overboard affair. At other times, children are described, but do not describe or speak for themselves: they are treated as 'speechless emissaries', to use the anthropologist Liisa Malkki's phrasing.[13] Of course, they are not silent but rather are silenced, and not listened to by those who write these documents. So I had to look at different documents in order to see what child refugees have said directly to government.

The archives I examined were initially produced in contexts of government and administration throughout the course of the twentieth and twenty-first centuries, but they are continually altered, changed, their meanings reconfigured as they are looked at by and through different eyes. In this rethinking sits a dialogue, variously involving the person whose life is documented, the government bureaucrat who created the archive, the archivists who set the conditions under which the documents are retained and read, the legislators who determine when documents will become available (currently, for most government archives, it is twenty years after their creation) and the researcher who reads the document, seeking to make meaning. Archives have an ethics in the way they are made and how they are used. Often as I was reading the archival traces of these policies and processes of policymaking, I found myself troubled by the words and ideas they contained. This should be no surprise, for they are the archives of a colonial government, testifying to governmental violence that has damaged people and communities. As such, they make an ethical demand on those of us who read and use them. I have tried to respond to these demands as I wrote this history.

This book is framed around a set of policymaking ideas and figures (legislation, the minister, politicians, the public service), and highlights some themes that move across them (the 'best interests of the child' and the language of 'crisis'). It investigates the intimate and public relationships and cultures that have created the current conditions for governing child refugees and asylum seekers in Australia. And it looks at how discussions of alternative possibilities have been narrowed. Through this, and through the stories which this book tells, it is my hope that we can all become more familiar with the emotional and discursive manoeuvres policymakers undertake. If we can, there is greater potential for opening up space for the creation of new languages, ideas and policies, as well as new types of relationships between all of us who live on this continent. To be utopian, we can usher in new understandings of the potential for freedom and justice produced by the global campaigns for no borders, no nation-states and no state control over the movement of peoples. We can collectively develop more tools to appreciate the illegitimacy of settler-colonial law, and to thereby undo the policies that successive governments have produced to control the people who have come to, or who have sought to come to, this country.

To be clear, though, this book is not aimed at providing definitive policy answers to how governments should approach child refugees and asylum seekers. Oftentimes histories of refugees conclude that with some changes to policy – granting so many visas, or the conditions of immigration detention being loosened – the problem of Australia's treatment of refugees can be solved. But this approach potentially

Introduction

becomes just another way to narrow the conversation around how we should treat those who come to these shores. More significantly, it is important to me to always remember that it is not my place as a coloniser on Indigenous land to say precisely what should happen with that land. Instead, we need to continue the conversations that already exist. And so I want to think through some histories and some questions, and illuminate where that can lead us. Let's begin.

CHAPTER 1

Starting Points

One day in September 2012, the president of the Indigenous Social Justice Association, Uncle Ray Jackson, led an Aboriginal Passport Ceremony in Redfern. The aim of the ceremony was, as Jackson explained to cultural studies academic Joseph Pugliese, to grant passports to 'migrants, asylum seekers and other non-Aboriginal citizens in this country', on the basis that '[w]hilst they acknowledge our rights to all the Aboriginal Nations of Australia we reciprocate by welcoming them into our Nations'. Pugliese explained that '[i]n the course of the ceremony, non-Indigenous Australians were required to purchase an Aboriginal passport and to pledge a formal acknowledgment of unceded Aboriginal sovereignty over the various Indigenous Nations that cover the Australian continent'. This Aboriginal Passport Ceremony functioned to both enact Aboriginal sovereignty and to welcome refugees and asylum seekers in ways which accord with that sovereignty.[1] It also recognised the many forms of deaths in custody that occur in Australia: in immigration prisons and in domestic prisons, police cells and police vans.

As First Nations peoples, activists and scholars consistently make clear, the presence of refugees (and migrants and all non-Indigenous people more generally) on Aboriginal land necessarily produces a relationship between the two. Interactions between people from these groups reveal their interconnections, as well as the ways that Australian governments approach, regulate, control and variously exclude and include both populations. The facts of enduring Aboriginal sovereignty and a persistent settler colonialism are inextricable dimensions of Australia's migration history.

Amangu Yamatji historian Crystal McKinnon explains that we must not see Australia's practices of border control as extraordinary, as to do so 'obscures the violence and horror of colonialism'. 'To see contemporary practices of incarceration and detention of asylum seekers as exceptional,' she writes, 'removes them from the historical and contemporary context of global systems of imperialism and racial capital ... It removes the local context and histories too, erasing the ongoing colonial violence against Indigenous people.' This context is important, and we can work alongside McKinnon's writings to comprehend that 'it is vital to understand detention, incarceration, and other forms of custody as central to colonialism in order for us to analyse these systems, fight against them, and build better societies with Indigenous sovereignty as the foundation'.[2] While McKinnon focuses on incarceration practices, in this book I use her work in order to think about the relationship between these colonial structures and practices and child refugee policies generally.

We do not need to be conscious of the histories and currents within our society for these histories to have powerful effects on our actions and decisions. It is not a matter of choice. We do not need to volunteer to be part of the settler-colonial project for it to affect us. In the words of legal scholar Angela Smith, 'for Australia as a settler colony in the Asia-Pacific region, forced mobilities are intrinsically linked to questions of belonging, possession, and sovereignty'.[3] But we should attempt to understand the past, because our present policy orientation rests on it.

Settler-colonial Australia

The landmass now labelled Australia was invaded and colonised by the British in the eighteenth century. At the time of this invasion, there were already people living on this continent, who had been here for thousands of generations. While this originary moment of invasion – of the physical landing – occurred in the past, colonisation continues into the present. Australia remains a settler colony: the settlers have 'come to stay'. In the late historian Patrick Wolfe's words, the settler colony 'strives for the dissolution of native societies' and 'erects a new colonial society on the expropriated land base'. This is its 'organising principle', and it is a project that is never finalised. It continues to be undertaken in diverse and manifold ways. Australia is structured by invasion.[4]

McKinnon explains that colonial power is everywhere, and it is 'exerted through multiple avenues, both informally through social actions and formally through explicit and state-sanctioned practices'.[5] These practices have existed as a series of controls on Indigenous and Pacific peoples' movement around Australia and the Pacific from the early moments of colonisation, as the late historian Tracey Banivanua Mar has shown.[6] Across this continent, the presence of Aboriginal people and Aboriginal sovereignties have been integral to the ways that, as the historian Ben Silverstein writes, 'settlers transit, in different ways, to become at home in Australia ... Practices of governing Aboriginal people were key to making and distinguishing different kinds of settlers'. Settlers have made claims for their belonging in Australia through 'the negation of Aboriginality'.[7]

In 2001, at the Liberal Party's campaign launch for that year's federal election, Prime Minister John Howard applauded Australia's border security efforts and talked about this country as a leader, a 'nation saying to the world we are a generous, open-hearted people taking more refugees on a per-capita basis than any nation except Canada'. Then he stated, to great applause, a line now infamous: 'But we will decide who comes to this country and the circumstances in which they come.'[8]

This line from Howard is striking, and it has been widely remembered. It is a refrain that regularly rings out in Australian politics and political commentary, even today. Howard was reminding his audience that his white-dominated Australian government had control over the borders and over who lives on the land. And he was asserting a malignant vision of Australia as 'generous'. This was a statement of both immigration control and population control. It was a statement of Australian settler colonialism.

Australian state-making is bound up in both of these things: in total control over the land, its borders and who lives within them; and in the perceived right to be magnanimous with that land. And so even though we like to think of ourselves as welcoming, that welcome is colonial in nature. As anthropologist Ghassan Hage has argued forcefully, the white settler population has always had control over who comes to this country and how, and whether they are allowed to stay.[9] It is the host who claims the right and the power to welcome. Howard's line was an expression of control.

In 1901, the year of Federation, the set of policies that we call the White Australia policy was ushered into existence, codifying a way of thinking about non-white individuals that long preceded the creation of the Australian nation. These policies ensured that immigration for non-white people was near impossible. Employing language tests, refusing visas and controlling which jobs a person could hold, who would be counted in the census, even what the postage system looked like: these were all part of the attempt to make Australia a white country.[10] And while the White Australia policy might be formally over – having been gradually ended in practice by the Coalition during the 1960s and formally ended by newly elected Labor Prime Minister Gough Whitlam in January 1973 – its practices and structures remain. They are embedded, for instance, in our migration laws and in the decision-making powers that the Immigration minister holds, including those that sit above judicial review. As legal scholars Peter Prince and Eve Lester have shown, one of the men who made the White Australia laws as a politician later became a High Court judge, ruling on the 1906 *Robtelmes v. Brenan* case that determined the legality of these laws and thereby who was an 'alien' and who a citizen, producing the 'authorisation [of] the mass deportation of the Australian South Sea Islander community'. This judgement set a legal precedent that still stands today. White Australia policy law is still in force, Prince and Lester make clear.[11]

There are 'shared strategies, policies, practices and rationales' that are 'deployed' to 'manage' both First Nations peoples and migrants.[12] Indeed, there has traditionally been a strong overlap in leadership between the government portfolios of Indigenous Affairs and Immigration. Clyde Holding and Gerry Hand – two ALP politicians serving in the 1980s and 1990s – both moved from being Minister for Aboriginal Affairs to Minister for Immigration, Local Government and Ethnic Affairs. The Liberal Party's Philip Ruddock and Amanda Vanstone successively held the portfolio of Minister for Immigration and Multicultural and Indigenous Affairs. Across his career, senior public servant Wayne Gibbons moved between numerous portfolios, most particularly Immigration and Aboriginal Affairs. Journalists have named him one of 'the brains' behind both the Northern Territory Intervention and the abolition of the Aboriginal and Torres Strait Islander Commission in the mid-2000s. He had previously been the coordinator of the Indo-Chinese Refugee Resettlement Program from 1978 to 1980 and had worked for successive Immigration ministers before, in the early 1990s, becoming deputy secretary of the Department of Immigration and Multicultural Affairs under Minister Hand, where he was 'regarded as a key architect of the Government's hardline response' of mandatorily detaining people who came to Australia by boat to seek asylum without prior authorisation.[13]

Going back further, in 1908 A.O. Neville was appointed Secretary for Immigration in the new Department of Immigration, Tourism and General Information within the Western Australian bureaucracy. In this role he organised a series of border reforms in 1910, including instituting conditions aimed at preventing anyone with a potentially contagious disease from remaining in Australia, and allowing migration of potential wives for farmers. He also developed tourism to Rottnest Island – a former prison island, incarcerating Aboriginal boys and men – and encouraged British people holidaying in Western Australia to migrate there permanently, to aid with the colonisation of that land. As Pat Jacobs, Neville's biographer, writes, in 1915 Neville was appointed Chief Protector of Aborigines 'against his will'. Jacobs asserts that 'he knew nothing about Aborigines [sic] except that they posed a problem for the Government ... In Public Service terms, it was a drastic reduction in status. In career terms, it was a disaster; a sidetrack going nowhere.'[14]

But Neville was, Jacobs writes, determined to 'make the best of it'. And he approached this new role with gusto. Perhaps most notoriously, at the 1937 Conference of Commonwealth and State Aboriginal Authorities, which approved the policies of removal and theft of children that produced the Stolen Generations, he asked, 'Are we going to have 1,000,000 blacks in the Commonwealth or are we going to merge them into our white community and eventually forget that there were any Aborigines in Australia?' Continuing, he asserted: '[W]e must have charge of the children at the age of six years; it is useless to wait until they are twelve or thirteen years of age. In Western Australia we have power under the Act to take away any child from its mother at any stage of life, no matter whether the mother be legally married or not.'[15]

Within a persistently colonial Australia, children are seen as bearers of the virtue of the nation. 'Rescuing' those who are deemed to be in vulnerable circumstances enables governments to stake a claim for themselves as Good Saviours. '"The child" is often invoked as a discursive category with which one cannot disagree,' gender studies scholar Barbara Baird has written.[16] Whether it is taking Aboriginal children from their families in practices framed by discourses of 'Aboriginal deficiency', as Chelsea Watego has shown, or arguing that refugees attempting to come to Australia by boat need to be turned back so that children do not drown, groups of children are routinely used within Australia to signal the imagined virtue of a nation who cares. Koori historian and writer Tony Birch has reflected on the 'bastardry and deliberate cruelty' of the stealing of Aboriginal children from their families. This cruelty has later been enacted on refugee children, also under the banner of care.[17]

When it comes to immigration, Australian governments have routinely defined Australia as benevolent, and the public has believed it. The historian Klaus Neumann writes that 'the assertion that Australia and Australians have traditionally been generous and compassionate has become something of a background chorus accompanying debates about public policy, particularly in the area of immigration and refugee policy'.[18] In Goenpul scholar Distinguished Professor Aileen Moreton-Robinson's framing, this is part of the 'possessive logic of patriarchal white sovereignty': a mode of government that centres on ownership, possession and control. It foregrounds and installs white colonial power over others.[19] It claims the right to determine and narrates its own correctness. It is cruel in its conception of care.

But First Nations sovereignties persist, regardless of colonialism. Crystal McKinnon writes powerfully, 'Indigenous sovereignty pre-exists and exists independently of colonial discourses of Aboriginality ... This is the simple truth of sovereignty; it is bigger and more powerful than the colonial structures which try to define, categorise and contain it.'[20] It is inextinguishable and omnipresent, marking one of its differences from European forms of legal sovereignty, which are impermanent. And so the creation of white government, of white sovereignty, remains a constant project, always being refined, with effects that reach beyond our physical borders. As Behrouz Boochani, journalist and former prisoner in Manus Island, has written of that place, stressing the wide-reaching impacts of colonialism: 'This space is part of Australia's legacy and a central feature of its history – this place is Australia itself – this right here is Australia.'[21]

How we create refugee children

This book is a history of discourse, of the way that governments and policymakers represent themselves, their interests and their ideas of Australia through the stories they tell about refugee and asylum-seeking children. Children in the period this book explores are variously imagined by politicians, public servants and non-governmental organisations as sources of hope, as pernicious threats, as innocent, as embodying progress, as violent and as invisible. But the children themselves talk of wanting freedom and justice. Refugee children imprisoned in Nauru who wrote submissions for the Australian Human Rights Commission's 2014 National Inquiry into Children in Immigration Detention repeatedly mentioned the oppressive heat, the short showers (only one- or two-minute showers allowed, when they are available), the lack of fans, the mould in their tents and marquees, the terrible food, the lack of proper schooling, the disastrous medical care, their feelings of being 'very sad'. They 'love freedom' and 'want freedom', they wrote. As one fifteen-year-old who had been imprisoned in Nauru for seven months put it, 'This is a bad life … I fled from war in Iraq but got stuck in harsh jail in Nauru where is nothing but cruelty. We want justice. This is not fair. There is no standard in Nauru. This is a hell for children.'[22]

Neither childhood nor refugeehood are inherent states: they are historically created and produced categories, and they are used for political ends. We can trace the production of the category of 'child refugee', by governments, politicians, policymakers and the public, to understand the moments when it becomes visible, and what it is used for. We can ask when, and why, refugee and asylum-seeking children become visible. While children made up half the world's refugees across almost the whole period this book considers, this is rarely reflected in the language used to discuss immigration: in Australia, we tend to speak about refugees and child refugees, rather than refugees and adult refugees, or child refugees and adult refugees. Therefore, when I use the term 'children', I am not referring to any natural category of person. Rather, I am referring to a created category, which shifts across time and space, and particularly across racial boundaries and citizenship positions. As we shall see, there are various age-based definitions of who is a child, and childhood is understood to be shaped by certain physical, emotional and intellectual characteristics. But given that these types of definitions are not stable, my focus is not on defining who is a child; instead, I am concerned with how the population category of child refugees and asylum seekers is produced and defined within policy discourse and practice.

Collective notions of what a child is – of who is signified by this word – are produced through an archive of diverse documents of policymaking. To provide one example: a report produced for the Australian Centre for Indo-Chinese Research in 1981 explained, 'The use of the word "children" contributes to the confusion of the situation [of how children will be treated]. In the West, the general comprehension of this term is those who are reliant on adults and who need traditional Western family type care to survive. The legal definition of children is those under 18 years of age.'[23] But, the report continued, 'Indochinese' communities can have different understandings of what constitutes reliance and how a family is comprised, leading to a situation where children are understood as requiring a specific formulation of help in Australia that the report's authors believed was not commensurate with 'Indochinese' life. And just one more example: the 2014 report on the care of unaccompanied asylum seeker and refugee children, produced by the National Council of Churches in Australia, was titled *Protecting the Lonely Children*. This emotive title, which foregrounds the concepts of 'protection' and 'loneliness', emphasises refugee childhood as shaped primarily by vulnerability and a lack of attachment or kinship. These are but two historical understandings of what the concepts of childhood, and refugeehood, can contain.[24]

It is important to pay attention to how refugee children – who sit in the intersection of these two categories – are uniquely understood and defined in relation to the Australian state and its policymaking. The Convention on the Rights of the Child, as Norwegian jurist Kirsten Sandberg articulates it, 'is based on the idea that it is useful to view children as a group'.[25] But what are the boundaries of this group? In 2019, the UN Committee on the Rights of the Child heard submissions from Australian groups and individuals about Australia's performance regarding children's rights, and found that Australian governments are sorely lacking in this arena.[26] In 2018, when I emailed Megan Mitchell, the then National Children's Commissioner at the Australian Human Rights Commission, to ask her to participate in an interview for this research project, I was informed by her assistant that Mitchell understood herself to 'not [be] a suitable candidate for your project as it is not something within in [sic] her scope of work'. She instead recommended that I speak with the Human Rights Commissioner or the Race Discrimination Commissioner.[27] Child refugees and asylum seekers were being defined as outside the remit of this commissioner's work; a border was established between citizen and non-citizen children.

We must also remember that 'refugeeness' is not something that occurs only at a precise moment of contact with the border (and also that there never is only one such precise moment). The border, or borders, stretch and twist, intersecting with people's bodies, lives, histories and archival documents in unpredictable, and often not completely traceable, ways. The border is spatial, and it is also temporal. It is rational, and it is also traumatic. And as US-based historian Rebekah Sheldon has argued, there is 'the vulnerable, innocent child whose rescue from harm appears tantamount to the future safety of us all'.[28]

Discourses of compassion rub against discourses of nation building, national security and border control.

For not all refugee children are seen as 'worthy' of rescue. Liana Buchanan, the Victorian Commissioner for Children and Young People, explained to me in August 2018 that in her work she has seen that for some 'it's almost as though being of a non-Anglo background is enough to cut out the protection. The desire to protect. Because the child, just by virtue of being an asylum seeker and a refugee and from outside of Australia, and from some kind of background that isn't well understood, that is enough to inspire that switch and that really negative response.'[29]

This analysis is shared broadly among those working within the official structures of international and national human rights regimes. Oliver White, a senior policy officer at UNICEF Australia whom I interviewed in April 2018, told me that the current policy framework for the different groups who are subjected to and controlled by Australia's migration regime is shaped by a 'growing anti-migrant sentiment, and increased xenophobia and racism and protectionism', as well as – for those seeking to come to Australia by boat – a desire to 'secure the border [and] prevent people arriving irregularly. And, in that instance, these special protections that exist for children, under international law, in practice are just completely disregarded.'[30]

If we look further back, we can see that in the aftermath of the Holocaust and World War II child refugees came to Australia from Europe, while those from elsewhere were excluded from Australia. Indeed, the United Nations Refugee Convention of 1951 allowed signatory states to decide who the rules would apply to: people affected by 'events occurring in Europe before 1 January 1951' or people affected by 'events occurring in Europe or elsewhere before 1 January 1951'.[31]

Starting Points

Australia, along with a number of European countries, had pushed for this choice. When Australia acceded to the Convention, they agreed that it would apply only to people affected by events in Europe. Australia did not sign on to the 1967 Protocol Relating to the Status of Refugees, which extended the Convention to cover the whole world, until Prime Minister Gough Whitlam formally ended the White Australia policy in 1973. Although, as historian Joy Damousi has noted, members of the Australian public did push for the children of white Australian soldiers and Japanese women – who had been conceived while the soldiers were stationed in Japan during the war – to be allowed to come to Australia in the 1950s and 1960s.[32]

As we will see in Chapter 4, when we journey back to the era after World War II to look at the foundational legislation for unaccompanied child refugees, the postwar period was also a time of highly emotional discussion about child refugees and migrants, which developed from the particularly sentimentalised idea of children as vulnerable that emerged during the interwar period. Australia's attitudes were a result of local and imperial histories of settler colonialism, but they were also part of international currents of thinking about child refugees and migrants through the lens of 'rescue'. Damousi explores this in her discussion of the work of UNICEF, which was founded in 1946 in New York, and Foster Parents PLAN (Plan International), founded in 1937 in Spain. She shows that the thinking about refugee and migrant children that held sway from these organisations' founding through to their work in the 1960s and 1970s in Asia included 'attempts to depoliticise and decontextualise war by framing child refugees in neutral terms, as objects of humanitarian assistance worthy of pity rather than as victims of a political conflict, to attract funds and also avoid a political analysis of the US and Australian foreign policy'. In doing so, they constructed 'a humanitarianism which framed white donors as secular heroes and saviours'.[33]

Refugee children are at times understood as an innocent group who require saving from the crises governments present them as facing (rather than the crises that they might see themselves as facing). This is a thoroughly racialised process: only certain groups of people are described through these particular discourses of innocence, and one's place in relation to the border and citizenship (and thus the way they are racialised) plays a key determining role.[34] What is of fundamental importance is how it shapes those who get to define who is innocent: US-based anthropologist Miriam Ticktin has explained that when this innocence is put onto people it 'also creates a savior class or subject and they too make claims to innocence. If the people one is saving are understood as innocent, outside time and place, and one is intervening only to stop the suffering, how can this not be considered innocent too?'[35] I am interested in examining when politicians, ministers and governments understand themselves as part of this circle of 'innocence' that brings them into a co-constitutive relationship with the figure of the refugee or asylum-seeking child. Cruel care is shaped by an understanding that 'stopping the suffering' is always an act of kindness.

Within the modern period there has been a shift in the ways that refugee and asylum-seeking children are imagined, talked about, remembered and understood to have been governed. In the stories that policymakers now tell about their work between the 1970s and the 1990s, children were not a significant focus of policy. While children were brought into, or arrived in, Australia in family groups or as 'unaccompanied' children, there was little discussion of them as a discrete group. When I interviewed the policymakers who worked during this period, they told me that they do not remember how children fit precisely into the policymaking. In 1990, the Convention on the Rights of the Child came into effect and, globally, discussions of children changed. This shift in representations and discussions of refugee children is perhaps exemplified by the death of Alan Kurdi, a two-year-old Kurdish boy whose body was photographed after it washed ashore on a Turkish beach in 2015. Kurdi and his brother and mother, along with others, drowned in the Mediterranean after the dinghy they were travelling in capsized. The image of Kurdi flew around the world, provoking outpourings of feeling about the plight of Syrian refugees, but little concrete action. People and governments felt his death deeply, but by and large they did not act. The focus was on the conversation and the concern.

In Australia, refugee and asylum-seeking children became subjects of discussion and emotion in the twenty-first century. While Australian governments have always exercised control over particular groups of racialised children – especially Aboriginal children, as typified in the Stolen Generations and in practices of mass incarceration – refugee children did not become the subject of similarly intimate and publicly discussed national control until the late 1990s and early 2000s. For the first fifteen years of the twenty-first century, child refugees were a key focus for governments. This was exemplified by the Howard government's focus on the lie of the 'children overboard'.

But in the final term of the Morrison government, from 2019 to 2022, there was little public talk of refugee children, besides the children of the Nadesalingam family. One of the rare times in which refugee children were discussed in Parliament during this government was telling. Liberal Party senator Mathias Cormann, in a December 2019 answer to the Dorothy Dixer of 'how is the Morrison government's plan working to make Australia even better?', remarked that, 'Every child asylum seeker has now left Nauru and Manus, and we've closed 19 detention centres since 2013.'[36] A few days earlier, in the parliamentary debates around retracting the Medevac provisions, Liberal senator Amanda Stoker had similarly pointed to the government's removal of children from detention. A couple of months later, so did Dr Fiona Martin, the Liberal MP for Reid, who asserted that '[i]t is the Morrison government who have removed all children from detention' in a speech she gave in February 2020 in the House of Representatives to assert the government's border control credentials.[37]

In December 2019, Prime Minister Scott Morrison also used this line, drawing on a discussion of Medevac legislation and children to tout his record on border control:

> Our government policies were supporting people who required medical attention and they were brought to Australia for that medical attention. It was our government that got every single child off Nauru. That was done under my Prime Ministership. We ensured that we delivered that. This mob on that side – this Labor Party – were the Labor Party that sent children to Manus Island. How do I know that? I went there as a shadow immigration minister and I sat with the mothers and children that they sent to Manus Island. So I will not take lectures from a Labor Party that showed themselves to be involved in the most outrageous treatment of women and children in sending them to Manus Island and then did nothing while we sought to stop the deaths at sea and we got every single child off Manus and off Nauru. The Labor Party's record on this issue is beyond a disgrace and, if this leader of the Labor Party ever got the opportunity to be in charge of border protection, he would set a new low.[38]

In discussions about the legislation to repeal Medevac, Labor politicians such as Josh Wilson, the Member for Fremantle, and Andrew Giles, the Member for Scullin and now the Minister for Immigration, Citizenship and Multicultural Affairs, drew on children as a way of heightening the emotion of what was at stake. Giles asserted: 'Regardless of what you think about the wider debates about asylum policy, Australia can and should show humanity. We should not fail to provide critically ill people in our care – in particular, children – with urgent medical treatment.' Wilson told Parliament, 'I know everyone in this place cares about the wellbeing of children. We all acknowledge the need to do better when it comes to mental health care, especially for Aboriginal kids. And we need to do better for those who are still in offshore detention centres.'[39] Indeed, children were the focus of many of the cases that lawyers took to court through what is termed 'strategic litigation': cases that are actively used to create change, in this case to push parliamentarians to do something about the vast numbers of sick people in offshore detention.[40]

Predominantly, however, Medevac has been described and discussed in public – during both its introduction and its repeal – in terms of its effects on the men who had been brought from Manus Island and Nauru for medical treatment, and who were then imprisoned in hotels and detention centres, mostly in the eastern states of Australia. An academic and journalist, Saba Vasefi, has written a series of articles in *The Guardian*, pointing to the continuing impacts of detention on refugee children and on refugee women, but she is one of the few pushing this perspective in the public sphere.[41]

How many refugee children are there in Australia?

Since the 1970s at least, it has never been clear how many child refugees were coming to Australia or living here. Refugee children have kept coming, in ways that the Australian government planned or in ways that the children and their families determined for themselves. An example of the former is Operation Babylift (1975), when a couple of hundred infants were airlifted out of Vietnam and brought to Australia.[42] But these were not the only Southeast Asian refugee children to come to Australia at this time, for we know that many others came by boat, for instance. Precise numbers were not tracked.

Indeed, this area of governance has historically been treated in an ad-hoc and imprecise manner. The way that Australian bureaucracies define and record 'child refugees' differs across parts of government, so it is difficult to form a reliable picture of how many have come. It was only from 1977 on that the Humanitarian Program visas – which include visas for refugees and asylum seekers – were documented in public statistics, and these statistics do not provide details beyond the top-line numbers of 'refugees', 'special humanitarian program', 'special assistance category' and 'onshore' visas granted, and they do not distinguish adults from children.[43] But, of course, refugees – both adults and children – had been coming to Australia for decades prior. The first major arrival of refugees to Australia was as a result of the Holocaust and World War II.

For the years 1989–2012, the numbers of children detained is listed in a publication produced by the Social Policy Section of the Parliamentary Library.[44] But it is just a list of numbers, with no other information.

The lack of public counting, of awareness of how many children have come and are living in Australia, continues into the present. Since the beginning of 2013, 'Immigration Detention Statistics' are released each month. These tell us how many children have been detained.[45] They are made available on the Department of Home Affairs website with a lag of around three months. These statistics break down the numbers of people detained in each location, and whether they are men, women or children. A separate section provides details about the numbers of children, explaining where they are detained and sometimes offering some notes on what the government's plans are for them. These numbers help us to understand how many people are affected. But given that some refugee children enter and live in the country without having been detained, the total number of refugee children in Australia is not publicly recorded.

This lack of counting is important to note, but I am not suggesting that the solution is to document child refugees more closely or to place them under minute surveillance. There is a movement towards increased strictness in the treatment of refugees in general, as legal scholar Anthea Vogl shows with regard to the ways that Australian authorities determine some documents to be 'bogus documents' and then subjectively designate the holders of those documents as 'bogus refugees', therefore not worthy of protection.[46] The increased role of governmental authorities in adjudicating who is to be considered a refugee and who is to be considered a child has sometimes had harmful effects. We saw this, for instance, in 2014, in the treatment of at least fourteen child refugees who asserted that they were children, but who were determined by the authorities to be adults and sent to Manus Island detention centre.[47] At one stage Australia was using wrist x-rays in order to determine age, before this was thoroughly discredited. This flawed process led to one child named Loghaman being erroneously determined to be an adult and sent to Manus Island in 2013 at seventeen years old, 'despite the fact he was carrying a photocopy of his national identity document that showed his birthdate, and told immigration officials he was under 18', as *The Guardian* reported. In 2015, when he was twenty, he was assaulted by a guard and then forced to pay for his own painkillers to treat his injury. Loghaman told *The Guardian*, 'I leave my country because I come to freedom. But here is the same. I am caged like an animal.'[48] The problem is best resolved by trusting in refugees' testimonies rather than by increased governmental and bureaucratic scrutiny, which often leads to punitive outcomes. Moreover, not everyone needs, or wants, to be known by the state and its apparatuses.

While we do not have the total numbers of child refugees and asylum seekers traversing Australia's borders, there is a little more information about how many children have been detained over the last thirty years.[49] But as part of the process of making things complicated and obscure, the government maintains many different forms of immigration imprisonment. There are immigration detention centres (such as Christmas Island Immigration Reception and Processing Centre or Villawood Immigration Detention Centre in Sydney), so-called immigration transit accommodation sites (such as Melbourne Immigration Transit Accommodation) and Alternative Places of Detention (which have not been publicly listed by governments but include sites such as hospitals or hotels). There is community detention, where people live in the general community but without Medicare, the right to work or other civil liberties. And then there has been the uncertain life on a Bridging Visa E, which is a temporary visa that bridges the gap while people go through the process of applying for asylum or awaiting forced removal, as well as various other forms of Temporary Protection Visas (TPVs), including most recently the Safe Haven Enterprise Visa.

In mid-February 2023, the Albanese government fulfilled an election promise and moved to end TPVs for almost 19,000 refugees who had been held on them for a long period, beginning the process of allowing them to apply for permanent protection. But, as many pointed out, there was another large group of people – nearly 12,000 – who had been denied refugee status in a flawed process conducted by the Coalition government and so this development didn't apply to them: they remained stuck on temporary visas, with all the limits on daily life and the ability to interact freely with their family and friends that this entails.[50] The government also decided to keep TPVs on the books, able to be used in the future. And Operation Sovereign Borders – the military-led 'border protection' operation – released a new video featuring the operation's commander, Rear Admiral Justin Jones. The video made explicit that this positive development would not apply to all. 'Let me be clear, anyone who attempts an unauthorised boat voyage to Australia will be turned back to their country of departure, returned to their home country or transferred to a regional processing country,' Jones says to the camera.[51]

So taking all of these forms of detention together, the numbers of children affected have shifted considerably over the years: from 62 in 1989–90, to 376 in 1994–95, 1344 in 2000–01, 206 in 2008–09, 2898 in 2011–12 and around 3800 in mid-2017. From mid-2021 until the present, all of the children were moved onto bridging visas or held in community detention. At the end of February 2022, 1705 children faced these forms of incarceration and uncertainty. By the end of that year, there were 1496 children.

But these are just government statistics. They hide human lives, individuals with all their histories and futures. Behind those statistics there are stories of children battling their way for justice and freedom, on their own, and with their families and communities.

Klaus Neumann has shown the important role that history has played in developing policy. He explains:

Those drafting a new policy often try to heed what they consider to be historical lessons. In order to construct such lessons, they might, for example, analyse the effectiveness of analogous previous policies. Contributors to public debates about government policy, be it within or outside the parliamentary arena, also regularly draw on the past in support or criticism of new initiatives. In discussions about new policies, however, relevant pasts tend to be invoked selectively.[52]

We all have and draw on ideas about what the past has contained, and those ideas are – necessarily – selective. The histories this chapter has sketched in order to situate the study of child refugee policy focus on Australia's settler-colonial past and present. This is the history that has had the firmest bearing on refugee policies in this country, and which we must look at straight on if we are to make the changes necessary to bring about justice at the borders.

CHAPTER 2

Best Interests of the Child?

On 14 February 2019, the Home Affairs Minister, Peter Dutton, told radio shock jock Ray Hadley on 2GB:

> from our perspective the most important thing here is to make sure that we get national security right, that we protect our borders. We've spoken to the sailors who pulled the kids out of the water, the half eaten torsos, those people, those sailors, members of Border Force, I mean they're people still to this very day with PTSD and they've never recovered and some never will. The most important thing for us is to make sure that boats don't start, don't get back through.[1]

Dutton's narrative here conveys a sense of Australia as a nation that controls people's movements *because they care*. But while 'stopping the boats so the kids don't drown' has been framed as an act of humanitarian governance, it is deeply harmful. It could also be considered illegal under international law, as turning back boats is *refoulement* (returning people to places they have fled and where they are in likely danger of persecution). The use of mandatory detention as a deterrence strategy might also be considered illegal, as the government imprisons groups of people arbitrarily and indefinitely.[2]

The story that Dutton is telling is used across party lines. To offer one example: at the 2015 ALP National Conference, Tony Burke – the Minister for Immigration, Multicultural Affairs and Citizenship from July to September in 2013 – stood up and told the conference that the party should change its policy position to support boat turnbacks *because of the children*. In a speech described by *ABC News* as 'passionate and emotional', during which 'some in the audience were moved to tears', Burke focused on his experience as minister to argue that 'Labor needs to be able to turn boats back'.[3] He said that there needed to be a deeper understanding of what it meant to be compassionate in this area of policy. He told the conference that

> the number assigned to my time as Immigration Minister is 33. I was there for fewer than 4 months and there are 33 lives that were lost on my watch. When I first got the list – the list was only of ages – but I noticed that one of them was 10 weeks old. And I remember asking my staff to go to the Department and get his name.

At this point he took a deep breath. Then he resumed, telling his audience that 'the staff came back and said "oh no, they can't give you his name, you can't use it in the media at the moment because the names can change and the details can change."' Burke raised his voice:

> I said 'can you just tell them I don't want to use it in the media.' He was ten weeks old, he died on my watch, I just want to know his name. His name was Abdul Jafari. I was given his name on a post-it note, and I kept that post-it note on my desk until we lost office. I kept it there for one very simple reason: we have to

show compassion not only to who is in our line of sight, but to everybody who is affected by our policies.[4]

The Labor policy was changed. The party, which is now in government, supports boat turnbacks. This position was reinforced by Anthony Albanese during the 2022 federal election campaign, when he asserted in April 2022 that a new Labor government would 'turn boats back': 'I was asked today about boat turnbacks – our position is clear, we continue to support them,' he told reporters.[5] There are few signs that this position will shift, despite the appointment of Andrew Giles – who led the argument at this same national conference against a policy of boat turnbacks – as Minister for Immigration, Citizenship and Multicultural Affairs. Giles's language was clear in 2015: he disagreed with the policy because he was 'unconvinced by the effectiveness' of boat turnbacks, which he regarded as an 'inherently unsafe' practice that ran 'contrary to our international obligations'.[6]

'Stop the boats so the kids don't drown'

Practically speaking, 'stopping the boats' in Australia has variously meant turning boats around at sea, disembarking passengers and transporting them back to their destination port, and taking passengers to immigration prison in Christmas Island, Manus Island and Nauru. The Manus Island Regional Processing Centre, located in a former Australian navy base, is an immigration prison in Papua New Guinea established by the Howard government in 2001, alongside the immigration prison in Nauru, as part of what was termed the 'Pacific Solution'. It was an extension of Australia's colonial relationships with Papua New Guinea and Nauru. Both sites stopped being used in 2003, and were formally closed by the Rudd government in 2008, but they were reopened by the Gillard government in 2012. This 2012 move was a result of the recommendations of a report by former Chief of the Defence Force Angus Houston, former Secretary of the Department of Foreign Affairs and Trade Michael L'Estrange and CEO of Foundation House Paris Aristotle. This report provided advice to the government as increasing numbers of refugees made their way to Australia by boat. It resulted in a range of punitive measures being instituted. It was also subject to sustained criticism from human rights groups, academics and some in the media.[7] On 19 July 2013, the second Rudd government announced that everyone who had been transferred to Manus Island would never be resettled in Australia. In practice, some people who came on boats after this date were able to live in the Australian community: arbitrary decisions were made as to where people would be sent.[8] But nearly a decade on, this decision remains in force. While the prison in Manus Island has been closed, the prison in Nauru continues – and was reauthorised by the government in February 2023. Many people continue to languish in Nauru, Papua New Guinea or Australia (some of whom were brought to the Australian mainland under the Medevac laws) without options for permanent settlement.

At a hearing of the Australian Human Rights Commission's 2014 Inquiry into Children in Immigration Detention, Greg Lake – a former department official on Christmas Island, responsible for 'preparing the criteria by which people would be selected to go offshore' – testified that in 2012 someone from the office of Chris Bowen, the Labor Immigration minister, called him, telling Lake that his 'responsibility' was to 'select the children that looked the youngest' to send to detention in Manus Island. Lake made clear that the government 'wanted to send a deterrent message' so 'it was important to send some children'.[9] Legal scholar Madeline Gleeson explains that children selected for this most punitive form of detention had to be at least seven years old 'since doctors had advised that it was not possible to vaccinate children younger than this against the diseases there'.[10] Thus the government was looking for the youngest-looking children who were over seven years old.

Despite the harms it causes, the narrative that the boats must be stopped has attained normative status across the twenty-first century. It is a nation-building and racialising story, which works to create the people who stop the boats as saviours who are fundamentally good (and white), and those who are being stopped from being on boats as lacking (and non-white). This narrative rests on an idea that the boats need to be stopped because it is in the children's best interests to do so. It seems to assume, patronisingly, that children and their caregivers would not already be acting in the child's best interests.

As sociologist Michelle Peterie has shown, 'discourses of compassion are a well-established feature of Australia's asylum seeker debate' in recent years. These discourses, she says, 'have gained traction … because they reconcile Australia's preferred self-image as a decent country with its underlying insecurities and need for control'.[11] Pointing us towards a longer history of such manoeuvres, historian Joy Damousi has written of post–World War II efforts to 'rescue' Japanese-Australian children, explaining the ways that this 'paternalistic' approach was embroiled in a 'major perception and investment in a particular image of Australia as a humanitarian nation'.[12] There is a long history of work to create an idea of Australia as 'caring', and this work has always been part of a project of maintaining control.

The discourse around 'stop the boats so children don't drown' sets up politicians, the media and the public as looking out for these children and their best interests in a way that their parents, families and communities do not. It establishes whiteness as responsible and non-whiteness as irresponsible. We see this consistently in the ways that Australian governments and institutions talk about refugee children. It is also a globalised understanding of children. In 1994, the UN High Commissioner for Refugees (UNHCR), Sadako Ogata, wrote in her preface to the UNHCR Guidelines on the Protection and Care of Refugee Children: 'children are vulnerable ... children are dependent ... children are developing' and '[r]efugee children are children first and foremost, and as children, they need special attention'.[13] In this formulation, which represents how the United Nations and its Convention on the Rights of the Child conceptualise the child, children 'are presumed to lack the competency and capacity to assist in the design and development of any measures or interventions to ensure their effective protection', as legal scholar John Tobin puts it.[14] We will see this sentiment and practice throughout this book, as we see the ways that these ideas have formed the basis of Australian government thought.

But before we look more at how – and why – the 'stop the boats so children don't drown' story operates, it is important to take a step back and understand it in a larger context, of discussions in Australia about the 'best interests of the child'.

What is the 'best interests of the child'?

In the late 1980s, the UNHCR made clear that all actions 'on behalf of refugee children' should be guided by 'the principle of the best interests of the child' (as well as 'the principle of family unity'). This 'requires that the child's welfare precedes all other considerations, that individuality be respected and that physical, psychological and social developmental needs be met'. In considering how this will be implemented, the UNHCR has said that '[t]he best interests principle further requires that those who make decisions and take action on behalf of refugee children be fully qualified and sensitive to their needs in the light of the children's particular circumstances'.[15] Legal scholars such as Jason Pobjoy have shown that this principle 'mandates that the best interests of the child shall be a primary consideration in all actions concerning children'.[16] It demands precedence over almost any other principle, requiring compliance from anyone dealing with children under any circumstances and in any timeframe. It asserts that children be understood as individuals with particular needs.

It is routinely ignored.

Many of us will be familiar with this basic concept of 'best interests of the child', or at least familiar with the phrase itself. It has become a widely deployed concept. It is often used in Australian human-rights discussions and by humanitarian organisations. Some people working in positions of care and responsibility for children understand themselves – and are understood by other people – to be acting in a child's best interests. Uttering this phrase has come to enable the speaker to stake a claim to expertise, to having undertaken due care and consideration, even as they may downplay its relevance in the order of priorities.

But as we will see in this chapter, when it comes to making child refugee policy in Australia, the 'best interests of the child' serves primarily as a symbol, a phrase that policymakers use to talk about the problems of implementing draconian policies, or a way to lay claim to doing the 'right thing' – even when they are prioritising perceived security concerns over justice. And it implies a hierarchy, a split between those who define what a child's best interests are and those who experience the repercussions of those decisions. That is, refugee and asylum-seeking children have decisions made for them, as policymakers assert that they are considering the children's 'best interests' in order to claim that they care about the children and that they are governing with empathy.

While in 1924 the League of Nations adopted the Geneva Declaration of the Rights of the Child, and in 1959 the United Nations ratified the Declaration of the Rights of the Child, legal theorist Jacqueline Bhabha explains that 'it was not until the 1989 Convention on the Rights of the Child', which Australia ratified in December 1990, 'that international human rights law seriously engaged the question, What sort of a human is a child?' The answer this law seemed to provide was that childhood is 'a status at once separate from adulthood because particularly vulnerable, and thus deserving of special protection, and at the same time similar but inferior to adulthood in its capacity for agency and entitlement to autonomy, subjecthood, and voice'.[17] 'Children' became understood as a special category of human who were deserving of this unique idea or form of protection.

So while the concept of 'best interests of the child' predates the Convention, this was its moment of formal codification in international law. And while there have been attempts to codify it in various ways in domestic Australian law, it remains simultaneously mostly unaccounted for within the *Migration Act 1958*, and regularly discussed by policymakers and legislators working within the realm of child refugees and asylum-seekers. The closest it comes in the Act is Section 4AA, Article 1, which asserts that 'a minor shall only be detained as a measure of last resort'.[18]

According to historians Nell Musgrove and Shurlee Swain, 'the phrase "best interest" first appeared in Victoria's child welfare legislation in the *Social Welfare Act* of 1960, and has gained increasing prominence in subsequent legislation'. But, they say, it has been difficult to pin down what exactly this should mean, and so it has operated primarily as a vague 'guiding principle', often being spoken about in the same breath as policies that 'do not serve [children's] interests at all'.[19] Or, as historian Max Liddell has identified, 'the interests of children have been, and still are, downgraded as other priorities dominate'.[20] This is often the pattern of child-refugee policymakers in Australia. And while, as literary scholar Margaret R. Higonnet has explained, it was in the aftermath of World War I that 'children came to the fore as the epitome of the vulnerable human being and thus as emblems for the violation of human rights', this notion of 'vulnerability' has come to be articulated in numerous different ways over the last century.[21] What they all have in common is that they presuppose a child who requires an adult to decide their future for them. The child is imagined as oblivious and incompetent. This idea is central to the vision of the child refugee that Australian policymakers have worked with.

Making 'best interest' determinations

There are many archival traces of determinations of the 'best interests of a child'. One instance from the mid-1980s, a file note now held within the settlement services archives of the National Archives of Australia, discusses a sixteen-year-old Vietnamese boy. The author, a worker in welfare services in Melbourne, notes that 'Catholic Immigration' wanted to sponsor his migration to Australia. According to the note:

> He has siblings ... in USA and a ... sister in Melbourne. She is married and pregnant. She and her husband live with another family. The boy is in Holland with a cousin ... ISS (Holland) feel that the child is well settled, adapting well, learning a skill but would like to see his sister again. The Welfare Officer on

the case thinks that this should be put 'on hold' as child's best interests might be served by remaining in Holland.

The note goes on to list a variety of reasons for this view.[22] The official recorded that the Melbourne office agreed with this approach, and that the case would be reviewed after some months. Numerous such file decisions and notations clutter the archives.

Through this example we can see that determinations of the best interests of the child are made largely by government officials. Decisions are at the discretion of the officials, working within their institutional guidelines, often taking into little account the ideas of the child whose 'best interests' are being decided upon. Even today unaccompanied refugee children living in the community need to receive permission from the Immigration department to undertake everyday activities, such as to go on excursions or sleep over at a friend's house.

Another aspect of best-interest determinations for refugee children sits at the population level. On 1 January 2023, Cabinet documents from 2002 were released to the public by the National Archives of Australia. From these we learn that on 4 April 2002, among a range of recommendations related to capping the 'onshore' and 'offshore' numbers of refugees taken by Australia – as well as determining who should be given permanent residence and who a temporary protection visa (TPV) – Immigration minister Philip Ruddock recommended that the English as a Second Language – New Arrivals (ESL-NA) Program be extended to include English-language lessons for 'refugee minors with temporary residence status', not just those with permanent residency status. He noted that '[d]ifferentiation in the treatment of refugee minors based on their residence status in Australia could be subject to criticism that the Government is not meeting its obligations under the Convention on the Rights of the Child, that all refugee children residing in Australia should be treated in the same manner as other children'. While '[a]llowing access to this aspect of post arrival services for TPV minors to fulfil Australia's international moral obligations will result in a minor increase in expenses', this was not a concern since there had been 'fortuitous savings' as a result of the creation of TPVs in 1998 and a corresponding drop in the number of refugee children who had access to the program.[23] Both Treasury and the Department of Finance and Administration opposed this recommendation on the basis of its cost, while the Attorney-General's Department was in strong support, noting that 'the implementation of this recommendation is intended to fulfil relevant obligations under the Convention on the Rights of the Child'. All other departments – including Prime Minister and Cabinet – supported it or had no comment.[24] In other words, the children would not receive permanent protection, but they would have access to English lessons while allowed here temporarily.

In this example – as elsewhere – we see an intersection between ideas of 'best interests of the child' and perceived national interests of border, security and population control, with government priority placed on the latter. Security, securitisation, border, crisis and control discourses have predominated over discourses and administrative practices of 'children's interests'. In Australian policymaking – and elsewhere in the world too – we see the needs of the child deprioritised when security or border control is being considered. 'Best interests' has been used by some policymakers as a political bargaining chip, weighed up against other concerns of state-making or other ideas about what governments want refugees and asylum seekers to be able to do.

In this vein, the 2014 'Resolving the Asylum Legacy Caseload' Bill brought about many cruel measures. For example, it reintroduced TPVs and created a 'fast-track' process for some asylum claims – a process that provided as little opportunity as possible for these asylum seekers to outline their refugee claims, leading to high rejection rates, and so in practice denied many people subjected to it their rightful access to asylum and to standard review procedures. In the Bill's explanatory memorandum, the Coalition government explained that 'in developing the policies reflected in this Bill, the government has treated the best interests of the child as a primary consideration'. 'However,' they asserted,

> it is Government policy to discourage unauthorised arrivals from taking potentially life threatening avenues to achieve resettlement for their families in Australia and this, as well as the integrity of the onshore protection programme, are also primary considerations which may outweigh the best interests of the child in relation to a particular measure.[25]

In an interview I conducted in October 2018, Chris Evans – a former senator who was the Labor Minister for Immigration and Citizenship from 3 December 2007 to 14 September 2010 – remembered himself as governing in a way that prioritised 'best interests of the child'. But he also recalled that this principle caused a difficulty for him: it raised a problem in deciding how to balance different facts, and thus in knowing what to prioritise and how to act. He told me, 'It was difficult. I mean, if you're a Minister and you got a report from ASIO that said this person is a security risk to the country, and you've got someone screaming at you "oh you can't have the kids in detention", [the question becomes] do you separate the kids from the other members of the family? People would scream at you about that too. So you've got to make the call – well, are we better off keeping the family together? Because quite frankly, the security advice is so strong, the security classification report is so serious that, you know, you can't in all conscience say off you go [out of detention]. But you've got a couple of young kids.

'… It was never simple. So we tried to manage that through one of those community housing type options but with some security. We had a few houses near Villawood that we could sort of subtly patrol and manage their access to the community. So you'd try and find solutions like that. But equally, you know, if something goes wrong, the Minister and the Department have got a real problem. So the easiest default position was leaving them in detention.'[26]

Others faced similar strains. A former ministerial adviser in the Immigration portfolio told me that issues arose when children self-harmed while in detention. 'In their best interests,' she said, 'we [would] need to move them' so they wouldn't be in the environment that caused them to self-harm. However, there 'was always more a practical consideration of, do we have the community detention placement and the supports available to move them in the timeframes that we could?' Moreover, there were other considerations at play. As she explained: 'if people were self-harm[ing] … that's difficult … you don't want to say, "Well, self-harm and then … you get to move", you know … One of the hardest things actually when I was in the detention space was when people would protest and we'd just have to be so hardline, you know, because the second you give in to a protest, the second that escalates into something else the next time because it's seen as a reward and stuff … that was really hard 'cause people were hurting themselves and you were like, "Nup, tell them to get off the roof" … and it was awful, you know, awful cases … [T]hat was one of the areas actually where the Department was absolutely firm in their advice, from the word go, like, just "do not, do not give in to this", which was pretty hardline ... it made sense because you just couldn't give into it, but, you know.'[27]

The importance of security is so heavily emphasised that policymakers see few other choices than to implement approaches that go against a child's (and adult's) best interests – even as they continue to use the rhetoric of the child's best interests. This rhetoric is often used (whether consciously or unconsciously) as a handy catchphrase that helps them to articulate the concerns of statecraft, the problems of being a policymaker. In this way, the very real harms produced by border control policies, which they participate in creating and implementing, are obscured from view. But never from the view of those targeted, of course.

The balancing act involved in making decisions about the best interests of children and national security spreads from government to non-governmental organisations. Mat Tinkler is CEO and director of policy and international programs at Save the Children, and a former chief of staff for Bill Shorten. He told me when we met in October 2017 that hard decisions sometimes had to be made within Save the Children. When we spoke about how the organisation managed its advocacy role alongside its service provision role – wherein it is reliant on government funding to execute many of its projects – he explained that there can be a chilling effect on what staff feel they can say publicly. Talking about their work in Nauru, he told me that

> we did a lot of individual advocacy for things like family reunification and health care for individuals who are in our care. We did individual advocacy with the relevant ministers on Nauru. But the biggest tension I think we had to manage was really the desire of our staff to be doing advocacy and to be seen to be doing something publicly. Because, you can imagine, particularly when

you're at the coalface, if you're a child protection or welfare office who sees a child sewing their lips together in Nauru protesting over their treatment, you want to talk about that. And managing the expectations and the desires of our staff versus our licence to operate was very tricky.[28]

For Save the Children, this tension would prove to be unmanageable. In October 2014, the nine Save the Children workers stationed in the Australian detention camp in Nauru were sacked and removed from Nauru, after the Coalition government accused them of 'coaching asylum-seekers to self-harm and fabricate stories of abuse' – allegations that were later found to be false.[29] Tinkler described this to me as the government using Save the Children as 'a bit of a scapegoat' in order to create a 'circuit breaker' in the disastrous situation in Nauru: creating a crisis in order to regain control at a time when 'the Government was really worried that they would lose control of the situation'.[30]

I will return to a discussion of the ways that governments imagine and produce such crises in the next chapter. But we can see that in these examples, children are presented as requiring governance, and the Australian government uses emotionally potent discourses of concern as a justification for harsh treatment. This points us to some of the deep problems with the materialisation of the phrase 'best interests of the child'.

But for Professor Gillian Triggs, former president of the Australian Human Rights Commission, the International Covenant on Civil and Political Rights and the UN Convention on the Rights of the Child were essential documents in prosecuting the case for the rights of the children in detention. Both rely on the concept of the 'best interests of the child'. In March 2018, she explained to me that, when the Commission was carrying out their inquiry into children in detention in 2014 – the second such inquiry they had undertaken, and one for which Triggs would face heavy criticism from the sitting Coalition government – 'we brought the media with us all the time'. 'We made that decision,' she said. '[T]he media really got the point about the children and it helped me as a lawyer to say that one of the great scandals is that Australia signed up to that treaty [on children's rights] but never implemented it in Australian law, and so that's a huge impediment to actually going to a court … in relation to children in particular, apart from very specific bits of legislation that deal with child welfare and so on. So we felt that by putting a focus on our international obligations, which is our mandate at the Human Rights Commission in any event, we were able to focus on those provisions but also have the benefit of the jurisprudence of the committee on children.'

I asked whether it was a strategic decision to focus on children, and she explained that 'it was a legal decision … [as] Australia's bound by those obligations'. But, she said, 'focusing on the children had a strategic advantage as well because we felt that that would move people more, that you can hold adults more morally responsible or ethically responsible for their actions but you couldn't do that to children, and it's common across every major legal system that you do not detain children other than for very, very specific reasons and for the shortest possible time'.[31]

The beginnings of 'humane deterrence'

In April 1975, as the Vietnam War was coming to an end, Australia, the United States, France, West Germany and Canada came together to airlift more than 3000 babies from Saigon (now Ho Chi Minh City). These mostly orphaned children were placed onto planes – the littlest were transported in shoeboxes, according to some accounts – and flown around the world to be adopted. This rescue mission was named Operation Babylift.[32]

On 4 April 1975, the Department of Foreign Affairs in Australia cabled representatives in Hanoi to tell them that a Qantas charter flight was being organised to land in Bangkok and bring back approximately 250 Vietnamese orphans who had been flown there from Saigon on Royal Australian Air Force aircrafts. Foreign Affairs told them that

> if you think it necessary, please explain to the DRV [Democratic Republic of Vietnam] and PRG [Provisional Revolutionary Government of the Republic of South Vietnam] authorities that over past years a great number of orphans have come to Australia for adoption, this present step is merely an acceleration of past practice. All orphans are coming for adoption by Australian families who had already applied to adopt a Vietnamese child. The adoption of Vietnamese orphans is a long-standing private expression of Australian concern at the suffering caused by war and the government, with the full support of all segments of the Australian people, is accelerating the movement of orphans.[33]

Four flights went between Saigon and Bangkok, with the planes ill fitted to transport these children. In his recent history of Operation Babylift, Ian W. Shaw reports that 'the older children did what they could to help the younger ones, but that first C-130 to land in Bangkok carried a cargo of traumatised orphans, now suffering from headaches, earaches and dehydration on top of whatever else was ailing them'. In Bangkok, on the next flight (a Qantas flight that came to be known as the Angel of Mercy), and then on arrival in Australia there was confusion amid the children and staff: proper documentation about the identities of all the children was not available, nor was there concrete information about their health needs.

Eventually records would show that there were about 194 orphans airlifted out at this time. These children were processed and held for a time at North Head Quarantine Station in Sydney. On 6 April, the day after the children arrived, Prime Minister Gough Whitlam and his wife, Margaret, visited them, talking to staff, touring the quarantine station and posing for photos holding 'a small Vietnamese orphan girl'.[34]

The children who came to Australia under Operation Babylift were adopted largely by white families. Interviewed by *SBS News* on Operation Babylift's fortieth anniversary, one of the children brought to Australia, Le Thi Ha – now named Chantal Doecke – described how she had been left at an orphanage by her birth mother. Doecke had been born premature and unwell. 'She had me and she fled. Obviously knowing that she couldn't run with a newborn baby who was quite fragile … I don't believe there was any paperwork. Unfortunately, a lot of us adoptees were in that same position. There's no time to think about passing over details, it was just, "Get my child out."'

The sudden move to Australia made for a disjointing experience. Doecke explained, 'Partly what I've struggled with now, now that I'm older, is that we've been plucked from our Asian heritage and then we've been placed in a Western background and we've had to assimilate into Western lifestyles. A lot of the adoptees' families don't realise that it has affected us in some way. I don't think it's intentional, but it has affected a lot of us in small ways, or large ways.' She and others, such as Dominic Hong Duc Golding, talked about experiencing racism growing up: 'I experienced quite a lot of racism … But I also experienced a lot of exclusion because I was not white, even though I was brought up to be white,' Golding explained. 'I was told so often at school that I'm different, I'm Asian, "you don't belong here", "go back to where you come from" – being called a "gook" or a "charlie" ... So there's these constant statements of otherness ... reinforcing the fact that I'm not an Australian has made me want to investigate and try to take some kind of ownership of my own Vietnamese heritage.'[35]

For them, as for many other refugee children who have come to Australia across the twentieth and twenty-first centuries, racist targeting has been a common experience. This racism is also part of Australia's overall approach to refugees – it shapes how refugees coming by boat are talked about and treated.

When Operation Babylift took place, refugees had not yet begun arriving in Australia by boat. While the Whitlam government started to hear about refugees making their way by boat out of Vietnam in May 1975, the first boat only came to Australia a year later, in April 1976.[36] As more people came on boats from Vietnam and surrounding countries in the late 1970s, public discussion became focused on concerns about Australia's sovereignty and the country's ability to respond to the plight of these asylum seekers. Historian Klaus Neumann has shown that there were also concerns expressed about the 'legitimacy' of some of the travellers' refugee claims – the idea of so-called 'queue jumpers' entered the discourse through the words of Moss Cass, Labor's Opposition spokesman on immigration.[37] There was also chatter about the robustness of Australia's *Migration Act*. While there were no claims to concern or any discourse around asylum-seeker children drowning, 'in 1977 the government for the first time defended its approach to refugees by drawing on the language of humanitarianism *and* by invoking Australia's responsibilities in the Asia-Pacific region. Significantly, its defence did not draw on the language of human rights and did not include prominent references to Australia's international legal obligations,' Neumann writes.[38]

From this late-1970s moment and into the 1980s, more refugees came, and sought to come, to Australia from Vietnam and Thailand, and the Australian government found itself with more and more people they were unsure how to manage. They commissioned numerous reports, and a range of community aid organisations formed around the country.[39] A particular focus was placed on refugee children. In February 1983, during the last months of the Fraser government, the Department of Immigration and Ethnic Affairs commissioned Elizabeth Lloyd to undertake research into the topic. Her report, '"The Children of Indo-China": A Study Including Policy Recommendations of Children Leaving Indo-China Without Their Parents', was produced that same year. Rod Plant was working in the refugee sector at the time, and in his 1988 book on Khmer unaccompanied minors living at Burnside, a refugee housing project, he explained that Lloyd's report was never meant to be made public. When it was released, it was heavily criticised by those in the sector.[40]

In Lloyd's report, we see the strands of 'humane deterrence' being formulated. After noting that 'insufficient is known about unaccompanied minors and this report should be regarded as preliminary to a more thorough and ongoing investigation', Lloyd writes that '[a]t least some of the recommendations may seem harsh and potentially unpopular. They have only been made after careful consideration and discussion with a number of interested people. The results of current "humanitarian" actions may also prove unpopular or even cruel in the long term.'[41] Invoking the idea of the 'anchor' child, who is imagined to be sent to a country perniciously, in order to set roots down and bring the rest of their family later, the report also explained that

> Most countries including the USA, are very unsure how genuine are the needs and claims of these minors or how much continuing acceptance of Vietnamese minors act as a 'pull factor,' attracting more such children to leave Vietnam in the hope of making a new life in a Western country.
>
> There is a consensus of opinion that longer stays in camps may act as a deterrent to others considering leaving their country, just as quick acceptance and rapid movement to third countries may act as 'pull factors' and encourage further departures.
>
> Matching the desirability of 'humane deterrance' [sic] through longer stays in camps, against the inhumanity of keeping children in less desirable circumstances in a refugee camp is part of a decision and policy making process that we must face, and then defend whatever decision we make.[42]

The language of the report is at times disconcerting. While it acknowledges that the unaccompanied children in Cambodia, who have 'survived the horrors of Pol Pot', were 'in this situation of physical danger, starvation, separated from their families', it notes that they 'are of course an emotive, needy, and appealing subject group'. Lloyd also asserts that the parents of Vietnamese children who had come to Australia were putting 'pressure' on their children 'by letter … to send money home. This is thought to account for poor performance in school, often jeopardising their education … Experienced teachers commented that they knew by the depressed expression and lack of concentration which children had just received a letter from home.'[43] Throughout her report no real evidence is provided for her claims.

The ideas Lloyd proposed are part of longer histories of Australian interest in – and support for – a range of deterrence strategies. When the

United Nations Refugee Convention was being drafted in 1951, the Australian delegation reported back to the Department of External Affairs (the precursor to Foreign Affairs), raising whether the draft convention 'prohibited the imposition of penalties upon refugees who unlawfully enter' and suggesting that Australia not agree to this, as 'the power to impose penalties on unlawful entry may prove a useful deterrent which we should not abandon'.[44]

While the Department of Immigration and Ethnic Affairs did not adopt all of Lloyd's recommendations, it did implement one of them, in modified form: a restriction on unaccompanied boys over the age of fifteen being 'selected' and brought to Australia. The report implied that these children were too difficult to assimilate or control. This decision was fought against and eventually – through the involvement of UNHCR – overturned.

Lloyd, who was brought on as a short-term consultant to write the 'Children of Indo-China' report, was afterwards 'given a permanent position in the department and made responsible for policy on refugee youth', according to Plant. There was, he recounts, at this time 'extraordinary resistance' in the immigration department to resettling 'these few unaccompanied minors': the department, in his description, was 'reluctant, obstructionist, and based mainly on refusal to acknowledge responsibility that would entail greater expenditure'. But those in the sector who lobbied for more were, he says, not willing to 'accept what had been the norm for refugee youth until then'.[45]

Plant was not the only one to comment on the problem of the lack of funding; other reports also made clear that refugee children's needs were not being attended to. The Standing Committee of Social Welfare Administrators, which included representatives from across the country, gathered together and in April 1984 produced a report which asserted that services for refugee children – and particularly unaccompanied refugee children – were provided haphazardly, with insufficient resourcing, and were not catering to the needs of the children who were in Australia.[46]

There is a clear through-line from these discussions that occurred in the public service and the bureaucracy – raising issues of a lack of care, promoting the idea that the parents of refugee children are negligent, and suggesting various harsh measures to deter refugees from making their way to Australia – through to the twenty-first-century use of humanitarian language in order to argue for the boats to be stopped. The overwhelming control of refugees' lives continued from the Fraser government of the early 1980s through to the Labor governments of the late 1980s and 1990s, which saw the introduction of mandatory and indefinite imprisonment for people seeking to come to Australia by boat without prior authorisation. The foundations – the language, the bureaucratic approach, the lack of attention to the details of refugee children's lives and their needs – were set for this new approach to be developed, implemented and embraced.

A brief history of 'stopping the boats'

From 2000 to 2001, an Iranian child refugee named Shayan Badraie was imprisoned in Woomera and then Villawood detention centres. Badraie had come to Australia with his family, seeking protection. He suffered stark trauma responses to what he saw and experienced in these prisons as a five- and six-year-old. This included violence perpetrated by Australasian Correctional Management guards and attempted self-harm by refugees imprisoned there.[47] Badraie was hospitalised numerous times over the course of 2001, both for dehydration and as a result of the 'psychological paralysis' he fell into. He had stopped speaking, had begun having panic attacks and was 'wasting away' as a result of being in detention. He was diagnosed with PTSD. Eventually, in August 2001, following a series of damning media reports – including on ABC's *Four Corners* television program and in newspapers around the country – Badraie was released from detention into the care of a foster family. Despite advice to Immigration minister Philip Ruddock that the family should be released together, the rest of his immediate family remained held in detention.[48] In January 2002, the minister granted bridging visas to Shayan; his mother, Zahra; and his sister, Shabnam. The three were reunited. His father – who had lodged a complaint about Shayan's treatment with the Australian Human Rights Commission in September 2001 – remained imprisoned.[49] It was not until April 2002 that the whole family were granted bridging visas. In 2003, Shayan sued the government for the damage to his mental health sustained while he was in detention. Three years later, the same year that his family was eventually granted permanent residency, he received an out-of-court settlement from the Australian government, who also paid his legal bills.

According to legal scholars Bernadette McSherry and Azadeh Dastyari, Shayan Badraei's story 'galvanised activists working toward stopping the immigration detention of children'.[50] His case helped lay the groundwork for a focus on children, both by the government and by those seeking to act for refugee justice.

This was in part because it came soon after a wave of controversy about Australia's immigration policy. On 24 August 2001, a wooden fishing vessel, *Palapa 1*, became stranded in international waters travelling from Indonesia to Christmas Island. On 26 August 2001, the Norwegian cargo ship *Tampa* rescued the 433 asylum seekers (and five crew) aboard. The ship's captain, Arne Rinnan, sought to disembark the passengers at Christmas Island – and a small group of distressed asylum seekers agitated forcefully for this too – but was prohibited from entering Australian waters, and told he may be prosecuted as a people smuggler if he did so. When he disobeyed his instructions and headed towards Christmas Island – the vessel did not have food or safety equipment for this number of passengers, several of whom were suffering from dysentery – the *Tampa* was boarded by Special Air Service troops and held in place while legislation was introduced into Parliament to prevent it moving further towards Christmas Island.[51] Although this legislation was ultimately defeated in the Senate, the asylum seekers were held on board for eight days.

Abbas Nazari was one of those child asylum seekers rescued by the *Tampa* – he was just seven years old at the time. He recalled the experience to *SBS News* in 2021: 'It was almost like a war zone ... You've got immense sea sickness and diarrhoea and every sort of illness and ailment. Many people, including myself, had really bad skin conditions from being sunburnt and from sleeping on damp wood for so long. We all had pus-filled sores and our skin was cracked and bleeding.'[52]

The *Tampa* captain, Arne Rinnan, later said: 'I have seen most of what there is to see in this profession, but what I experienced on this trip is the worst. When we asked for food and medicine for the refugees, the Australians sent commando troops on board. This created a very high tension among the refugees.'[53]

At the end of September the government excised Christmas Island from Australia's migration zone, introduced a policy of boat turnbacks and created 'the Pacific Solution': the system for imprisoning asylum seekers on islands in the Pacific, such as Nauru. Some of the asylum seekers on the *Tampa* were forcibly removed to Nauru, while others (including Nazari) were taken to New Zealand.[54]

Some members of the public immediately picked up on the politics of emotion the government was leveraging. In a letter to *The Canberra Times* on 10 September 2001, Stewart Homan wrote that Howard's 'strategies' with regard to the treatment of refugees and asylum seekers 'show definite leadership and will no doubt save many parents and children from watery graves'.[55] This letter praised the government's politics, using humanitarian vocabularies to shore up support for punitive policy, at a time which gender studies scholar Barbara Baird has identified as marking the beginning of 'a particularly intense period of "child politics"' in Australia.[56]

Within weeks of the *Tampa* affair, on 6 October 2001, the HMAS *Adelaide* stopped SIEV 4, which was carrying 223 passengers and crew towards Australia, most of whom were seeking asylum. SIEV is an Australian designation, and it stands for 'Suspected Illegal Entry Vehicle'. There is power in naming: describing something, or some*one*, as illegal is to imbue them with a certain illegitimacy, to imply criminality. After first attempting to turn the boat around and facing opposition from those on board, the *Adelaide* attached itself to SIEV 4, seeking to drag the vessel to Indonesia. On 7 October, some men jumped from the deck or fell overboard. On 8 October, SIEV 4 began to flounder and sink. People were evacuated into the sea and photos were taken, which were subsequently spread through the Australian media, shared as evidence of what the government and Defence personnel began to call the 'Children Overboard' incident.[57] In what would later be termed a 'great untruth' by reporter Virginia Trioli, Prime Minister John Howard and Defence minister Peter Reith promulgated the idea that parents had thrown their children into the sea in order to 'blackmail' Australia into granting them entry.[58] In a radio interview, Howard remarked that he felt there was something 'incompatible' about someone being a refugee and also throwing their children into the sea. 'It offends the natural instinct of protection, and delivering security and safety to your children,' he said.[59] While the figure of the child was mobilised in the naming and sentimentality surrounding the Children Overboard affair, the children themselves were almost never discussed. Regardless, this was an exemplary instance of when the child refugee was made to carry particular moral freight in a set of highly charged debates about border control.

These moments draw attention, too, to the powerful force in Australian culture and politics that is the ocean. Cultural studies scholar Suvendrini Perera has made clear that determining the meaning of the waters around Australia, and the ways that refugees engage with those waters, is a fundamental way in which Australian claims for sovereignty are produced.[60] The waters – how they are imagined to carry boats and people, and the ways that colonial governments narrate their force – are an important element in this story. The fact that Australia is 'girt by sea' has played a large role in Australian political emotions and stories.

The focus on preventing child drownings was developed further during this Children Overboard affair. In one example of the media's response, *The Sydney Morning Herald*'s editorial on 10 October accepted the government's false story of children being thrown from boats by their parents and asserted that 'there is no doubt that the pitching of children into the sea, even wearing life jackets, is distressing'. Drawing on the script of control, deterrence and border protection – wrapped up in the language of concern for the safety of 'genuine' asylum seekers – the editorial asserted, 'While the Government has the right and responsibility to protect Australia's borders, there is little evidence that the new measures have been an effective deterrent.'[61]

More was to come. On 19 October 2001, the devastating sinking of another fishing boat, the SIEV X, in international waters when it was on its way to Australia, and the drowning deaths of some 353 people, including many children, led to increased scrutiny on the perils faced by child refugees.[62] 'X' here was used by the Australian authorities because they had not allocated this boat a tracking number. The sinking occurred during a high-profile federal election campaign and the people on the boat received tributes in Australia, with one memorial in Canberra and another on Christmas Island.

Alongside the profusion of discussion about children drowning was an associated conversation about children being held in detention. The two are intimately linked, as policymakers debate their preferred way of governing and controlling refugee and asylum-seeking children. Many across the beginning of the twenty-first century have constructed the problem of children in detention as an insoluble governmental quandary: how can children be released from detention if their release will encourage other children to come by boat? This is a rhetorical strategy that keeps the government at the centre of the concern and narrows the possibilities for action. There is a foreclosing of the political imagination.

We can see this project of producing limitations in a column written by conservative newspaper columnist Andrew Bolt in December 2003, when he described letters that schoolchildren had sent to the Minister for Immigration and Multicultural and Indigenous Affairs, Liberal senator Amanda Vanstone. These letters, sent from schools in Melbourne, called on Vanstone to release children from immigration detention. Bolt took exception – both to the letters being written and to their assertions – and declared, 'In no letter I've seen did a child hint at having been taught the other side of this story – that to free the children you must also free their parents. And that would encourage the people smugglers who have already drowned so many children in their lethally overstuffed boats.'[63]

This was the same year that Shayan Badraie sued the government over his grievous mistreatment. It was reported that the government spent $1.53 million in legal costs alone fighting the case – far more than Badraie received in compensation.[64]

In 2007, as the Howard-led Coalition government – a government that many believed had profited politically from destructive refugee policies – was in its dying days, increasing numbers of people began taking boats towards Australia.[65] At this point, it seemed, the Australian Labor Party rediscovered the political utility of the discourse around child drownings. In an op-ed published in *The Daily Telegraph* on Anzac Day in 2007, Tony Burke, the Shadow Minister for Immigration, Integration and Citizenship, argued that the Howard government 'seem[ed] determined to endlessly repeat the claim that under Labor the floodgates would open for people seeing asylum in Australia'. He asserted, 'Deterring people smuggling is important. When the number of boats arriving reached its peak under Howard, hundreds of women and children drowned at sea. The operators trade in human misery. People smuggling must be shut down.'[66] A clear link was made between 'vulnerable' people and the need to exert control over them and their lives. Negligence was located in granting 'permission' to set sail, care in 'shutting down' routes to Australia. No other options were imaginable. The notion of the child's 'best interests' had by now been thoroughly overtaken by concerns over 'deaths at sea', 'national security' and 'queue jumpers'.

It was from 2007 on that the story of children drowning, and the need to 'stop the boats' to prevent this, gained bipartisan currency and so became a permanent fixture in our political vocabularies.

Proving a remarkably resilient discourse, it has now become normalised in our political discussions.

In these examples, as in the countless others with which the Australian public is familiar, 'children' are useful as emotional currency, with a value that can be extracted to buttress the arguments of policymakers and achieve the desired policy outcomes. Children are differentiated from adults, understood to carry some distinct power to signify meaning, and used narratively – and materially – to produce a collective understanding of the importance of border control. But while policymakers may frame border control as resulting from a desire to stop harm to children, it can be better understood as part of maintaining racialised projects of population control. This is Australian nation-building, creating both the population who will live in Australia as citizens, and the sense of what kind of country Australia is.

In 2019, we saw the result of the vision behind 'stopping the boats' articulated precisely by Major General Craig Furini, AM, CSC – the Commander, Joint Agency Task Force Operation Sovereign Borders, Department of Home Affairs. In his appearance before the Senate's Legal and Constitutional Affairs Legislation Committee, he stated:

> Since its inception in September 2013, Operation Sovereign Borders has utilised a multilayered approach of deterrence, disruption, detection, interception, return, regional processing and denial of a settlement pathway in Australia to successfully stem the flow of illegal maritime arrivals. While the illegal maritime people smuggling threat is currently suppressed, it is definitely not defeated. As recent ventures highlight, Australia remains a highly desirable destination and people smuggling remains an enduring threat to Australia's borders, with criminal people

smugglers continuing to prey on vulnerable people with false promises of offering illegal passage to Australia.

The Migration Legislation Amendment (Regional Processing Cohort) Bill 2019 gives full effect to the government's longstanding policy that people who travel to Australia illegally by boat and are transferred to regional processing countries will never settle here. The proposed legislation is designed to strengthen measures to make it difficult for people smugglers, to deter potential illegal immigrants from attempting needless dangerous voyages and to encourage people to pursue regular migration pathways ...

The department considers the proposed legislation is consistent with Australia's obligations under international law ...

Australia is a generous resettlement country and we have a long history of welcoming migrants, but we want people to come to Australia safely, utilising regular migration pathways. This bill will help keep our borders safe and save lives at sea. It will make it more difficult for criminal people smugglers to convince vulnerable people to part with their money and risk their lives in a bid to travel to Australia by boat.[67]

The political use of feelings and emotions

When policymakers and politicians have publicly discussed their reasoning for why they think the boats must be stopped, they have often used hyperbole and deliberately emotive language. In a 2014 reply in Parliament regarding Budget spending, Treasurer Joe Hockey used the image of children drowning to add an emotional punch to his claims about the government closing detention centres and saving money:

There were more boats coming in than there were planes at Sydney airport. I tell you what, as the boats came in under [Labor] the boats stopped under this minister for immigration. The boats stopped, and not only that; because the boats have stopped we have saved the budget $2½ billion and we have closed nine detention centres. But most of all, as a result of the actions of this government there are no children floating in the ocean between Australia and East Timor, as occurred under Labor.[68]

In September 2015, arguing against calls from the Coalition leader in the Senate, Eric Abetz, to prioritise Christian refugees in Australia's intake, Bill Shorten asserted, 'If you're a woman facing terrible crimes committed against you, if you're a child, a little child potentially drowning at sea, I'm not interested in their religion, I'm interested in their safety.'[69] And in October 2015, in response to calls from the Australian Medical Association 'to heed concerns at Melbourne's Royal Children's Hospital about discharging asylum seeker children back into detention', Peter Dutton told the *Herald Sun* that while he 'understood' the 'concerns', 'the Defence and Border Force staff on our vessels who were pulling dead kids out of the water don't want the boats to restart'.[70]

Policymakers aren't ignorant of this emotional power game. Anna Burke, former Labor MP and Speaker of the House, told me in November 2017 that by focusing on children 'you can attract everybody's attention' because 'people then do get concerned' about the situation they face. It has become, she said, 'almost evangelistic', whereby people can say that 'we're doing the right thing by not letting them drown at sea and we're protecting ourselves and ra-ra-ra. Yeah, but we've actually dropped the numbers that we're taking in, you know, and there's a worldwide crisis out there, and just saying we've stopped the boats isn't dealing with the issue, you know.' So much is made permissible, Burke told me, by the sustained focus on children drowning. She told me that she's 'sat with Labor ministers who've sat there going, "Well, you know, this is the right thing to do"', that the boats need to be stopped. But for Burke 'it's like yeah, gee, I'm not feeling it. I'm not agreeing. "We've got to stop the drownings at sea." Well, you can pacify yourself with that but … I'm not sure, you know, being this brutal is the only way of achieving that.'[71]

The need to control children

Philosopher Joanne Faulkner has explained that 'as representative of human futures, governments see childhood as a site of management, expropriation, and intervention' and as 'a "resource" valued in so far as it is able to articulate a viable future' within settler colonialism.[72] Children, that is, are a screen onto which fantasies of the future can be projected. For anthropologist Miriam Ticktin, 'the child represents a mode of experience that is protected, controlled – it performs the part of tabula rasa, and as such it offers proof that as humans we can be anything'.[73] Or, in the words of literary scholar Rebekah Sheldon, children (who she also described as a 'resource') are regularly 'freighted with expectations and anxieties about the future'.[74]

In the colonial Australian mindset, Aboriginal children almost always require removal, policing and control. We can see this in two key examples that pervade the twentieth and twenty-first centuries: the Stolen Generations and the Northern Territory Intervention. Noongar woman and social work academic Jacynta Krakouer noted in October 2019 that she 'wonder[ed] if the stolen generations never ended, but instead, just morphed into child protection':

Many contemporary Indigenous child removals are unwanted, many are legitimated by state-sanctioned power – such as police jurisdiction and court orders – as was the case during the stolen generations. And in another striking parallel, Indigenous children today are still removed for their 'best interests', the same language that was used to justify forcible removals in the 20th century. The similarities between past and contemporary Indigenous child removal practices raises a host of questions. On whose values do we determine the 'best interests' of the Indigenous child?[75]

In the twenty-first century, refugee children coming to Australia by boat experience a similar kind of subjection to assumed knowledge: the discourse that originated in the settler state's violent control of First Nations children has been transferred in adapted form onto refugee children. The imagined 'need' for children to be controlled is understood through colonial frameworks to be absolute. Following Chelsea Watego, we can understand that figuring children as requiring care and rescue in these ways is part of the process of racialising them, of making them into racial others, different from – and dependent upon – the white state and its bureaucracies for saving.[76] Their 'best interests' are understood to be determined through this vocabulary of racialised vulnerability, a vocabulary which was formulated through the treatment of Aboriginal children and which has since been adopted and adapted onto refugee children.

The project of settler-colonial nation-building – of shaping the population who live in Australia – is ongoing. The discourse of 'stop the boats so the kids don't drown' has become an important rhetorical tool for governments in pursuing this project in the twenty-first century, which is also the project of producing an imaginary of Australia as caring and humanitarian. This is a discourse that creates a crisis, a catastrophe or a disaster – children being thrown overboard and drowning – that, due to its emotional resonance, requires a specific response. As Barbara Baird writes, in the discussion about both the Northern Territory Intervention and the Children Overboard affair, 'a crisis in child protection is [treated] like a natural disaster, it is outside politics, outside anyone's control or representation'.[77] In response, the lexicons of international humanitarianism are drawn upon to depict politicians and bureaucrats as rescuers, and refugees – and child refugees in particular – as always needing to be rescued. As Joy Damousi notes, the plight of children is rendered 'emotional, sensational and sentimental'.[78] And the emotion induced by watching children (potentially) drown becomes the key means through which policy responses are formulated.

The histories of the people on a boat, the reasons why they are there, are ignored, made irrelevant, even as refugee and asylum-seeking children have spoken back to commissions of inquiry and through social media. The question of what will happen to them if their boats are turned back, of what violence they may face as a result, is erased from political discussion in Australia. What is made relevant is how politicians imagine their suffering, feel for their plight, care for their future. There is, in anthropologist Liisa Malkki's words, a 'vision of helplessness [that] is vitally linked to the constitution of speechlessness among refugees: helpless victims need protection, need someone to speak for them'.[79] Politicians narcissistically imagine themselves as being both able to and required to speak for child refugees and their desire to stay alive and safe. These discourses depersonalise refugees, transforming them into populations to be moved, controlled, traded, punished and articulated at will. These discourses reiterate a well-worn colonial idea: we know better than you what is better for you.[80]

In this there is, as historian Francesco Ricatti has explained, a 'fantasy of white moral superiority' at play.[81] This fantasy has an emotional basis, when politicians who articulate it deliberately use emotional language to mount their argument. Indeed, as Ticktin has explained, 'while humanitarianism is often understood as driven by emotions – compassion, empathy, benevolence, pity – in fact, it relies on a very narrow emotional constellation, and this in turn constrains our responses ... [It provides] little impetus to animate political change'.[82] A different sense of the emotional possibilities is needed: we need 'to make way for feelings that fit with different projects for equality, with different political visions'.[83] For within the political vision created by the emotional register currently on offer, the focus is on the feelings of politicians, on their desires and ideas, on their conceptions of care and protection. The saving of children makes government better. More profoundly, the relationship of saving and being saved forms the categories of 'us' and 'them'. This creates a totalising, frightening logic of 'stop the boats'.

Let us turn now to another piece of the puzzle: to examine more fully the ways that crisis has been mobilised as a technique of government, a lens through which to govern and control.

CHAPTER 3

Crisis

In September 2017, I interviewed a senior figure within the Australian Labor Party in his office in Canberra. At one point in our discussion he told me: 'The biggest contest in Australian politics is essentially around which issue you can make ascendant, so if you're [a] conservative Opposition leader, you want to make border security or the lack thereof and debt and deficits the issues that are ascendant in people's minds, and then the carbon tax. But certainly in 2010, prior to the hung parliament and the cross-party agreement on climate, it was all about border security and debt and deficits.'

He continued, explaining to me: 'So what you're doing every day, the whole contest is about can you make sure that that's the story in the newspapers the next day, and then if it's the story in the newspapers the next day, is it what the radio's talking about in the morning, and then if it's what the radio's talking about in the morning, is it what the TVs pick up or it's what the leaders get asked about at their media events and therefore that informs the TV news in the evening, and then you have a new revelation at some point in the afternoon that you push out or that someone uncovers that starts the cycle again.'

This, he argued, was a tactic that the Liberal Party embraced in the 'latter period' of Chris Evans's time as Immigration minister, when 'every time [Labor] thought they had been successful in moving the conversation on to some other topic, either events would catch up with them or Abbott or Morrison would go out and say something really outrageous that would inflame the conversation about border security and it would shift the conversation back onto that'. He described this as 'the Lynton Crosby thing of if you drop a dead cat on the table in the middle of a dinner party, no-one's going to like it. Everyone's going to think you're a bit weird, but they're going to spend the rest of the night talking about the dead cat on the middle of the table in the dinner party.'[1]

The Lynton Crosby being referred to here is a former federal director of the Liberal Party, who, with Mark Textor, co-runs a political campaigning consultancy firm, C|T Group. Crosby oversaw the Liberal Party's campaigns for the 1996, 1998, 2001 and 2004 federal elections, all of which were won by the Howard-led Liberal–Nationals Coalition. People who have worked for C|T Group also played a role in more recent Coalition campaigns: the 2022 federal election campaign included someone from C|T Group as a pollster, and an 'alumnus' as a consultant.[2] And so many did not feel it was a coincidence that on the final day of that campaign, with clear signs that the Coalition would lose, there was an announcement that Border Force had intercepted a boat carrying refugees which had been heading towards Australia.

Crosby himself has subsequently run elections for the Conservative Party in the United Kingdom, including for Boris Johnson and Theresa May, where his 'dead cat' strategy gained some notoriety thanks to a *Telegraph* column by his former star politician. Writing in 2013, Johnson revealed: 'Let us suppose you are losing an argument. The facts are overwhelmingly against you and the more people focus on the reality the worse it is for you and your case. Your best bet in these circumstances is to perform a manoeuvre that a great campaigner describes as "throwing a dead cat on the table, mate".' He continued: 'The key point, says my Australian friend, is that everyone will shout "Jeez, mate, there's a dead cat on the table!"; in other words they will be talking about the dead cat, the thing you want them to talk about, and they will not be talking about the issue that has been causing you so much grief.'[3]

While at times the strategy is used to distract from potentially more damning political conversations, in Australia we have also seen controversy being created to direct attention to the political games being played over matters related to national security and our borders. Creating a crisis is a means of controlling the media and the narrative, controlling people's emotions and controlling people's lives. For we should never lose sight of the asylum seekers at the borders whose lives are subjected to these political games.

'A shock through the system'

We have already seen that the *Tampa* came to epitomise highly charged debates about border control. It occurred in the lead-up to the 2001 federal election, which has subsequently become known colloquially as 'the *Tampa* election'. And it was discussed by the government using the rhetoric of crisis. It was a 'dead cat on the table' moment, using the historically common targets of refugees and border control in order to perform and exert white Australian sovereignty, or the power of the federal government to dominate and control.

On 29 August 2001, as the *Tampa* was boarded by Special Air Service troops and held in place, emergency legislation was introduced into Parliament to prevent it moving further towards Christmas Island.

The Border Protection Bill 2001 sought, according to its explanatory memorandum, 'for more abundant caution, to ensure that there is no doubt about the Government's ability to order ships to leave Australia's territorial waters'.[4] It allowed Australian officers to use force if necessary to remove any ship in Australian territorial waters, without the fear of prosecution under criminal or civil law. It was written to apply retroactively if brought into law.

While this legislation was quickly passed in the House of Representatives, it was defeated in the Senate. And while supportive in general terms of this approach to the *Tampa*, Kim Beazley, the Leader of the Opposition, told the House that the legislation was inappropriately broad in its effects, that he was unhappy with the limited time given to consider it, and that the Coalition was playing 'wedge politics', even though he agreed that the *Tampa* needed to be managed.[5] Senator John Faulkner, the Leader of the Opposition in the Senate, echoed these concerns, telling the Senate that 'we are prepared to consider whatever legal action the government may wish to propose to deal specifically with the MV *Tampa* situation' but this Bill was 'another example – another desperate gambit from an unpopular Prime Minister about to face the electorate – of wedge politics'.[6]

Despite the Bill's fate, the government very quickly excised Christmas Island from Australia's migration zone and created the Pacific Solution in order to detain asylum seekers in Nauru. Soon after, those waiting on the *Tampa* were forcibly removed to Nauru. While this set of actions was carried out by the Coalition government, it was overwhelmingly supported by the Labor Opposition, who, as historian James Jupp has written, 'had no policy on immigration worthy of the name and followed … behind the Coalition when the *Tampa* crisis broke'.[7]

The introduction of the Border Protection Bill 2001 and the controversy surrounding it raised the situation of the *Tampa* to the status of a crisis. The Children Overboard affair in October – and its false claims around what refugee parents will do to their children – created another crisis, heightening the feelings for some of a national emergency. These were crises created for clear political ends. They were a success for the government, and a disaster for these asylum seekers and all who would come after.

One former ministerial adviser in the Immigration portfolio explained to me that she understood that successive governments – particularly from the *Tampa* on – would routinely identify 'a need to put a shock through the system': '*Tampa* was a shock through the system, I think … the governments get to a point where it's just like (a) we're not managing and (b) this can't continue. [And they start thinking] What can we do to jolt it? [T]hat might be a very benevolent view of *Tampa* – *Tampa* could've just been just a really evil thing, I don't know… but I suspect that was part of the thinking … It's very much the sort of language that the Department used: well if we do this it'll jolt something upstream. You used to talk about sort of upstream, so it's like, you know, migration flows – migration flows upstream.'[8]

Creating a 'jolt' would, it was perceived, enable the government to control what was happening and the terms in which events would be discussed. It would enable them to 'stop the boats': to control the movement of people across the borders and the stories that would be told about this movement. Such language is radically, shockingly, devoid of the recognition that there are humans at the centre of what is being talked about. And we can also observe that these 'jolts' and 'circuit breakers', which successive governments have devised, have leaned towards the punitive, rather than towards open borders and a greater emphasis on settlement support, justice and solidarity.

These moments tell us how political parties and political operatives can work, and open up the possibility of understanding how a shared language around crisis has developed. Policymakers have taken on this idea that unsanctioned immigration events are crises, or can be communicated as crises. The deployment of this language of crisis is dehistoricising, as it works to strip people of their histories – of the reasons they are on the move.

The language of crisis is used not only by politicians and political parties, but also by bureaucrats. The notion of a 'jolt' was echoed by Sandi Logan in an interview with journalist James Button. As Button wrote in 2018,

> Sandi Logan had been the [Immigration] department's media spokesperson for nearly 10 years when the offshore [immigration detention] centres were reopened in 2012. 'My fingerprints are all over it,' he says. 'I thought the policy was designed to put *a short-term jolt* to the people-smuggling model. In the short term, I could live with Manus and Nauru, as detestable as they were. All these years later, I don't sleep easily at night at the thought that people are still there, having their lives destroyed.'

Logan continued, 'Immigration is not just about asylum seekers but that is what it has become. That is the greatest tragedy of my time there.'[9] It is notable that Logan frames his concern around what he could live with, rather than what those in these immigration prisons could be expected to live with.

This form of crisis-making has a broader history within settler-colonial governments. The Northern Territory National Emergency Response – more commonly known as the Intervention – was created and sustained by a moral panic around child abuse. It followed the June 2007 release of the *Ampe Akelyernemane Meke Mekarle: Little Children are Sacred* report, co-authored by Rex Wild QC and Patricia Anderson, members of the Northern Territory Board of Inquiry into the Protection of Aboriginal Children from Sexual Abuse. In the lead-up to the 2007 federal election, the Howard government exploited this report to enact the *Northern Territory National Emergency Response Act 2007*, which imposed harsh measures around alcohol use, pornography and access to welfare payments in Indigenous communities, and was exempt from provisions of the *Racial Discrimination Act 1975*. Many have written about how the government leveraged imaginaries of a crisis around child abuse, and racist discourses centred on the idea that the government should offer protection for Aboriginal children from 'bad parents', to implement a range of colonialist practices targeting Aboriginal communities in the Northern Territory.[10] The government used concern for children to institute a range of measures, most of which had little to do with children, but impinged on the lives and freedoms of Aboriginal people in an attempt to control them, and which through their use of incarceration (among other measures) have severely hampered Aboriginal children's lives in the Northern Territory. There was no process of community consultation prior to the Intervention: these measures relied on the ideas of Aboriginal communities put forward by the 'White Witness', rather than the 'Black Witness', as Darumbal and South Sea Islander journalist, writer and academic Amy McQuire explains it. Within this schema, 'Aboriginal people in remote communities are either victims or perpetrators – they are never afforded any complexity, despite the diversity of histories, languages, cultures and traditions.'[11] Importantly, the Intervention and the treatment of refugee children used similar languages of colonial control – the assertion was that both Aboriginal and refugee children lived in crisis conditions, faced harm and required the state to intervene in their lives.[12]

The leveraging of this moral panic discourse, alongside a discourse of deficit, continues into the present. It crops up regularly in the media. For instance, on 19 June 2022, when Opposition leader Peter Dutton was asked on ABC's *Insiders* about his thoughts on an Indigenous Voice to Parliament and constitutional change, he responded in part: 'I want to see the reduction in the violence against women and children, particularly the sexual violence against children in Aboriginal communities. I don't want to see little kids in Indigenous communities in our country in the year 2022 locking themselves in shipping containers to get through the night to save themselves from being sexually assaulted. And that is what's happening. So I want to see that practical effort.'[13]

In the Intervention, as with the *Tampa*, and as with the other examples we will see in this chapter, a crisis was produced, and a securitised response – one aimed at controlling the conversation and restricting the lives of the people subjected to the crisis narrative – was employed. In this way, the political mobilisation of crisis has become thoroughly normative in Australia, as a settler-colonial practice aimed at maintaining control over the population. Again, the constant work of population control is a fundamental part of settler-colonial projects.

When it comes to refugees, the language and practice of government has been inclined towards crisis particularly since the *Tampa*. But this builds on a much longer history of the imperial institution of borders, colonial control of movement across those borders, and the use of incarceration as a form of control from the very beginnings of the colony that would become Australia.

What does a 'refugee crisis' look like?

Many around the world talk about 'the refugee crisis' when describing the movement of people seeking asylum. But, as Glasgow-based historian Benjamin Thomas White has shown, the use of this terminology of 'crisis' is inaccurate and 'misleading, but also counterproductive', as 'talking about the unprecedented scale of current displacement reduces the complexity of many different displacements, with many different causes, to a single and impossibly huge "crisis"'. That is, it is dehistoricising, dehumanising and obfuscating.[14]

One way of understanding successive Australian governments' apparent fixation on a refugee crisis on our shores arose for me from the interview with the senior Labor figure that I discussed at the beginning of this chapter. Walking away from that interview, I found myself thinking about the ideas of crisis Naomi Klein offers in her book *The Shock Doctrine*. That is, thinking about crisis as a space to build from, in a colonial, capitalist and patriarchal fashion. Crisis, in this formulation, can be mined for gain, whether consciously or unconsciously: political gain in the form of election wins, or gains in the form of moulding Australia into the kind of place these politicians desire. *The Shock Doctrine*'s epigraph comes from Milton Friedman, whom Klein terms 'one of the original shock doctors': 'Only a crisis – actual or perceived – produces real change. When that crisis occurs, the actions that are taken depend on the ideas that are lying around.'[15] Both of these points are crucial for my exploration here: that crisis (actual or perceived) creates the basis for manufacturing change, and that existing group languages, discourses, understandings of society and feelings about people and their modes of interrelationship determine what change will occur.

In a discussion of responses to Hurricane Katrina, Klein explains that she 'call[s] these orchestrated raids on the public sphere in the wake of catastrophic events, combined with the treatment of disasters as exciting market opportunities, "disaster capitalism"'.[16] I want to adopt and adapt this approach, to understand more acutely something potentially uncomfortable to confront: despite their claims to always be acting out of generosity and care, some (not all, but some) policymakers perceive, describe and use crises in ways that take advantage of suffering. Some (again, not all, but some) use crises as a tool of government practice that relies on exploitation and extraction in the service of building a new approach. Some, we must recognise, use crises in violent ways. The immigration prisons are an example of this, as are restrictions on access to healthcare, education and work rights for some refugees. But there are many more examples. Klein talks of the shock doctrine, and Friedman's tactic, as a way 'to advance a fundamentalist version of capitalism', and I think we can see the approaches to child refugee policy in Australia in the twenty-first century as being part of this vision of capitalism, and part of the growth of the carceral border regime around Australia and internationally. It is a mode of governance and policymaking that 'exploit[s] crisis and disaster', building a 'vast, clean canvas' from which to develop, in Klein's terms.[17] It has generated large amounts of income for private companies. It has yielded large numbers of votes for those most willing to exploit it politically. Seen through this lens, for policymakers there is a utility in understanding and creating moments as crisis events, narrated as problems and cast as opportunities. Through this thinking, the 'dead cat approach' becomes even more troubling.

Miriam Ticktin explains that the timeframe of emergency acts as a dehistoricising agent. An emergency, or a crisis, seems to 'require immediate action'. 'With this temporal perspective,' she says, 'there is no way to understand events in a larger historical context, no time to think of the past or plan for the future'.[18] Crisis collapses time. Brian Massumi, a social theorist, argues that in the twenty-first century we are in a time of fear of 'future threat' – of the feeling that there is future danger that we need to be protected from. Threat is 'affectively self-causing' ('if we feel a threat, there was a threat') and permanent ('if we feel a threat such that there was a threat, then there will always will have been a threat. Threat is once and for all, in the nonlinear time of its own causing.')[19] A key example that Massumi uses is to show how the feeling of a potential threat was all George W. Bush needed to invade Iraq.[20]

Through these three writers, we can understand the productive power that language and feelings about crisis hold – the potential they contain for policymakers to tell stories about the kinds of governance and control they feel they are required to create and authorise. We can understand that policymakers seek to build a future for the Australian nation-state – a project that is always being undertaken, for a nation-state is always being made – but they do so through the production of 'no future' for many refugee children (and 'no future' for First Nations children).[21] And they do so through a limited repertoire of ideas, actions and languages.

Crisis controlled and refused

On 15 December 2010, a boat carrying asylum seekers crashed at Christmas Island, in a maritime tragedy that made news around the country. *Janga* was carrying Iranian, Iraqi and stateless asylum seekers, as well as an Indonesian crew, when its engine failed and propelled it towards a dangerous outcrop, where it was dashed against the rocks. Both those on board and residents on Christmas Island had called the Australian authorities to report a vessel in distress, but the authorities were remarkably slow to respond. Christmas Island residents watched from the cliffs as passengers screamed for help when the hull broke apart and they were catapulted into the water. Residents threw lifejackets and safety equipment into the water to help the drowning passengers, but for many, it was to no avail. *Janga*, which the Australian authorities labelled SIEV 221, was carrying ninety-two people, and only forty-two survived.

Footage captured by Christmas Island residents was shown widely on Australian television. It is horrific. One survivor, Hassan, told researchers Linda Briskman and Michelle Dimasi:

> If the Navy could have come a little bit closer to the rocks to save people ... I don't know what happened but one speed boat it came to save only one of the people, one person, then going back to the Navy boat, smoking and looking, but then staying there for a while before they came back. They could have picked up seven or eight people at one time [but] they didn't do so. It seems they didn't care about us. If they had been quicker, only by two or three minutes, they would have saved the people ... We owe our lives to the people of Christmas Island, not the Australian Navy. The life jackets they threw us made us to survive.[22]

Another survivor lost his wife and three-month-old son: he told the 2011 coronial inquest into the disaster that he saw his son's body floating in the water six metres away from him, but his wife had disappeared. Her body was never recovered. 'We have suffered enough and we can't sleep during the night because as soon as we shut our eyes, all these scenes and memories come to our eyes … Who's going to answer for that?'[23]

When I discussed this crash with a former ministerial adviser, she told me, 'You can't underestimate how shell-shocked [government] people were. Some of the ministers that went up to Christmas Island were just traumatised by what happened.'[24]

Numerous other interviewees mentioned this to me as a key event that shaped their feelings about refugee policy. It has had a profound effect on those in the Australian Labor Party in particular, as Labor was in government then. Matt Thistlethwaite, Member of Parliament for Kingsford Smith, told me that he was deeply affected, as someone involved in the lifesaving community. 'I was just looking at it thinking, geez, get in there and save them,' he told me. 'You could just see these people drowning. Jump in and bloody well save them. That's the natural reaction that someone as a lifesaver has. But I understand that that couldn't be done because it was quite a dangerous situation and a lot of those people wouldn't have had the skills that a lifesaver has or the devices that a lifesaver uses … but that really changed a lot of my view of that. It was just a tragedy that so many people could drown in front of everyone's eyes really, in front of the nation's eyes.'[25]

This moment, he told me, had 'a massive effect in changing a lot of people's views'. 'It certainly did within the Party. So, we then started to try to work on well, how do you – how do you still become compassionate, how do you take your fair share of refugees, given what's happening internationally, but stop people from putting themselves in those dangerous situations, because a lot of the evidence that we were receiving was that they're vulnerable people. Because they might get to Indonesia, they're told that – [by] the UNHCR – that well, you're going to have to wait eight to ten years if you want to go to Australia. If you've got kids that's your kids' education, gone,' he said.

'So they're vulnerable and they're manipulated by people who can say, "Well, I can get you there in the next six months." They don't tell you that it's going to be on an overcrowded boat and you're going to – there won't be lifejackets, travelling across a rough stretch of sea, you don't swim, you don't know how to swim, and you're risking your life. So that was the policy dilemma really for us: how do you make it safe but still show compassion and generosity?'

I am not aiming to adjudicate on whether claims to emotional stress, sadness and desperation on the part of those in power are genuinely felt. But I am trying to understand what work the description of these feelings – whether they are being discussed in an interview with a historian, or in a caucus meeting, or with a journalist – does. Here, the problem is identified as people (including children) boarding boats and risking death on the seas – 'putting themselves in these dangerous situations'. And the solution is understood to rest in the governmental management of people's movements and access to border crossing, to balance restriction with 'compassion and generosity' in a formulation determined by the policymakers. It is always a government's ideas, a government's understanding of the events and the possible solutions, which become pre-eminent. We need to question why governments are so rarely seen as being responsible for creating the conditions that allow for such tragedies to occur.

In 2017, I discussed with a former ministerial adviser in the Immigration portfolio the role of ministerial decisions in removing people from detention, or other forms of ministerial intervention into people's claims for asylum. She explained some of the different situations and factors. There was a reluctance in both the Immigration minister's office and the department to release those who were self-harming, as they believed this would be considered a 'reward'. The best response was a refusal to engage, they believed. For her, this constituted a particularly difficult part of the job: '[T]he hardest job in the office were the people who answered the phones: people would be ringing up abusing you saying, "You're all hard arses and you're this and you're cruel and you're horrible," and other people are ringing up and saying, "You're not being hard enough," and you didn't know which phone call you were taking every day, and that would happen. When there was something blowing up it would just come in. We'd be getting it from both sides, which was horrendous.'[26]

I have thought a lot about this comment. She had been incredibly welcoming: hosting me in her home, buying lunch, looking through her files for information, talking with me at length and generally being engaged, interested and supportive of my research. We were two white, middle-class women chatting. Yet in this moment she describes people self-harming – inscribing on their bodies the depth of their need for asylum in ways that those of us who have never experienced such trauma can scarcely imagine. She describes the dreadful emotional impact of allowing people to self-harm and the effects on staffers of taking phone calls. And reiterates the wisdom of doing nothing. I think of this as a moment of crisis refused. Many of those who are self-harming are also attempting to force a crisis, but this crisis is of a fundamentally different nature to the Friedman notion that Naomi Klein critiques and that policymakers work to institute. Refugees are attempting to force a response that recognises their claims. But those with the power and authority to intervene too often turn away. The department refuses to see an epidemic of self-harm as a crisis, denying the historical context and discourse these asylum seekers and refugees claim. Instead, senior staffers tell a story of suffering also endured by politicians, advisers and staffers.

We see this pattern again and again. In 2016, the so-called 'Nauru files' – a collection of 'more than 2,000 leaked reports from Australia's detention camp for asylum seekers' in Nauru – were published by *The Guardian*. The journalists explained: '*The Guardian*'s analysis of the files reveal that children are vastly over-represented in the reports. More than half of the 2,116 reports – a total of 1,086 incidents, or 51.3% – involved children, although children made up only about 18% of those in detention in Nauru during the time covered by the reports, May 2013 to October 2015.' The release of these documents, some of which 'contain distressing examples of behaviour by traumatised children', led to a parliamentary inquiry, but no substantial policy or practical changes.[27] The desire to provoke a crisis was clear, but the cry went unheeded.

The former ministerial adviser informed me that she cannot imagine any government allowing asylum seekers who arrive without permit to be granted free entry on arrival any time soon. She has 'had arguments with plenty of advocates', and her view is 'get over mandatory [detention] … no government's ever going to get rid of mandatory detention … particularly in the current environment. No government is going to put themselves in the position … that someone has arrived on a boat or arrived on a plane and three weeks later blows up the Sydney Opera House. They're just not going to do it. They're not going to leave themselves wide open for that. And that's actually what the Australian people want, so, that's the political reality … It's a really challenging space.'[28]

Stories of national security – that is, of the 'risk management' needed to avoid a potential 'crisis'– dominate the media headlines. Yet my interviews also tell of the brutality of the society in which this border regime exists. They tell of the fundamental problem that is woven into the fabric of a settler-colonial government.[29]

In 2015, paediatricians Professor Elizabeth Elliott and Dr Hasantha Gunasekera conducted a 'monitoring visit' to the detention centre at Wickham Point in Darwin, in order to report to the Australian Human Rights Commission on 'the health and well-being of children in immigration detention'. As part of their visit, they asked children and their parents what they would like reported to the AHRC. One sixteen-year-old boy told them, 'The Prime Minister of Australia says he is saving our lives but at the same time he is killing us.' A fifteen-year-old boy said, 'I honestly don't see [a] future. I wish I had died in the ocean.' An eighteen-year-old boy told them, 'I think for dying. I don't see any future. I feel sadness I see no future.' A father of three teenage boys said, 'I have not come to this country to teach my children how to commit suicide.'[30]

When I interviewed Elliott in November 2018, she distinctly remembered the father telling her this. She related more stories of what she had seen, and the conversations she had had, impressing upon me, 'It is not normal for a woman with a young baby to try and kill herself. It's not normal for a seven-year-old child – or not just one, many seven-year-old children – to say they want to kill themselves. It's not that these people realise, you know, what might be manipulative behaviour.'[31]

People become, in queer theorist Sara Ahmed's formulation of the work of emotions, orientated towards certain other peoples, histories and ideas.[32] In my interview extracts with the government staffer, we can see that she is broadly sympathetic to those ringing in with complaints and to those who self-harm, but she identifies strongly with the members of the department who provide advice on how to respond, or with the staffers in the offices receiving the angry phone calls. She expresses sympathy for them while remaining keenly aware of the broader tragedy of the situation. But this may create a false equivalence, whether intended or not.

Indeed, the idea that the governing of refugees is a 'challenging space' for policymakers has a significant history. Refugee policy has long been seen as a difficult 'question' with no ready answer. In a 1978 speech given by Liberal Immigration minister Michael MacKellar, for instance, he affirmed: 'The truth and seriousness of the matter is that Australia is being faced with a massive social, economic, and humanitarian question. The way in which we, as a nation, respond to the challenge will affect not only the internal situation, but our international reputation and relationships in the foreseeable future.'[33] A perplexing question can act as a framework for determining policy creation for the nation. Defining something – or someone – as a question or a problem is to circumscribe how they will be approached.

Crisis and child refugees

Because child refugees are a group imbued with emotional potency, the mobilisation of narratives of crisis have a certain political power and potential. The category of 'refugee children' and the notion of crisis are co-created and interlinked over decades, as ministers and governments pursue their policy goals. There is a fantasy of control – it is imagined that by producing the crisis or disaster, policymakers can direct policy outcomes, as though governments can ever fully command people's movements. This fantasy sits alongside a repudiation of refugees and asylum seekers because they are cast as deliberately and negligently 'willful': 'The willful character insists on willing their own way, without reference to reason or command. Willfulness could be described as a character perversion: to be willful is to deviate, to will one's own way is to will the wrong way,' Ahmed writes.[34] For as political journalist Laura Tingle has explained, 'Howard's greatest political moments came when he persuaded Australians that they – and their government – were in control of events that they didn't feel in control of. His famous battle-cry about asylum seekers arriving by boat – "We will decide who comes to this country, and the circumstances in which they come" – remains the best encapsulation of this.'[35]

In October 2014, the case of Baby Ferouz came before the Brisbane Federal Circuit Court. Baby Ferouz was the pseudonym given to an eleven-month-old born to parents who were asylum seekers in detention in Brisbane at the time of his birth. By the date of the trial they were in detention in Darwin. Born in Mater Hospital, Baby Ferouz was determined to be an 'unauthorised maritime arrival' under the governing legislation, inheriting the status from his parents. As a result, he was due to be sent to detention in Nauru, along with his parents, who were being returned there. Baby Ferouz's lawyers – one of whom was Murray Watt, now Minister for Agriculture, Fisheries and Forestry and Minister for Emergency Management in the Albanese government – sought a ruling from the court that would prevent him and his parents from being sent to Nauru.[36] This ruling would have additionally provided the basis for 100 children born in Australia to asylum-seeking parents to remain. The Brisbane court, however, ruled in favour of the government: Baby Ferouz would not be given a visa to remain in Australia. As *The Guardian* reported, the judge ruled that it was 'clearly the intention of parliament to establish a regime whereby the immigration status of a non-citizen child born in Australia followed or aligned with that of his or her parents'. He accepted the government's argument that otherwise 'there may be more incentive for pregnant women to engage people smugglers and make the dangerous journey across the seas in the hope of a perceived advantage that their child might become entitled to a visa once born'.[37]

The language of stopping boat journeys and deaths at sea, and the ideas of negligent parents and mistreated children, are all part of the production of crisis: it refers back to the lies of Children Overboard, as well as to the discourse that has developed over the last twenty or so years, of the 'need' to 'stop the boats so that children do not drown'. The outcome of this judgement was that Baby Ferouz and one hundred other children were not given extended permission to stay in Australia. They remained at risk of being moved from detention in Australia to detention in Nauru.

Later that year, in December 2014, the Tony Abbott–led Coalition government sought to pass punitive legislation – the Migration and Maritime Powers Legislation Amendment (Resolving the Asylum Legacy Caseload) Bill 2014 – which would entrench this 'classify[ing of] children born in Australia to asylum seeker parents as unauthorised maritime arrivals'.[38] The legislation involved reintroducing temporary protection for people seeking asylum (in the form of Safe Haven Enterprise Visas); introducing a fast-track process that would limit judicial review of applications for asylum; and providing the Immigration minister with extended powers to control and turn back people arriving by boat, among other provisions.

Integral to the passage of this legislation was the Coalition's agreement that children would be removed from detention: it was promised that 'all children in detention on Christmas Island would be out of detention by Christmas Day'. *The Guardian* reported that 'crossbench senator Jacqui Lambie called on [Assistant Immigration Minister Michaelia] Cash to resign if children were not out of detention by Christmas'.[39] Shalailah Medhora, also in *The Guardian*, reported that Clive Palmer, then of the Palmer United Party, told the Senate in voting for the Bill: 'All I care about as a father is that these kids are out of detention.'[40] In a parliamentary speech, Senator Sarah Hanson-Young, the Greens Immigration spokesperson, explained that Scott Morrison, the Minister for Immigration and Border Protection, had organised for children detained on Christmas Island to call Ricky Muir – another crossbench senator, from the Motoring Enthusiast Party – to 'beg that senator to let them out'. 'If that is not treating children as hostages, what is it?' she asked.[41] Hanson-Young described this as an act which 'only a sociopath' would commit, while her Greens colleagues, Senators Christine Milne and Scott Ludlum, echoed her distaste over the use of children as bargaining chips in the passage of this punitive legislation.[42]

While Muir and Morrison denied that such a call had been made, Muir provided the final vote the Coalition required for the passage of the legislation. In doing so, he told the Senate – in a speech characterised by Medhora as 'emotional' – that 'this has been an extremely difficult process for me ... There are many aspects of this bill that I am not comfortable with'.[43] Muir told Parliament that he had 'spoken with people who have worked closely with detainees on Christmas Island' and 'while [he] was speaking to these people and they were informing [him], they started to break down and cry as they were speaking about children who have been in detention since they were born who are two years old. They speak about the word "out". To them "out" means going to church on occasion, and that is it. When they hear the word "out", they cannot begin to associate it with freedom.'[44] Muir made clear that he resented being put into the position of having the casting vote on this Bill, but that the question he faced was, 'if I am to vote this bill down because it is not perfect, am I making a worse decision for the people who desperately want to be processed?' He was, he felt, 'forced into a corner'.[45]

Reportedly as part of the deal with Muir that enabled the passage of the legislation, Morrison agreed that babies born in Australia to parents who had been in detention in Nauru would be allowed to stay and apply for refugee status. Baby Ferouz was one of those. But this agreement had very particular circumstances, applying only to babies born before 4 December 2014 – so it was a political concession used to grease the wheels, rather than a policy change.[46]

In this situation, the Abbott government, and its Immigration minister Morrison, used the grammars and emotions *produced by creating a crisis* facing child refugees in order to buttress the border regime. They relied on the potency of emotional discourses around child refugees – which Muir and others participated in – to reinforce multiple prongs of the refugee policy framework. Indeed, the next year Muir told the Senate: 'Last Thursday I attended an event hosted by [legal firm] Maurice Blackburn to celebrate the release of Australian-born asylum seekers and their families from detention. I met with the children and families that I helped prevent from being deported to Nauru. It was an emotional night and one that I will treasure forever.'[47] Here is an important example of the way that policymaking around child refugees has operated through the production of crisis, pitting people against one another, drawing on the potent emotions around children and the use of the shock doctrine.

Choices in crisis

In the 2005 parliamentary committee discussions regarding the Migration Amendment (Detention Arrangements) Bill – which was designed to alter the conditions under which children could be held in detention and to introduce community detention for them – Liberal Minister for Immigration and Multicultural and Indigenous Affairs Amanda Vanstone asserted, 'What the government want to do is maintain strong border protection. We are very pleased that we have largely stopped people coming on boats. We hope that no more lives are lost by people taking a chance on those rickety, stinking, unsafe vessels to come in monsoon time, or at other times, and put their lives at risk.'[48] Vanstone went on to talk about the 'choices' that politicians are forced to make between 'policy alternatives' – whether to face the 'crisis' of boats arriving, or to keep child asylum seekers in detention – when 'you do not want either of them but you have to have one. Or you are forced to choose between alternatives when you want both of them but you cannot have both'. 'Government,' Vanstone said, 'is not about the luxury of writing on a whiteboard what is the ideal world ... It is not about the luxury of sitting in academia and saying, "what would be ideal?" It is about what must be done in the national interest at this time and what is fair.'[49]

There is, we have seen, a routine rhetorical deployment of discourses of fears of boats, drownings and the problems of detention. There is also the deployment of discourses of crisis and what we could call 'being stuck in a bind'. As we shall see in more detail in subsequent chapters, these binds are of politicians' making. A crisis is created, and that crisis then limits the possible responses. It is a kind of path dependency: 'choosing between alternatives', as Vanstone framed it, is a frame of mind in public policy, not a universal truth.

This approach to public policy is part of a broader approach that relies on mobilising successive crises in order to continue the work of colonising Australia. The maintenance of the border, and control over the population of this country, is ongoing. Discourses of crisis – the understanding that governing through crisis is a way to maintain control, the embracing and refusal of different crises, the production of an emotional community that understands crisis in certain ways, the limiting of options through the timeframe of emergency produced by a crisis, and the use of refugee children as a potent mobilising force – are integral to this project.

CHAPTER 4

Legislation

Writing to the Australian Human Rights Commission's National Inquiry into Children in Immigration Detention, an unaccompanied child detained in the Australian immigration prison in Nauru penned this poem:

> I want freedom.
> I need freedom.
> What is my future. I am 17 years old. I don't have my mother.
> I am U.A.M.
> I want freedom.
> I need freedom.
> Please consider my loss of human rights.
> and who took these from me.
> Thank you For Listening. very much.'[1]

Unaccompanied refugee and asylum-seeking children are primarily controlled by two pieces of legislation in Australia: the *Migration Act 1958* and the *Immigration (Guardianship of Children) Act 1946*. The former controls all migrants, all refugees and asylum seekers who seek to come to these shores; the latter only those children who travel without parents or guardians. It gives them a guardian: the Immigration minister. Currently this means that Andrew Giles is their legal guardian. Before that, Alex Hawke; before that, David Coleman; before that, Peter Dutton; before that, Scott Morrison. And so on.

But what does it mean in practice? And why is this legislation so important?

Government bureaucracies aim to contain, control and define. By writing about children in certain ways, using specific vocabularies and controlling them through legal instruments, government bureaucracies can create a body of knowledge around a population or a category of person. In this chapter we can understand this legislation as being part of the bureaucracy that creates the legal category of the 'child refugee or asylum seeker'. The *Immigration (Guardianship of Children) Act 1946* functions as what migration theorists Suvendrini Perera and Joseph Pugliese have termed 'law as an apparatus of biopolitical governmentality', or a tool for governing, regulating and administering the health and life of the population.[2] Law is central to government. As criminologist Maria Giannacopoulos explains, 'In Australia, as in many other settler-colonial countries globally, it is law that imposes colonial ordering over stolen territories while disguising the inherent violence of these practices by deeming them lawful.'[3] In geographer Jennifer Hyndman's phrasing, we can understand that the Act is one mechanism for 'disciplining displacement', a way of organising people who are on the move.[4] Attached to this, we can understand that childhood, as Katy Gardner, an anthropologist, has framed it, is 'discursive rather than an empirical fact': it is created through stories and narratives or, more broadly, through various ways of describing. This Act, with its various permutations over time, is one site for the creation of these categories in Australia. This Act, and its history, is uniquely Australian: no other country has legislation like it.

The Act produces a kinship relationship between child and guardian. In doing so it draws on histories of who Australian governments have seen as fit parents, and propels those ideas into the future. And so the Act helps to create the idea that the unaccompanied child refugee is dependent on the Minister for Immigration. The minister is seen as the responsible figure and social workers and government bureaucracies are corralled into supporting this relationship of guardian and dependant. This flows on from the histories we have seen in previous chapters, of how governments interact with Aboriginal and Torres Strait Islander children, or how refugee and asylum-seeking parents were imagined in the Children Overboard affair.

A brief history of the Act

While Australian state and federal governments have been acting as the guardian for child migrants since around World War I, the post–World War II era ushered in the modern period of governing unaccompanied child migrants. In 1946, as the National Security (Overseas Children) Regulations came to their conclusion with the end of the war and its accompanying legislative framework, the governing Labor Party introduced a Bill to cover some of the gaps they felt would be left. This proposed legislation, the Immigration (Guardianship of Children) Bill 1946, would 'enable the Immigration Minister to continue as the legal guardian of overseas children who remain in Australia and also as legal guardian of children brought to Australia under any governmental or non-governmental organisation',[5] and had been suggested by a meeting of the state and territory migration authorities held on 20 August 1946. This meeting had 'resolved that the Commonwealth should continue to be the sole authority for migration activities overseas and that the States and territories would carry out the function of reception on arrival in Australia', with these functions often delegated to private agencies.[6] This legislation, then, would cover the mostly British unaccompanied children who had been brought to Australia during or soon after World War II, enabling their guardianship arrangements to continue while also providing a mechanism to ensure that any future unaccompanied children would be provided with a guardian.[7] The legislation was framed as a means to 'prevent exploitation' of the children and their labour, and it was noted in Parliament and by newspapers that the powers of guardianship would be 'delegated to officers of welfare departments in each state, but could be terminated at any moment in respect of any child'.[8] These facets of the legislation would then become the Act, creating a situation where the Minister for Immigration was the guardian for those child migrants who were unaccompanied by any parent or immediate relative who could act as a guardian, until such time as they reached the age of twenty-one, left Australia or became citizens. The responsibilities of this guardianship could be delegated, and provision was put in place for the minister to exclude, by regulation, a class of migrant children from the Act, if they so desired.

While by the mid-1970s the Act would be applied to all unaccompanied migrant, refugee and asylum-seeker children, in this post–World War II period the Act was primarily aimed at providing guardianship for the British migrant children who were 'brought to Australia under voluntary migration schemes sponsored by social welfare organisations and church bodies'.[9] These children, legal scholars Mary Crock and Jacqueline Bhabha explain, faced 'appalling conditions' wherein they were 'subject[ed] to systematic abuse' by the organisations that housed them, as they were used 'as a source of cheap and easily exploitable labor': 'Vigorous campaigning about the plight of these victims ... led to [the scheme's] abandonment in the late 1970s, with a renewed emphasis on governmental control over all aspects of the child migration program'.[10] In 2009, the Australian government apologised to them for their mistreatment.[11] During this era though, as historian Klaus Neumann has noted, 'Australia's DP [Displaced Persons] program included surprisingly few unaccompanied minors, and discriminated against large families. Australia's resettlement of DPs favoured workers.' Of those refugees and Displaced Persons who came through the postwar International Refugee Organization scheme, Neumann explains, 'it was not until the arrival of the *Castel Bianco* in April 1949 that the first unaccompanied minors arrived in Australia'.[12]

The then Immigration minister, Arthur Calwell, heavily favoured an expansive migration program for Australia – an important step, he believed, to create the much-needed 'bigger population if we are to hold this land for ourselves and our children'.[13] This, it should be clear, is coloniser talk: taking Aboriginal land and holding it by populating it with white migrants is key to Australian settler colonialism. Using a range of evocative bodily metaphors, Calwell later told Parliament: 'We Australians are a young and virile people and our national heart beats strongly. But the body, of which that heart is the motivating force, is a huge land mass, an island continent of some three million square miles with 12,000 miles of coastline. Before a body of such vast dimensions can be operated at full efficiency, its heart must beat strongly and be fed by the extra lifeblood which only new citizens can supply.'[14]

As well as expounding the virtues of increased immigration, Calwell discussed the financial functioning of the Act, explaining that costs would be split between the Commonwealth and the states. This ensured that the whole country was invested in the growth of Australia's white European migrant population.

In the 1946 parliamentary debates for the Act, Liberal MP Thomas White raised concerns on behalf of himself and Dame Enid Lyons that the legislation 'lacks a provision for the adoption of children by private families'. White was married to Vera Deakin White – daughter of Alfred, Australia's second Prime Minister, and greatly involved in the Red Cross – which perhaps influenced his perspective. In his speech, White expressed his feeling that '[w]elfare workers and sociologists, who have been in close touch with this work, agree that the principal need of children is human affection, which is found more in the home than in any institution. The present scheme will "institutionalize" the children.'[15] This sentiment was picked up by others over the following years, with amendments introduced in 1948 to allow private individuals to act as carers for these unaccompanied migrant children. Other amendments provided for the minister to be the guardian of the child's estate as well as their person, and specified that any child covered by the Act would need to receive permission from the minister before leaving Australia. These amendments, Calwell explained, were based on the experiences of those working with the Act and were made on the advice of 'officers expert in child welfare administration' – not, it should be noted, on the advice of the children governed by the Act. Calwell further explicated that '[t]he purpose of the act is to ensure that immigrant children shall be provided with the care and supervision which they would normally expect to receive from their parents or next of kin'.[16] The provision allowing private individuals to act as a custodian for an immigrant child was referred to in the press and in Parliament as necessary, for 'a second-rate home was often better than a first-class institution'.[17]

Legislation

Within the Act there is, like any other Act, the scope to make orders and regulations. In 1950, Harold Holt, the Minister of State for Immigration, directed under Sections 4 and 11 'that the provisions of the *Immigration (Guardianship of Children) Act 1946–1948* shall not apply to any immigrant child, selected by the Commonwealth Government as a displaced person or a refugee under its current agreement with the International Refugee Organisation, and who has or had attained the age of eighteen years at the time of disembarkation in Australia'.[18] That is, the Act was now specifically to exclude refugee children over the age of eighteen, as a class, from its considerations. Those children who were refugees or Displaced Persons would be treated differently to other immigrant children, who would be covered by the Act until aged twenty-one. By 1956, however, this would no longer be the case, as all the Hungarian refugee children who were brought to Australia were provided with guardianship by the Immigration minister.[19]

From this point on, the Act was applied to refugee children who came from Europe, including Jewish children in the 1940s and Hungarian children in the 1950s. But, crucially, in accordance with the requirements of White Australia policies, it was not until 1974 that non-European children were covered by the Act.[20] At this time, with the arrival of larger numbers of refugee children from Vietnam and surrounds, the Act began to be applied in earnest to unaccompanied non-European refugee children. In 1983, amendments to the legislation replaced 'immigrant' with 'non-citizen' in specifying who was covered by the Act. The work of categorising people is never done.

Other amendments have altered the group of children governed by the Act, as well as who could be considered a guardian. These changes have included the age-based definition of a child, which changed in 1983 from those under twenty-one to those under eighteen.

Since 1985, a non-citizen child who is governed by this Act has also been a person who 'intends, or is intended, to become a permanent resident of Australia'; these amendments enabled the Immigration minister to 'direct that a person under 18 years of age shall be a ward of the Minister notwithstanding that that person entered Australia' with a guardian. The amendments required that the 'relative who is charged with caring for the person consents to the Minister assuming guardianship'.

Amendments in 1994 altered the legislation so that the Immigration minister was no longer responsible for children entering Australia for the purposes of adoption, while amendments in 2008 – which came as part of the *Same-Sex Relationships (Equal Treatment in Commonwealth Laws – General Law Reform) Act 2008* – provided new gender-neutral definitions of 'parent' and 'relative'. These changes expanded the definition of who was eligible to provide legal guardianship to children – meaning these children would thus then not be considered as covered by the Act.[21] Amendments passed as part of the *Migration Legislation Amendment (Offshore Processing and Other Measures) Act 2012* – which amended both the *Migration Act* and the *Immigration (Guardianship of Children) Act* – allowed the government to assert the primacy of the former over the latter. This meant the government could make and implement 'any decision to remove, deport or take a non-citizen child from Australia', enabling the offshore detention and processing of all child asylum seekers.[22] This significant measure was further strengthened by amendments made in 2014 to the powers held by the government under the *Maritime Powers Act 2013*.[23] Interestingly, the introduction of the foundational migration legislation, the *Migration Act*, in 1958 produced no amendments to the Act.

Since the creation of the Act, the Immigration minister's guardianship obligations are considered to have ended when the child reaches adulthood, becomes a citizen or leaves Australia permanently. Since 2012, 'leaving Australia permanently' was considered to have occurred if, among other things, the child was 'taken from Australia to a regional processing country'.[24] That is, if they were taken to immigration prisons in Nauru or Papua New Guinea. These regimes of detention are uniquely Australian – nowhere else in the world has a program of indefinite offshore detention for all asylum seekers, including children, who come by boat. However, the United Kingdom – influenced by Australia – is in the process of trying to establish a system to remove some refugees to Rwanda, and Donald Trump, when President of the United States, applauded Australia's treatment of refugees in a phone call with then Prime Minister Malcolm Turnbull, and later on social media.

The Immigration minister has also always been able to delegate some of the responsibilities of guardianship and has regularly done so, to departments of Social Service or Community Service or similar bodies, and to private companies running immigration detention centres in each of the states or territories. As just one example of how this all plays out, with the Australian Immigration minister no longer the guardian for children in detention in Nauru, in 2015 Save the Children was delegated as the guardian by the Nauruan Minister for Justice.[25]

This brief history demonstrates a broad consensus among successive governments that unaccompanied child migrants in general, and, for our purposes, child refugees and asylum seekers in particular, require forms of support from the government. As we saw in Chapter 2, the Convention on the Rights of the Child, introduced in 1989 internationally and in 1990 in Australia, emphasises the 'best interests of the child' and proposes that children be primarily regarded through the lens of considerations of rights, but this Act demonstrates a different approach to decision-making.[26] Australia's accession to the UN Convention on the Rights of the Child did not result in any amendments being made to the Act. The explanatory memorandum for the 2014 amendments to the Act, when weighed against the Convention, explicitly states that

> in developing the policies reflected in this Bill, the government has treated the best interests of the child as a primary consideration. However, it is Government policy to discourage unauthorised arrivals from taking potentially life threatening avenues to achieve resettlement for their families in Australia and this, as well as the integrity of the onshore protection programme, are also primary considerations which may outweigh the best interests of the child in relation to a particular measure.[27]

So, this is an Act that has been amended in various ways, each time – in Harold Holt's words – to 'strengthen the administration' of this aspect of the 'immigration programme'.[28] Yet as the Act began to apply to increasing numbers of Vietnamese children, the provision of services became increasingly difficult to administer: the bureaucratic and service infrastructure was not in place to properly account for all the children covered by the Act, or to provide the settlement services and support they required.[29] Throughout the Act's existence, however, there has been one constant: guardianship was vested in the Commonwealth minister, while it was the responsibility of the states and territories to provide the day-to-day services. So while the minister might have delegated the functions of guardianship, they remained the legal guardian. This point is crucial: throughout the history of this Act, the children who were subject to its control – whose lives in

Australia were, I argue, in some ways both discursively and materially constructed by its control – were considered to be both children and migrants, travelling alone across borders and requiring the guardianship of the Immigration minister.

These children have not been, of course, passive recipients of care and control. There are important stories to be told about the ways in which these categories are lived and contested; those stories, however, are not to be found in government archives or storytelling. They are also not my stories to tell.

So how has the Act functioned? How have, as historians Shurlee Swain and Dorothy Scott described, children subjected to these types of government care and protection legislation been seen 'as both victim and threat, savage and waif'?[30]

How long does one remain a migrant (and so need a guardian)?

In 1975, the Act faced its first challenge at the High Court. In *R v Director-General of Social Welfare (Vic); Ex parte Henry*, as legal scholar Michael Coper explains, an Australian husband and wife – Raymond Maxwell Henry and Joan Olive Henry – 'arranged for the transfer of a four-year-old South Vietnamese girl from South Vietnam to Australia', but 'on her arrival in Australia she was placed under the control of the Director-General of Social Welfare for Victoria with a view to her adoption by a couple other than the applicants'.[31]

The child, named as Nguyen Thi Nhung, had arrived in Australia on 18 April 1975 and was taken to the Infectious Diseases Hospital at Fairfield, 'where she stayed for some days under the control of the Director-General before being placed with temporary foster parents'.[32] In authorising the child's adoption, the Director-General was acting as a delegate for the Immigration minister, who, following the provisions provided by the Act, was the guardian of the child. The Henrys 'disputed the validity of the Act, and therefore of the Minister's guardianship, and sought custody of the child by habeas corpus proceedings'.[33] The case focused on Section 6 of the Act, querying whether it breached Section 51 of the Constitution. That is, whether the Act breached the Immigration powers. Or, to put it another way, whether the child was to still be understood as a migrant.[34]

This case sat within a large and complex history of judicial deliberations regarding the make-up of the category of 'migrant' produced by the Australian Constitution. The Henrys were not victorious: the High Court ruled that the child remained a migrant and was thus governed by the Act.[35] While the judgement was unanimous, a range of opinions were voiced as to why the Director-General maintained the authority to decide who could adopt the child. All of them centred on a discussion of how long, and why, the minister remained the guardian for such children.

Justice Gibbs explained that he

> consider[ed] that a person who has immigrated to Australia will pass beyond the range of the [Immigration] power when the act of immigration is at an end – that is when that person has become a full member of the Australian community. It follows, in my opinion, that the Parliament can attach to the entry of an immigrant who is a child the condition that the child have a suitable guardian and can ensure that the guardianship subsists until the child has been fully absorbed into the Australian community.[36]

Justice Stephen noted that 'it is now well established that the concept of immigration extends beyond the actual act of entry into Australia to the process of absorption into the Australian community'.[37] But, he queried, how can a child, travelling alone and 'without legal capacity', become absorbed? This process, he affirmed, could only be gradual. But this raised a question for him about the process of absorption for those children – such as British children – who 'encounter[ed] no obstacles to absorption', particularly after they had been in Australia for a long time. How, Justice Stephen asked, can the Immigration power 'still reach' such a child?[38]

Similarly, Justice Mason expressed his opinion that the 'power extends to the making of laws for the general welfare and protection of immigrant children so long at any rate *as they continue to possess the character of immigrants*'.[39] Comments such as these, which testify to a particular 'character' held by 'immigrants' (in Mason's phrasing), or to the different experiences of migration (as Stephen articulates), are but one example of how refugee children are repeatedly, across a long period of time, made into refugees. Legislative and judicial determinations racialise children, making judgements about someone's assimilatory processes on the basis of their country of origin.

In his judgement, Justice Murphy focused on the Act's 'protective' function. That is, the Act aimed 'to provide for the supervision' of an immigrant child and to act 'in her best interests'.[40] Referring to the United Nations Declaration on the Rights of the Child, Murphy argued that the Act provided the proper protection and support for unaccompanied immigrant children. Elsewhere, Stephen noted that these immigrants 'being children, lack full capacity'.[41] In this 1975 High Court case, therefore, we see the raising of a range of considerations as the justices sought to grapple with how far the Immigration powers extended; what the Constitution, and the Act, could tell us about how long these children remained immigrants; and what precisely that would mean in terms of their refugee status and their imagined deficiencies as children. But this question of how long unaccompanied children remained immigrants – and thus how long they would be subject to the minister's guardianship – had been present since the very beginnings of the Act.

In his Second Reading speech in 1946, Arthur Calwell told Parliament:

> It is believed that the Commonwealth Government, in encouraging and financially assisting child migration by way of contributions towards passage money and payment of child endowment to organizations caring for the children, accepts a responsibility which does not end with the children's arrival in Australia. It is, therefore, incumbent on the Commonwealth to see that child migrants are properly accommodated and cared for until they reach 21 years of age. The only way in which this can be achieved is by vesting in the Minister for Immigration an overriding legal guardianship in respect of all such children.[42]

This idea that the minister was responsible for caring for the children throughout the stages and processes of absorption and childhood was reported on by newspapers and reiterated by Calwell when discussing the amendments to the Act in 1948.[43] Indeed, over the course of the early years of the Act, these issues would be a focus of discussions surrounding the work conducted by the Act.

In 1952, Senator John Spicer, while discussing amendments to the Act, noted that '[a]part from the desirability of a uniform policy throughout Australia in regard to child immigrants, it is considered that in granting financial aid, the Commonwealth accepts a responsibility which must continue after their arrival in this country'.[44] While in these early years of the Act this applied to immigrant, rather than refugee, children, by the 1975 High Court challenge, the Act's guardianship provisions – and its construction of ideas of the length of time a child remained governed by the Act – had been expanded to include refugee children. Thus, the Act was never intended to provide guardianship for only a brief period. From the Act's inception, the government believed that it was its responsibility to provide care for unaccompanied immigrant children for the full amount of time it would take them to be considered absorbed, or no longer migrants, or until they reached the age of majority.

In discussions surrounding this aspect of the Act, the language used was both highly bureaucratic and highly emotive. There was, it would seem, a sense of care being expressed: a desire for the children's future as Australians to be shaped by their early experiences of guardianship. Senator Robert Clothier, in his Second Reading speech in 1948, noted, 'The Minister is to become the legal guardian of migrant children, and that should give to the parents of overseas children who contemplate sending their children to this country as migrants every assurance that they will be properly cared for'.[45] 'Care' was articulated through assimilation discourse: guardians would help them assimilate. The fact that the Act continued to work on children long after the moment of arrival demonstrates that these children continued to be produced as migrants requiring a guardian. And thus produced as continuously involved in the project of being assimilated. In this way, they were produced as being a different category of person, both different to citizen children and different to children who migrated with their families and guardians. This conceptualisation of their relationships to others determined how they would be governed.

The discussions of the Act very deliberately produced a relationship between children, the future and Australia. This is crucial, for as literary theorist Lee Edelman writes, 'we are no more able to conceive of a politics without a fantasy of the future than we are able to conceive of a future without the figure of the Child'.[46] Historian Jayne Persian explains that in the post–World War II era, Displaced Persons were chosen for Australia on the basis of their perceived assimilability: for instance, Christians from the Baltic states were deemed preferable to Jewish refugees.[47] This was true of child migrants too. Children were seen as preferable to adults due to a perception that they would assimilate more quickly and easily. We can see this view, for instance, in the words of John McEwen, then deputy leader of the Country Party, who asserted in 1948:

> It is generally agreed that it will be to the advantage of Australia to have child migrants, because they are more likely than adult migrants to absorb Australian sentiments to fall into the Australian way of life and, upon reaching adulthood, to be indistinguishable from natural-born Australians. We are, therefore, disposed to favour child migration as against adult migration ... It will be good to have the right kind of children brought here. It would also be good to have the right kind of cattle and sheep brought here. But children should not be brought here merely for the economic benefit of this country. If there is one right to which a human being is entitled, it is the right to the nationality of his native land ... I hope that we shall give priority of consideration to the human aspect and not to the economic aspect of this matter. I know that much can be said in favour of child migration as against adult migration.[48]

This pitting of child migration against adult migration also occurred in Queensland, in a discussion of a children's accommodation, the Shaftesbury Home. A local newspaper claimed in 1949 that 'the Federal Government regards children as the best migrants because they do not present the same accommodation problems as adults and are more easily assimilated into the community'.[49] Harold Holt, then Minister for Labour and National Service, echoed these sentiments in 1953, asserting, 'Generally speaking, these younger people are assimilated more rapidly than people of more mature years and are in a state of mind to accept naturalization after a shorter term of residence than people whose roots have gone down deeply into the countries of their origin.'[50]

The relationship between children and an assimilated future in Australia was developed by the newspapers. Here is *The Sydney Morning Herald* in 1948: 'Mr Calwell said to-day: "Many Australian couples, some of them childless, are anxious to adopt British children – the best migrants Australia could possibly receive."'[51] Later that year the paper again quoted Calwell: '[w]e appreciate that the child migrant is one of Australia's greatest assets, and that family life is the basis of a contented and well-ordered community'.[52] This sentiment in many ways solidifies what the preceding has sought to demonstrate: that through the Act and its accompanying legal procedures and discourses, migrant and refugee children are understood as a specific category of person, not-yet-citizen but moving towards being fully assimilated Australians, whose presence is important in shaping the country in line with what its politicians seek it to be. They are deemed to require the provision of particular legislative and social care, and the Minister for Immigration is viewed as the person best able to provide guardianship to help these children become Australians, or best able to control them.

How does this legislation understand the child?

Of course, while this legislation was being created and amended, the children who would be subject to it were not consulted. They were, like children generally at this time, understood as incapable of asserting their own needs, wants and desires. As I have stressed, this notion of the child as particularly unable to care for themselves and in need of protection echoes across Australian history. For instance, parliamentarian Enid Lyons in 1948 asserted, 'It is probably beyond question that, until a child reaches his majority, his guardian should control his estate as well as his person.'[53]

Lyons – described as an exemplary mother, or caretaker, to the nation – saw herself as an authority on what migrant and refugee children required in order to develop full lives as Australian citizens. 'The institutions and organizations that have undertaken this work [of caring for migrant children] have done it admirably, but there never can be within an institution the intense and personal affection that is necessary to bring a child to its optimum development,' she said in 1948. 'After many years of personal experience and study of this problem, I believe that to every child personal affection and human love are greater needs than good food. A child must develop within its own personality before it can become a happy citizen.'[54]

Through these words Lyons articulated a set of pervasive beliefs about the care and emotional needs of the child. And the force of her sentiments, along with those articulated by others, produces a naturalisation of these historically based ideas. Parliamentarian Annabelle Rankin, for example, expressed a similar view in 1948, asserting, 'we all realize that it is preferable for a child to be reared by a family rather than by an institution. Children need love and affection and a sense of security.'[55] The same ideas are evident in the words of

John Ignatius Armstrong, who told Parliament that '[o]ne difficulty associated with any large attempt to attract migrants to this country is the provision of adequate reception facilities. Whilst that is serious with adults, it is more serious with children.'[56]

These discourses creating an idea of children as distinctly lacking, or as requiring particular care, have pervaded all discussions of unaccompanied child refugees over the course of the life of the Act.[57] While the examples here point us to their origins in the late 1940s, we can also see them emanating from the High Court in their 1975 ruling. Justice Stephen asserted that children 'lack full capacity'. As such, their place of residence 'so long as they remain under disability' must be determined by 'their father': 'For them no change of domicile by the exercise of their own volition is possible.'[58] Stephen refers here to a sense of 'legal capacity', Justice Murphy relies heavily in his judgement on the idea of the 'incapacity' of the child,[59] and Justice Jacobs asserts in his ruling that 'the Parliament has taken the view that there is a speciality in the situation of persons under the age of twenty-one years who enter Australia as immigrants not in the charge of, or for the purpose of living in Australia under the care of, a parent or a relative not less than twenty-one years of age'.[60]

This is perhaps unsurprising – the view that a child is unable to make decisions for themselves remains widely held in Australia today. We can see the effects of this long-held discourse in the narrative that produced Children Overboard, for instance. But it is useful to trace this history, to remember that these ideas are culturally constituted and to understand the work parliamentarians, judges and other figures in power have undertaken to actively foster the idea of children as incapacitated and requiring particular forms of care.

What some may find surprising, given the focus on refugee children needing care, is that the support for refugee children under the Act has been consistently attenuated. In 1978, the Department of Community Welfare Services in Victoria produced a confidential report, 'Services to Isolated Refugee Children', which made clear they felt the federal government was not providing enough financial support for the delegated Victorian government agency to properly look after the children.[61] This problem rang through the 1970s and 1980s. Diane Zulfacar's 1984 report, *Surviving Without Parents: Indo-Chinese Refugee Minors in NSW*, was just one of a series of reports (or notes in meeting minutes) that explained no one knew with any certainty precisely how many unaccompanied children were in Australia.[62] The bureaucratic invisibility of, and lack of proper support for, unaccompanied child refugees is a theme throughout the archives. It is evident, in tracing paperwork sent backwards and forwards within agencies, and in examining reports produced by social welfare administrators and community groups, that decisions about children's care were often made on an ad-hoc basis, with little federal government direction. In July 1976, the Associate Director of Regional Services wrote to the Deputy Director-General of the Immigration department and argued, 'There would appear to be a fairly urgent need to clarify a range of policy issues related to defining responsibility and effective case planning for refugee children.'[63] It was not until 1985 that a cost-sharing agreement between state and federal governments was established – an agreement that remains in place, unaltered, today.[64]

In an interview I conducted in August 2017 with Ian Macphee, Minister for Immigration and Ethnic Affairs from 1979 to 1982, he noted that while he could not remember the work of being a guardian under the Act, he was 'sure that whatever happened if anyone had recommended to me that action be taken in accordance with that I would have, of course, gone along with that. In fact, I would have gone out of my way.' He and other senior officials, he said, took time 'to investigate and weigh up what was in the best interest of the person' because 'they cared. The senior officials cared and I cared.' It was, Macphee explained, 'just a process based on our humanity'.[65] To me, this comment is revealing of how successive ministers tend to think of themselves, foregrounding their compassionate motivations and the 'care' they believe they offered to refugee children.

In a hearing of the Commonwealth Parliamentary Joint Select Committee on Australia's Immigration Detention Network in September 2011, Mr Alan Noel Thornton, the deputy principal of the Christmas Island District School, gave evidence that some of the children would not have known who to approach if they had a problem; they were unaware of which adult they could go to for help.[66] In October 2011, speaking to the same committee, Mr Greg Kelly, the First Assistant Secretary in the Department of Immigration and Citizenship, responded to questions from Senator Sarah Hanson-Young where she argued that members of Serco with whom she had spoken had not been told who the children's guardian was in the detention centre in Darwin where they worked. Kelly was unable to point to specific notification procedures.[67] And Karen Zwi and Sarah Mares, working as part of the Australian Human Rights Commission's 2014 Inquiry into Children in Immigration Detention, noted that while the Department of Immigration and Border Protection provides unaccompanied children guardianship – on Christmas Island from a local 'Delegated Guardian'[68] – it was evident from the children's interviews that they were unaware who their guardian was. Further, children in the detention centre on Christmas Island told them that 'DIBP do not routinely contact families of unaccompanied children to inform them of their children's whereabouts and processing of asylum claims'.[69]

Such testimony provides another angle on the ways refugee children subject to the Act have been defined: they are seen as a group who are not expected to understand their place within the social fabric. They are, we could say, infantilised and made an indeterminate, governable, mass.

But isn't the minister being guardian a problem?

Some have long recognised the challenges of the Immigration minister also being the guardian of unaccompanied children, and the complicated relationships of intimacy and control this creates. In December 2002, Julia Gillard, then the Shadow Minister for Population and Immigration, told Parliament:

> Formally, the Minister for Immigration and Multicultural and Indigenous Affairs is the guardian of unaccompanied children. There clearly is a conflict of interest or, at the very least, a perception of a conflict of interest, and we believe that ought to be addressed by moving the guardianship to an appropriate other entity. Under Labor's suggestion, that entity would be the children's commissioner, which Labor policy would introduce to deal with children's issues broadly from the perspective of the federal government.[70]

Such a shift in responsibility – from the Immigration portfolio to the children's commissioner – would have meant that unaccompanied children would be considered within the realm of the child, rather than the realm of migration and border control. This would, as a 1984 report from a working party on refugee children convened by the Standing

Committee of Social Welfare Administrators made clear, serve to make these guardianship arrangements accord with those of citizen children.[71] The Coalition did not express any interest in changing guardianship arrangements.

But concerns about the border continued. In a discussion later that month about a bill to amend migration legislation, aimed at encouraging the government to release unaccompanied children from detention, Gillard reiterated that 'nothing in [the relevant subsection] requires the taking of any action which would cause a health or security risk to Australia'.[72] As we've seen in other instances, these vague notions of 'risk' continue to circulate, and are often considered Australia's pre-eminent concern, highlighting the importance of the minister's role in ensuring control of the nation's population.

Concerns about the dual role of the Immigration minister have been voiced for decades. In 2005, legal scholar Mary Crock wrote:

> The Immigration Minister's protective role under the *IGOC Act* stands in stark contrast with the obligations and powers conferred by the *Migration Act* and Regulations ... The simple and devastating problem for the young asylum seekers is that the Minister is both legal guardian, by virtue of s 6 of the *IGOC Act*, and their prosecutor, judge and gaoler within the complicated matrix of the *Migration Act*.[73]

Similar concerns were articulated by Senator Chris Evans when he was Immigration minister. In October 2008, he told the Standing Committee on Legal and Constitutional Affairs: 'I am responsible, for instance, under the act for unaccompanied minors and the guardianship of children, but I am also making decisions about them. I just think there are some really unsatisfactory arrangements in the way the legislation deals with children, and that is something we have got on the agenda.'[74] In 2012, Greens senator Sarah Hanson-Young likened the dual role to being 'both the jailer and the legal guardian'.[75]

From at least November 2012, Labor made clear that it no longer saw a need for an independent guardian, but the idea that change is necessary has been widely shared.[76] In 2013 and 2014, Hanson-Young introduced Bills to create a specific 'Guardian of Unaccompanied Children', explaining in 2014: 'This Bill sets up a Guardian who will be responsible for ensuring that the best interests of the child are always the paramount consideration'.[77] In a March 2018 interview I conducted with Gillian Triggs, the former president of the Australian Human Rights Commission, she recalled that she had tried to press for change in these guardianship arrangements around 2014. The Commission was 'concerned because we wanted an independent guardian for the children in detention'. But, she said, they were 'going around in circles all the time'. This was evidenced by, in her memory, her meetings with the then Immigration minister, Scott Morrison, whom she recalled as having said, 'What's the point in having an independent guardian because the final decision will come back to me and I'll do what I want anyway'. 'That was the answer,' she told me. 'He said, "There's no point because the decision's mine in the end." In front of about six people.'[78] I invited Morrison to participate in an interview in June 2018, but he did not respond.

Some refugee children themselves have made clear that the minister as their guardian does not address their needs. In response to a question about the guardianship arrangements for unaccompanied minors during the Australian Human Rights Commission's 2014 National Inquiry into Children in Immigration Detention, one child who had previously been in immigration detention wrote: 'Being without my family, I was very alone and sad. At 14, I didn't know what to do. I had to find an Iranian family who I got friends with. They helped me. If they didn't help me I would have been sick and sad.'[79] An unaccompanied child submitting to the inquiry from imprisonment in Nauru wrote:

> I have a tooth ache almost 4 months but there is no one to solve my problem … we are living under the tents sometime we have insects, crabs, spiders … we need someone to support us, but we don't have it … We are in a very tough condition. Every one of us killing their hopes. We don't have sleep at night because we are worried about our future. What will happen to our future? We are by ourselves and alone … We are thirsty for freedom … Please do something for us. We are getting crazy in here. Please! … Can anybody hear us. Can anybody solve these issus.[80]

Another young woman imprisoned on Christmas Island submitted a poem, 'I Will Rise', echoing Maya Angelou's 'Still I Rise':

> You now lock me in detention
> and damage my hopes
> but it's like dust
> and one day i will rise…
> You may hide the reality
> and break my heart
> but one day i will rise.
> You may send me to somewhere else.
> why cant you help me?
> I may be female of under age

who needs assistance from you.
You may send me to other countries
and shoot me with your words.
but one day i will rise
You may punish me
by saying lies
but one day i will rise
You may kill my with you hatefull action
but its like air
and one day i will rise
You may never care about my awful past
and enjoy my tears
but one day i will rise [81]

Parenthood and the ideal family

Alongside the construction of the immigrant or refugee child, the Act also constructs an idea of the Immigration minister as guardian, or a type of controlling parental figure. This construction works to shape the individual level of the person of the minister, as well as the category of the Australian parent, as worthy of acclaim. For the white family is a crucial building block of white Australia, with governments routinely demonstrating their 'anxiety', in gender studies scholar Erica Millar's terms, that there are not enough white children and families to maintain their hold over the country.[82] Building white families is crucial to Australia. In an article in the *Australian Women's Weekly* in February 1946, it was noted that the British children who were brought to Australia during World War II – the precursors of those children who would come under the control of the Act – returned to England 'saying nice things about … Australian mothers': 'That ticketed evacuee child, who arrived one day over five years ago from Britain, paused on the doorstep and looked a bit scared, is doing his foster parents credit now he is back home again.'[83] These words identify Australians as exemplary parents, and set the tone for the sentiments that would follow over the coming years. As historian Anna Haebich has made clear, in 1950s Australia, like other places around the West, 'the potent iconography of "family" was used ... to represent the *heart* of the nation, with the gendered nuclear family as the norm'.[84]

In 1948, during the discussions of the amendments to the Act, Arthur Calwell was referred to as 'Father Calwell' by the *Courier-Mail*, as it noted that the Immigration minister would from that point on be responsible as the guardian of both the estate and person of the unaccompanied child migrant, as well as having the authority to approve private individuals to act as carers for the children.[85] This depiction of Calwell as the father figure arose in parliamentary discussions too, with Neil O'Sullivan referring to the minister 'exercis[ing] ... parental care',[86] and Leslie Haylen proclaiming, 'The Minister for Immigration has been called all kinds of names in his time, but now he is to be the beneficent and legal godfather of the thousands of children who will pour into this country.' At that Calwell interjected, exclaiming 'the legal father'.[87] The title, and notion, of godfather was seemingly too far removed for Calwell.

Ideas of the ideal family swirled throughout discussions of the Act. The focus on the qualities of parenthood was reiterated by Senator Robert Clothier, who, in affirming Calwell's ability to care, asserted, 'The Minister is to become the legal guardian of migrant children, and that should give to the parents of overseas children who contemplate sending their children to this country as migrants every assurance that they will be properly cared for.'[88] Similarly, Haylen noted, 'It would be ungallant of honorable members on this side of the House not to pay tribute to the honorable member for Darwin [Dame Enid Lyons] for her thoughtful and very human appreciation of the bill. It is not very often that a measure is accepted so gracefully by a member of the Opposition. The honorable member's approval is rendered more important by virtue of the fact that she is, in her own right, one of the splendid mothers of Australia.'[89]

As the Act related to children who had travelled on their own, its very name – *Immigration (Guardianship of Children) Act 1946* – indicated that its subjects were children understood to be bereft of family, bereft of support. As such, conversations have abounded regarding the appropriate or ideal way to construct a family that would support these children. These discussions arose during debates over the 1948 amendments to the Act, where there was a bipartisan sentiment that the home provides the 'proper' type of family environment, disciplining, caring for and producing the child in the 'correct' manner. Neil O'Sullivan, for instance, speaking in the House of Representatives, asserted that there was a need to encourage unaccompanied children to be privately adopted. This was because, he said, it is only in 'private homes [that] they acquire a proper social outlook and enjoy the affection and intimacy which they need'.[90] Similarly, Clothier noted, 'Although the institutions that I have mentioned and other similar organizations do a magnificent job for the migrant children who come to this country, every one agrees that where possible children should be reared in private homes.'[91] Annabelle Rankin asserted that

> [a]s one who has had something to do with the many fine institutions in this country which care for migrant and orphan

children, I am aware of the splendid services which they are rendering both to the children and to the nation. At the same time, we all realize that it is preferable for a child to be reared by a family rather than by an institution. Children need love and affection and a sense of security, which can only be properly supplied by a private home.[92]

Through these words, we can see the ideation of the 'private family' over the communal institution. In raising this point, I am not interested in whether these parliamentarians' words are accurate. Rather, I highlight them because they illustrate the various discourses within which the Act sits. While the Act was designed, and amended, to provide guardianship, care and facilities for unaccompanied immigrant and refugee children, it led to the creation of a series of social institutions surrounding these children. None of these institutions are natural. The 'private family' is a constructed ideal, and it is not inherently 'preferable' – we know that families have the potential to be sites of great violence. And what of the place for extended families and kin, the role of communities, and so on? Of importance here then is the way this Act serves to help create an Anglicised hierarchy of ideas of family, with the minister seen as a father figure, the Australian parent as the ideal parent and the 'private family' as optimal. As Haebich writes, 'the family was the goal of an assimilated nation and the vehicle to help achieve it'.[93] Let's recall here the ideas of the refugee family that circulated through the Children Overboard affair and of Aboriginal and Torres Strait Islander families in relation to the Stolen Generations. The creation of the figure of the immigrant or refugee child who will be subject to the Act, then, is embroiled in the creation of racialised parental and familial ideals. The category of the ideal private Australian family was invoked to sit alongside the category of the unaccompanied migrant/refugee child created through the Act.

Producing relations of intimacy

Successive governments have made clear that the Immigration minister's responsibility to act as guardian for unaccompanied children is secondary to their responsibility to national security. This can be seen in the moments when assimilation is held up as a key marker of the success of the Act. It can also be seen in the twenty-first century, when governments are explicit that control of who crosses the borders is the minister's first priority. While this focus on the borders is not unique to the Immigration portfolio, it is useful to examine this political expectation. Doing so allows us to foreground an aspect of Australia's refugee history that has not been well understood and enables a more nuanced understanding of the broad effects of a focus on 'border protection' over ideas of settlement. Mainly, it enables us to understand in more depth the textures of the ideas of 'guardianship' as held by the Immigration minister, and the notions of family and intimacy produced by the Act.

In 2011, a series of amendments were proposed that would allow the government to institute the offshore detention and processing of unaccompanied child asylum seekers. They were created in response to the High Court of Australia overturning the so-called Malaysia Solution (which would have seen refugees without visas who wanted to settle in Australia be sent to Malaysia).[94] In a parliamentary speech about these amendments, Chris Bowen, the Labor Minister for Immigration and Citizenship, proclaimed they were necessary 'to assert the primacy of the *Migration Act* over the *Immigration (Guardianship of Children) Act*'. There was, he claimed, 'national importance' to these amendments; they represented a moment 'when we, as a parliament, must collectively do our job' to 'act in the national interest'. This was needed because 'a blanket inability of the government of the day to transfer unaccompanied minors to a designated country provides an invitation to people smugglers to send boatloads of children to Australia'.[95] Here we see the idea of crisis that echoes throughout all child refugee policy discussions.

Such rhetoric is fundamental to the ways the Act has functioned to produce certain notions of child refugees and refugee families as incompetent and uncaring. The message being reiterated is that the government knows better than the parents. This is why guardianship – or the regulation of who acts as guardian, carer or parent – becomes such contested terrain. Vulnerability is assured; what it means to act in the child's best interest, and what place that 'best interest' has in the hierarchy of interests, is what is contested.

What does this guardianship relationship entail, in the day-to-day? The responsibilities of guardianship are delegated to social welfare organisations, international bodies such as the Red Cross, and detention centre operators, among other institutions and individuals. And so we need to understand how some of these holders of guardianship responsibility have understood their task.

Control through description

Maintaining refugee settlement services in Australia has, over the years, resulted in a vast bureaucracy, with the production of mountains of reports describing those who were 'settled'. Often social workers played an integral role in documenting the lives of refugees in holding centres – the sites where refugees have at times first lived after arrival in Australia – as they began the process of settling into their new lives.

The records from the 1970s and 1980s that these workers left behind in their files, now held in the National Archives of Australia, provide a vital glimpse of the ways that governments, and those who help create and implement government policy, thought about the people whose lives they were describing and controlling.

Beyond the simple category of 'unaccompanied', the Act has also led to the categorisation of refugee children into smaller groupings. From the 1970s, all children governed by this legislation were known as 'isolated'. Under this umbrella term they fell into one of two groups: 'unattached', which meant that they had no relative in Australia to look after them, or 'detached', which meant that they had a relative who was over twenty-one but who was not a parent. These two categories translated into different funding schemes, housing arrangements and modes of care from the government and social services, a problem that was always debated by those responsible for the day-to-day care of these children.[96]

All of these descriptors position the child in relation to family or lack of family, and define the guardian as providing a form of family. These refugee children are grouped and managed based on the description of their relation to a caregiver and their relative perceived vulnerability. The descriptions of them in archived reports are a further testament to this positioning. Minute details of their behaviour are recorded, indicating it was thought that they required both care and surveillance, housing and monitoring, schooling and documenting. Guardianship, in this formulation and in these documents, enacts control at the level of the everyday.

This control came about due to the vast majority of refugee children coming to Australia in the late 1970s – children predominantly from Vietnam and Timor – being housed in migrant hostels on arrival.

These hostels were sites that provided access to food, English classes and medical care, and acted, as historian Sara Wills has framed it, as 'frontiers of assimilation', holding together ideas of Australianness and creating, as historian Glenda Sluga has put it, sites of 'material and cultural *discomfort*' for many.[97] While in these hostels, unaccompanied children would have their lives documented. There were three instrumental reasons for this. Firstly, as noted earlier, governments were unaware of how many unaccompanied children were in each city. Reports on children at each hostel were a type of census exercise. Secondly, given that the Immigration minister delegated the responsibilities of guardianship to the local Department of Social Services, the departments sought to gather certain information about each child in order to provide services. Thirdly, there was the question of funding: as each child was recorded, their funding needs and pensions were noted.

While some workers at the hostels would provide simple lists, other times welfare and settlement officers reported stories about the children. Some of these were full-page reports, containing information such as name, sex, place and date of birth, address, nationality, ethnic origin, details about their natural parents (such as whether they were alive or where they lived), sources of financial support, relatives in Australia, relatives in country of origin, relatives elsewhere, and current circumstances, with supplementary sections for an expanded background and comment. Others were short paragraphs, headed by a name and birthdate. Of recurring focus throughout the reports were questions of finance, housing and the child's temperament.

Throughout these reports, the voices of the workers dominate, with the chance rarely, if ever, provided for the children to report about themselves. As Shurlee Swain asserted in her study of 'the vignette' as featured in nineteenth-century child-rescue documentation: 'case records … do not give the historian access to any truths for they are products of the discourses of their time. They need to be understood as representations of their subjects rather than the voices of the subjects themselves.'[98] We need to approach them as evidence of the discourses that flourished, rather than as speaking truths about the children. We can gain a sense of the ways the social workers and administrators imagined and catalogued the task of managing the migration and settlement of refugee children in Victoria, how they – in the words of historians Catherine Kevin and Karen Agutter – expressed their 'expectations, curiosities, frustrations and sympathies'.[99] These descriptions are, as scholar Ann Stoler puts it, crucial to a government's population-control project: a necessary part of managing a group is to describe them.[100] Or, as historian Mahmood Mamdani has asserted, 'the management of difference is the holy cow of the modern study of society, just as it is central to modern statecraft'.[101]

Within the surveys of the children, there were rolling reports on their present and future housing situations. This began before the children arrived in Australia, with cables being sent from overseas to the Department of Immigration branch in Melbourne, noting the settlement officers' decision as to where the children should be placed upon arrival.[102] Once a child was in Australia, the housing arrangements were under constant scrutiny and discussion. It was reported of one child, 'He would be happy to live in a large communal house if his friends were also living there, if this cannot be arranged he has a twenty year old friend … [in Oakleigh] with whom he could live.' Another boy was reported as 'preferr[ing] living with his sisters to any other accommodation arrangement'.[103] Of a set of siblings, it was written that a settlement officer from Midway Hostel, together with a worker from the department, 'agreed that the best solution is to try to obtain a flat for them, but we believe that economically they cannot afford to pay for one'.[104]

A focus on the financial position of the children recurred throughout the reports, as social workers documented how much money the children had, needed and earned, and what this would mean for their living situations. In an April 1976 report on Timorese unaccompanied children at the Midway Hostel, it was noted that the circumstances of a group of boys was 'fairly stable': 'They have caused no problems. They are the boys who are receiving $4.80 per week after the hostel tariff is paid. Financially their situation is inadequate because from $4.80 they need to pay school requisites, clothing, other personal items and medical expenses.'[105] Some children, it was written, 'reject any form of communal living' and sought employment in order to live together, while others were described as 'not presently receiving any financial support'.[106] In the lists of the children, careful notes were made to explain precisely which government benefits were received.[107]

Workers were also keen to describe the behaviours of the unaccompanied children. The description of one child noted that 'the Welfare Officer feels that [she] has suddenly been allowed too much freedom and needs welfare follow-up. It would also be beneficial if she found lasting friendships outside of the hostel in the community.'[108] In 1976, one welfare officer working at the Enterprise Hostel described all the refugee children living there. Of one child it was noted, 'This girl is attractive and very shy, at school she is withdrawn and rarely speaks up.'[109] For another, an extensive note documenting her family's life in Timor was included, highlighting, 'All of their property was occupied by various Army forces during the war, and resulted in considerable loss of property.' Since her arrival in Melbourne, she had been found to be 'shy to the extent that she was unable to say her name'. This report concluded by noting that

> At the hostel M socialises well. The only time M and her family were upset, was during the time when her uncle was under a deportation order – This however has now been withdrawn and the family hopes that permanent residence will be given.
>
> M has applied for permanency <u>and</u> nominated her parents to come to Australia.
>
> <u>Comment:</u> This family could serve as a model in many ways.[110]

Another child, this time at Midway Hostel, was described as being bound to 'have many problems settling in Australia':

> She is functionally illiterate. She has little or no concept of time, and combined with a very short concentration span, she has great difficulty in keeping appointments and performing any kind of organised work. [expunged section] Many efforts have been made to help and support her. Catholic Family Welfare had arranged for her to live in a hostel with five girls, but she rejected this, she also has rejected any other form of alternative accommodation. [She] has always lived a 'free life', not bound by any restriction. I do not believe institutional care is the answer, but I am unable to offer any other alternative.[111]

The description ends there, with the last sentences covered by tape reading 'expunged', before the document was photocopied and the copy placed in the archival file, presumably by the archivist at the National Archives of Australia, where these documents are now housed.[112]

Legislation

These expungements give pause, compelling the historian in me to note the potential ongoing force of the documentation of these children's lives. Through these lists, information is acquired and certain forms of knowledge produced about these children, and where they can live within society. Where once these names and descriptions sat within confidential government files, today they sit in the archives, publicly accessible. This notation was created on 7 July 1976, relatively recently, and we can presume that this girl, or people who know her, remain in Australia. This is a description saturated with racialised ideas of personhood, 'appropriate' migrant living conditions and settlement, but it also contains expunged sentences. Some descriptors are, it would seem, judged too sensitive to be available to the public.

Indeed, this expunging is part of the process of racialisation of these children. The archival records of citizen children are withheld from public access for 100 years. The files and papers I am exploring in this chapter are publicly accessible, I would guess, because they sit within the record-keeping of Immigration, rather than of Social Services. And while archivists might repeatedly inform me that anything to do with personal, medical or sexual information is withheld from public viewing under exemption reason 33(1)(g) of the *Archives Act 1983*, the records I have seen suggest that this is not always the case. Personal, as well as medical, information – sometimes highly detailed – is often freely available in these archives, and appears in almost every National Archives file I have seen that holds documents dealing with the implementation of this Act.

While we cannot know the mindset of those who ruled these records open, the fact that these files are publicly accessible requires us to ponder the layers of ethics in using them to write histories. As I utilise them, then, I am forced to sit with an ambivalence over their usage.

Perhaps this ambivalence is essential to the work of the historian – for we are always confronted with materials the authors may not have anticipated would one day become public – but in this present moment, when the topic of refugees remains a political battleground, it imbues a potent feeling. These are affective archives, we could say. As I put them to work to craft a narrative, they do emotional work within me, as they do within the Australian nation. There is a discomfort, an unsettling. At the same time, my emotional response is irrelevant – this is not about me.

But does the public availability of these documents tell us something vital about how the various arms of government imagine, and manage, refugees within Australian society? These documents, it would seem, testify to an idea of child refugees as outside the realm of citizenship. If citizen children's archives are kept from public view for longer than those of non-citizen children, these differences illustrate the idea that the personhood of child refugees is substantively different to that of child citizens. While this might be obvious when considered as a question of legal categories – of course a citizen is different to a non-citizen, some may say – I am interested in what it means when thought about through the lens of a history of bureaucratic writing, or governmental practices, or interpersonal relations. What can this tell us about how these children are imagined, and their lives noted down, described and understood? It produces simultaneously both a distance from citizenship and a life lived under government control and surveillance. Refugee children are produced as a group through the collection of this information by social workers and the like, and its retention and availability in archives. Bureaucratic processes of description, collection and retention help to produce a population that can be known.

These instances of refugee children's lives being intimately – and now publicly – documented repeat and repeat. Another child at the Enterprise Hostel was described in the following language: 'His relationship with his aunt ... is not good. Amongst the complaints that he lists are that no friends are allowed to visit him in his room, he receives no pocket money.' The next few sentences are expunged. While certain intimate details are determined suitable to be seen, a line is drawn somewhere. The logic for this is, for those of us who access these documents today, inscrutable. But we know that we can read about other children described as 'likeable', as 'more mature than her age would indicate, readily displaying responsibility and sensibility', as having a 'well mannered, pleasant personality' and as 'attractive and very shy'.[113] A school was asked to provide a report on two siblings. Of the brother they report that he 'wears very corrective glasses', while the sister 'has no physical problems, in fact she has a most affectionate smile'.[114] Another child's report states, 'At the beginning he wanted to go back but with the time, he gained friends and his happy go lucky attitude is infectious. He has changed his mind and is definitely FOR AUSTRALIA.'[115] We can see here the anxiety around assimilation that parliamentarians and High Court judges pondered too.

All of these stories were collected as the result of the existence of the category of the 'child refugee', and in the service of the production of that category of person. Some refugees were described as 'models' for others: certain ideas of what it meant to be a refugee were created through these reports, in order to be held up or followed by others. These descriptions of the children exist as both a product of surveillance and to help bureaucrats and public servants lobby different branches of government to provide funding and support. For example, a July 1976 report from the Victorian state government utilised case file reports written about unattached children in order to support their claims for greater assistance and regulation in policy and practice. The reports included descriptions of children's housing and financial arrangements, as well as their state of mind, and served as 'illustrative of the difficulties being encountered in effectively planning for these refugee children'.[116]

These documents provide us with an insight into the genealogy of these categories of person and the ways in which their histories can be written. While the case file notes propose to outline the stories of the children, to provide seemingly vital information about them, they instead offer a set of discourses about how these refugee children were thought of and written about, how they were surveyed, described and categorised. Certain aspects of their lives were deemed important to document, other aspects discarded. These traces sit within the government archive, providing us with the means to understand the work that government discourse does when relating to, describing and producing certain categories of person through legislation and through bureaucracy.

CHAPTER 5

The Immigration Minister

Mehdi Ali tried to come to Australia when he was fifteen, before being intercepted and imprisoned. In February 2022 he shared his story with freelance journalist Zoe Osborne and wrote an open letter to Australia's Immigration minister, which was published in *Al Jazeera*:

> I spent the first nine months on Christmas Island, an Australian external territory located 1,550km (963 miles) northwest of the mainland. Then I spent about six years on Nauru, a tiny island nation to the northeast of Australia. It was a journey of trauma, tragedy, misery and frustration. I witnessed terrible, terrible things – children being detained, a man setting himself on fire, and so on.
>
> I was not treated like a human being, like a person. You treated me like I was dangerous.
>
> How could you take a child and lock him up for almost nine years with nothing?
>
> It feels bad. I couldn't get an education. It is a basic right for kids in any country but I didn't get any education. All I got is suffering, diseases, mental health problems.

[...]

Minister, I have served my time in a cruel system, and I have tried to ask for justice. But there is no justice for me. No one is answering my questions. No one is telling me what is going on … Minister, the law in Australia says that 'children must only be detained for the shortest appropriate period of time'. So why are you turning away from the law?

I'm angry, I'm frustrated, I'm exhausted.

I am exhausted.

[...]

Minister, if you have any sense of humanity release me, release us. Let us go.

From a desperate young man, who lost his childhood in detention.[1]

A key figure – perhaps *the* key figure – in child refugee policy is the Minister for Immigration, as we have seen. While the minister's power and authority can on occasion be challenged, including by the Prime Minister, the position wields a great deal of control in the policy process and, more significantly, over people's lives. The scope to intervene in people's claims for asylum – to determine whether they will be granted asylum and what type and length of visa they will receive – is an extraordinary degree of power to invest in a person. And yet, this is the system within Australia's immigration program.

While control over the movement of migrants to Australia began at the time of Federation, with the *Immigration Restriction Act 1901*, the *Pacific Island Labourers Act 1901* and the *Naturalization Act 1903*, its modern codification dates to the *Migration Act 1958*. And while Gough Whitlam formally abolished the White Australia policy's restrictions on immigration, control over who could come to Australia and under what circumstances has never lost its racial overtones.

Both the Immigration department and the position of the Minister for Immigration were created in the aftermath of World War II. Before this time, immigration controls were managed by the Department of Home Affairs and then the Department of the Interior. The first Minister for Immigration was Arthur Calwell, who held the position from July 1945 to December 1949.

It is important to know the perspectives and experiences of those who have held these ministerial roles, for they are just people, after all. They are people speaking, thinking and acting within histories – both personal and communal – and they create possible futures for themselves and the country as a result of these histories. And so, as we will see in this chapter, many Immigration ministers have come to understand themselves as one link in a chain of officials who approach their serious task with deep care and in search of the ability to be in control. Often they see themselves as being in a difficult position and ask the public for their empathy and consideration.

I interviewed some former Immigration ministers for this project, but far from all. I approached Amanda Vanstone, Kevin Andrews, Philip Ruddock, Tony Burke and Scott Morrison, all of whom did not reply. Chris Bowen and Peter Dutton declined to be interviewed. Chris Evans, Ian Macphee and Nick Bolkus participated in interviews. The other ministers in the period covered by this book have either passed away or were known to be frail (some, such as Chris Hurford, have since died), or I was unable to source contact details for them. So in this chapter – as throughout this book – I rely on a mixture of sources to help us understand the role of the Immigration minister in child refugee policy, and the different ways that such ministers have acted over time. My intention is to understand them as human actors – to gain insight into how a vital cog in the political machine operates.

Ian Macphee

In my August 2017 interview with Ian Macphee, he opened with an anecdote.[2] He told me that when he was around ten years old, he looked at a map of the world and noted how far England was from Australia, commenting to his parents that he was surprised so many Australians saw England as their home. His education and early working life were focused on an engagement with the world: he attained a law degree and was interested in thinking about Australia within 'our region'. He told me that he had 'an interest in both the Pacific and the Atlantic', and after spending time working in the 'Public Solicitors' Office in Sydney', he spent two and a half years working as a defence counsel at the Office of the Public Solicitor of Papua New Guinea, working on 'over a hundred murder trials'. On his return to Australia, he acted for the unions in industrial relations negotiations, before moving to Hawaii to study, on a scholarship provided by the East-West Centre (a US organisation formed by Congress in 1960 with the aim of promoting cross-cultural diplomacy between the United States, Asia and the Pacific), to 'complete' his 'understanding of our region'. While studying for a Master of Arts at the University of Hawaii, Macphee spent a significant period at Yale.

After graduating, Macphee became involved in the Liberal Party. He found a political role model in Malcolm Fraser. He told me that he 'realised, or we both realised, how much we shared in terms of our abhorrence of racism, our desire to have Australia integrated into our region and be amongst the leaders, but not [the] leader, and to become very much involved'. 'So that's what motivated me to go into politics and continue there,' he said. 'And, of course, when I finally lost the support of the Liberals it was because they'd turned inwardly and against all those things and Howard had returned to the racism and so forth. And so that was it.'

Given the way he described his biography – including noting that he worked with Bob Hawke, whom he came to know and once stayed with, while Hawke was at the Australian Council of Trade Unions (ACTU) – I was curious about what drew Macphee to the Liberal Party. He told me that it was primarily 'because I was a non-believer': 'I found the Liberal Party had a greater tolerance for ideas. The Labor Party had heavy dominance by the Catholic Church.' He explained that he had long known senior figures within the Liberals, and while he admired Whitlam 'in many many ways' and 'agreed with many of the things that he was trying to do', he 'still thought the way to do things was through the Liberal Party'. 'And so that's what motivated me then,' he told me. 'And when opportunities arose I stood in the electorate of Balaclava, as it was. It became Goldstein and I got that in preselection and away it went.'

Serving in the Fraser government, Macphee held the portfolio of Minister for Immigration and Ethnic Affairs from 8 December 1979 to 7 May 1982. Having that portfolio was his favourite part of being in Parliament – a sentiment several other Immigration ministers also expressed in my interviews with them. He told me that he was proud of the work that he had done in the Productivity and Industrial Relations portfolios, including funding the bionic ear and working on industrial relations reforms. But he liked Immigration because it enabled him to 'help integrate Australia into the region': 'And, especially because Malcolm and I, we'd discussed all these issues many times and he knew the Vietnam War was a mistake. He'd been Minister for the Army at that time and so we knew we wanted to bring, had to bring, a lot of refugees from Vietnam and Cambodia. So there was no question, we did that. And I reached across to the Labor Party at that time. I'd always had an affinity with the Labor Party ... and Mick Young, who was the shadow minister, he and I became very dear friends. And Bill Hayden was the opposition leader and he was happy for me to address the backbench committee of the Labor Party on the issues and so we got a bilateral position and we supported each other all the way through. It was bipartisan policy. So, that was very critical.'

Ending a policy in words doesn't mean that it ends in practice. And so given the continuation of race-based migration policies, Macphee identified 'ultimately abolishing the White Australia policy' and 'having a humanitarian approach not merely to refugees, but to those that were on the cusp of being officially, or legally, refugees, especially a humanitarian program' as important policy changes that he worked on. Macphee told me that John Menadue (then Secretary of the Department of Immigration) organised for the two of them, plus Mick Young (then Opposition Spokesperson for Immigration) to travel around the country holding meetings in capital cities and major towns, where they 'genuinely listened': 'we genuinely argued for a humanitarian approach, the Australian sense of a fair go, et cetera. And, frankly, we overcame the phobia that Howard and company have capitalised on.' For Macphee, as he explained to me, refugee policy 'has to be ... primarily humanitarian. It has to be. I am now ashamed to be Australian, frankly, the way they carry on.'

Macphee faced a preselection challenge in his seat of Goldstein in 1990, after the Liberal Party moved further to the right on matters of race and immigration. He lost that challenge to David Kemp and retired. In the 2022 federal election, Macphee supported independent

Zoe Daniel in her successful campaign to unseat Liberal MP Tim Wilson.

When I asked Macphee about his approach to child refugees while in Immigration, he responded that he had no memory of dealing with children particularly, including in his role as their guardian under the *Immigration (Guardianship of Children) Act 1946*. He explained: 'The reality was that we wanted all refugees and their age was of no consequence, although I suppose the younger they were, especially if they were orphaned, the more important, the more humane, it was to bring them, but ... I don't recall any particular discussions about children ... It was just something that was a consequence of a humane refugee program. And, again, if there was a displaced person not strictly fleeing tyranny and in fear of their lives, et cetera, but nonetheless (and not being economic migrants) being people in genuine need, poverty, et cetera, [and] with a desire to contribute. Anyway, certainly if there were children, and there were children, of course, there was various orphanages all over the place which we took, but I think they were just simply a consequence of the total policy.'

The focus of the 'total policy', as Macphee remembered it to me, was to bring 'people who were desperate enough to be genuinely fleeing the tyranny in their own country', recognising that Australia had a capacity to resettle people that more densely populated countries in Asia such as Thailand did not, and to complete 'the abolition of White Australia'.

Children could factor in when they were born to refugees in Australia. Macphee told me of 'going to hospital in Parramatta and seeing one Vietnamese mother who had been holding her child and the next thing the child is taken away to be cleaned after it was born and she had no idea what that was about. That's not what they did in Vietnam and she was screaming and carrying on and so that led me to ensure that we'd introduced telephone interpreter services and translation services, but to make sure that they extended it everywhere, including the hospitals, so people understood what was happening, the child would be brought back. And all these sort of basic things. And I have a myriad of memories of those humane issues as they arose. And so age wasn't a crucial thing, but if it was a child it was bleedingly obvious you had to look after the child. How else would it go?'

I asked him for his reflections on immigration policy, specifically whether it is useful to have different policies for children and adults. He told me that he thinks 'to the extent that there are kids who are indeed orphans, then they need special protection. The future is so vital to them. They need education, health, of course, and they can integrate easily, being children, and they can integrate in Australia and elsewhere. So there should be, perhaps, a special emphasis on children, but as I've implied I was not conscious of it in my day.'

The recollection that children did not play a large role in refugee policymaking and delivery at this time was shared by public servants who worked in the Immigration department while Macphee was minister. Derek Volker, who was First Assistant Secretary and then Deputy Secretary, and responsible for the migration program, told me that he had 'to be quite honest and say that I don't remember … I was certainly aware of it, you know, and I can remember several cases where I was involved, but it wasn't a big issue. I'd say, you know, less than 0.05 per cent of my time would have been involved in [looking after children] … But I was certainly aware of it.'[3] Later in the interview he commented, 'As I say, I'm not really an expert on that *Immigration (Guardianship of Children) Act*, but – and I didn't have a lot of cases that came to me or anything like that – but we were always concerned that if we had children that we do the right thing by them.'

Similarly, when I interviewed John Menadue, he told me that he had a 'vague' memory of doing work with children in this field. Menadue's main memory of his work with children was not of any 'specific policy', his policy approaches 'would've been in response', he was sure, to the UNHCR saying, 'We've got these large numbers of young kids. Will you do something?' And they 'often did', he told me. He also did not remember doing any work around the fact that the Immigration minister was the guardian for unaccompanied children, telling me that it was not an issue when he was Secretary, even if now he recognises that 'it's clearly inconsistent to have a minister as the guardian and decision-maker. You can't combine both of those.' But 'we were pretty naive in those days', he told me.[4] 'Those days', of course, were before the United Nations Convention on the Rights of the Child came into effect in 1989 and began to play a determinative role in child policy globally.

I want to draw attention to two things here. Firstly, we can note the sharp contrast between ideas of children during this period, the early 1980s, when Macphee controlled the portfolio and Menadue and Volker worked in the public service, and ideas that have proliferated in more recent decades, and particularly the pre-eminence of children in Australian refugee policy discussions since approximately 2001. Secondly, we can note the way that Macphee, and those working in the bureaucracy around him, recall their motivations as care and kindness. They had the task of determining who should be allowed to immigrate to Australia. They acknowledge themselves as in control, and remember their impact as positive, thinking about actions as being shaped by their own good intentions. I am not interested in evaluating their care – in determining the objective truth of their memories – but I am interested in tracing this belief that the right response from Immigration ministers is to articulate a form of control shaped by practices of benevolent care. These politicians understand themselves to be doing good things; they remember their impact fondly. At the same time, as we saw in the previous chapter, those with day-to-day responsibility for unaccompanied children were struggling under the lack of proper infrastructure, planning and financial support.

This trend of Immigration ministers and those around them exercising their ability to control people's movements, while understanding themselves as compassionate, is evident across their careers, not just in the way that they look back on their time in charge. Macphee's words while he was Immigration minister are revealing in this sense. In a speech he gave to Parliament on 16 March 1982, when he reported on a review that the government had undertaken of Australia's refugee and special humanitarian programs, he explained that the 'guiding principles' of the review followed those 'embodied in the government's stated refugee policy of May 1977', which were that 'Australia fully recognises its humanitarian commitment and responsibility to admit refugees for resettlement; [t]he decision to accept refugees must always remain with the Australian Government; [s]pecial assistance will often need to be provided for the resettlement of refugees in Australia; [i]t may not be in the interests of some refugees to settle in Australia.' Macphee highlighted that 'humanitarian' concerns governed his and the government's approach, but also insisted on the necessity of ensuring that those who came to Australia were 'genuine' refugees. He asserted:

> The purpose of the review was to ensure that Australia's response to refugee situations was appropriate to the needs of the people caught up in those situations. Another important consideration was the need to reassure the Australian community that people being brought to Australia for resettlement as refugees under

generous arrangements are indeed refugees. During my visit last year I reached the conclusion, commonly held by many involved in both the Indo-Chinese and Eastern European refugee situations, that a proportion of people now leaving their homelands were doing so to seek a better way of life rather than to escape from some form of persecution. In other words their motivation is the same as over one million others who apply annually to migrate to Australia. To accept them as refugees would in effect condone queue-jumping as migrants.

Macphee concluded his statement by asserting that '[o]ur policy is a most humane one and it is administered most fairly'.[5] While this is only one speech, it is representative of an approach that existed at the time and crosses across Immigration ministers since.

In between Macphee and Nick Bolkus – the next minister we will focus on in this snapshot history – there were seven other ministers. First was John Hodges (Liberal), and then, with the change of government, a string of Labor ministers who served under Hawke or Keating: Stewart West, Chris Hurford, Mick Young, Clyde Holding, Robert Ray and Gerry Hand.

Nick Bolkus

Immigration ministers of the 1990s and 2000s have been keen to describe themselves as having a very difficult, troublesome job to do. Over these decades, interlinking stories of refugee children with narratives of difficult decision-making and the desire to enforce border control has proved to be a bipartisan affair.

In an interview I conducted in June 2018, Nick Bolkus, the Labor Minister for Immigration and Ethnic Affairs from 24 March 1993 to 11 March 1996, told me that 'there's no black and white answers. There's always a matrix of complex issues that need to be put together. So you know where you want to go. You need to develop strategies to get there and you might have to do trade-offs along the way.'[6] But he was clear that – as he asserted in a 2002 parliamentary speech discussing the aftermath of the *Tampa* – 'as a former immigration minister, I know the importance of keeping the system under control; I know the importance of protecting borders'.[7]

Bolkus explained to me that 'growing up in the 1960s, it was hard not to be connected to politics'. For him, 'the issue of race was always important'. He was attracted to the Australian Labor Party because of its commitment to ending the White Australia policy. Bolkus is of Greek background and so, he told me, events in Greece in the 1960s, as well as the events of the Vietnam War, had a profound impact on him.

In sharing his perception of Australia, Bolkus told me, 'we've always had the underpinning in this country of being a frightened country. And whether it's economic and trade or whether it's human migration, it's been consistent. Just scratch the surface, it's there.' He ascribed this to the idea that 'we stuck out like a sore thumb in a sea of Asia. So it was a white settlement imposed on Indigenous people who were repressed from the start. And we were always afraid of the invasion, the Asian invasion.' The response could have been to have 'embraced the outside world and built a nation' but 'we built a frightened country'. I asked him what his thinking around cultural diversity and difference had been when he was Immigration minister. Taking a legalistic stance, he asserted that 'cultural diversity I think for me is – the rule of law's always been important. So instead of sitting back and waiting for issues to blow up in court, we did things like bring in some community legal centre type people to help in the formulation of regulations and for legislation to get a balance right.'

In this interview, Bolkus rehearsed a common line: that there is a logistical problem in managing people coming to Australia without visas and a need for a solution that 'works'. As he explained, the previous Minister for Immigration, Labor MP Gerry Hand, had made a decision to implement mandatory detention for all those who came to Australia by boat seeking asylum. 'It wasn't just mandatory detention on its own, [as a first step],' Bolkus told me. 'He'd built up to it, tried, [but] other approaches weren't working.' This was important to Bolkus, as was the fact that people did not drown. As he framed it: 'I think we found a way to do it without drowning people, which was also satisfying ... So I maintain that we had pressures of illegal arrivals, we had Cambodians all over Australia, we had the asylum seekers in the pre- and post-Tiananmen here. We had a whole lot of major issues. But we kept a lid on the program. It was managed. And in the process we didn't have to sink boats.' Other interviewees indicated to me that they believed Hand was not as hesitant to take this decision as Bolkus believed.

The management of potential 'problems' was an angle Bolkus returned to in his discussion of child refugees. He explained that during his tenure as Immigration minister, a number of Cambodian asylum seekers came to Australia with their families. 'We decided that our starting point would be that we would not separate the kids from the parents,' he said. 'I think Trump has found the perils of doing that' – in reference to the reports that were circulating at the time about then President Trump's moves to separate refugee and migrant children and their families at the US–Mexican border. But, Bolkus told me, 'by not allowing separation you had to put up with the reality of children being in detention. Now, our way to handle that was to work with the United Nations High Commissioner for Refugees and make things as comfortable and as educative as possible. So in Port Hedland I think with the UNHCR we developed an environment where the kids were taught how to – and remembering this is the mid-90s – how to use computers. The food was ethno-specific; rice, for instance. Ways of engaging with the local community. For me the main objective was to get them out of detention, all of them.'

He explained that the department worked with the local Cambodian community, but the impulse was to keep the families together because 'the minute that you separated them there'd be all the issues of separation and then they become your responsibility and you have to be concerned about child abuse and so on in the outside communities. So that's why I say they're never black and white issues.' Ideally there would be 'a fast process' to grant people asylum, 'but the reality is you can't get one … because [of] the creativity of my colleagues in the law'. Bolkus argued that even when there were limits placed on the length of time it could take to process applications, lawyers could appeal decisions and thus extend the time limit. This was one reason, he asserted, why deadlines were pushed out, or in the case of time limits on people being mandatorily detained, abolished: because the government wanted to wrest back control, and one way they did so was by making it possible to indefinitely imprison people who were making refugee claims.

In his discussion of the introduction of mandatory detention, Bolkus told me that 'part of the problem' Hand faced – 'and I don't identify it as a target that I would criticise emotionally and try and score points out of it' – was that 'our legal system's such that once a person is in the country then they've got a right to natural justice': 'They've got a right to go to court, right to go to the High Court in fact. And that makes it hard for more efficient fast-track policies to work. So for instance when I took over the portfolio I think the Department was involved in court appeals in every state in the Commonwealth. And my good friends in the legal profession would not let go. So there were cases where we'd get a ruling in a court in Victoria, the plane would have to stop for refuelling in WA and more appeals would be lodged there, and so there was a frustration that had built up that any other alternative was not going to work. And so I remember when Gerry introduced it, it didn't go down well but it was – there was an understanding that he had a shit sandwich there.'

This bind was because, Bolkus believed, there was a necessity for a cap on the number of places available within the migration program. And the 'migration program', he asserted, 'balances humanitarian and professional migration [a]nd family reunion' in a manner that is fair and 'sustainable'. 'You can't,' he said, 'have a bleed at one end and not the other. And it's never been an endless supply of opportunities. It's a fixed number.' This is indeed a practice that recurs throughout recent migration history: a cap is created, pitting migrants and refugees against each other in their attempts to secure a place within that cap.

Bolkus felt that children should be treated differently to adults as 'they're much more susceptible to all sorts of abuse and torture'. While 'being contained in an environment in itself is one or another of those two', it's 'a choice of if you let them out, that raises all sorts of other problems'. Immediately, he said, the pressure was, 'if you let them out, let the parents out. And then that impacts on the sustainability of your overall refugee and humanitarian and migration. It might sound hardline, but I'd rather have them learning computer skills in a farm-like detention centre than drowning.'

A cap is placed on possibilities, too.

Bolkus told me that he enjoyed celebrating child migrants and child refugees, and that he also saw importance in 'protecting' them. In his description of this protective drive, he also invoked women in the form of 'mail-order brides'. He explained that large numbers 'finish up in Australia'. 'They're the victims of domestic violence. And you've got to give them – while they are insecurely based here waiting for visa decisions they're even more susceptible, so you've got to find a way of giving them more security and recognising the court legal system is either too slow or too insensitive.' His movement from child refugees to women refugees – and then on to a discussion of his 'problem with illegal migrants' – demonstrates some of the slippages that occur in thinking about refugees, reinforcing criminality and that imagined vulnerable category of 'womenandchildren', as Cynthia Enloe famously framed it.[8] Similarly, in a conversation about settlement services, Bolkus talked about the virtues of 'family migration', asserting that 'families become much more productive much quicker if grandparents can look after the kids'. There is a quick movement to viewing people through the lens of productivity.

Towards the middle of our interview, I asked Bolkus what he thought the ideal policy would be for child refugees. This was a question I asked in most interviews. Bolkus told me, using the euphemism of 'containment' to describe immigration prison: 'It's got to be culturally sensitive. It's got to contribute to their development. Got to recognise that being contained is not good for their development but being productively engaged while in [containment] – can be. So a physical containment but a mental and interconnect with the outside world. And you can do that these days … Ideally you wouldn't want kids contained but being separated from their parents is, for me, not the answer … Family integrity is really important.'

Here Bolkus drew a connection somewhat similar to one I am making in this book. He told me, 'We actually separated one group of young kids from their parents and we're still paying the price and so are they. It's the Indigenous Australians.' I asked him if this connection was one he had considered before, and he said it was, as 'we still don't recognise what that dislocation has done to not just one generation but a number of generations'. While superficially it might appear that Bolkus and I are drawing a similar parallel, we are not. Where I identify a continuing colonial form of government, which reveals the Australian government and its bureaucrats as believing they know what is best for refugee and migrant children, Bolkus articulates a connection in order to argue for a different form of control: the continued imprisonment of refugee children *with their families.*

For Bolkus, refugee policy has a 'two-prong objective': '[O]ne is to help people and extract them from life-threatening situations. And the definition of refugee is still pretty broad enough. And the second part is to make them much more productive citizens.' His general understanding of child refugees was a group of people who carried 'a sense of helplessness because they're kids basically and they don't know why they are where they are'. 'For most of them [Australia] was a pretty calm environment compared to their recent experiences,' he said. 'So you get floored by their naivety in many ways. So I met a few of them in WA mainly. I met some in camps in Asia and Hong Kong and it was a much harder experience to endure. Met a few people in the Middle East – camps in the Middle East.'

When I asked him about the emotions involved in holding this portfolio, he was candid: 'it's a challenging portfolio for all sorts of emotions … And sometimes you're tempted to overreact and you shouldn't, you know that. But for me, I'd channel most of my priorities through getting the macro settings right and on the whole that probably worked. But you can show – you can show sensitivity.' He said that it was important to him to be understood as a compassionate Immigration minister, but that 'some would disagree obviously. And sometimes they were probably right. 'Cause you're not infallible.' Thus for Bolkus, as for Macphee, child refugee policy was understood as a means of control, driven by a sense of himself as caring and compassionate, negotiating complexity, and ensuring that people were useful. The similarities between the two men – both of whom located themselves on the left of their respective parties – are notable.

With the change of government, Bolkus ceased being minister, and Philip Ruddock took over for nearly eight years, before handing over to Amanda Vanstone.

Amanda Vanstone

On 7 October 2003, Senator Amanda Vanstone had the distinction of being appointed the first female Minister for Immigration, with the portfolio of Minister for Immigration, Multicultural and Indigenous Affairs (there was a shift in the Howard era from categorising portfolios as 'ethnic affairs' to 'multicultural affairs'), as well as Minister Assisting the Prime Minister for Reconciliation. The Prime Minister she was assisting, of course, was John Howard. Vanstone took on the Immigration portfolio in the aftermath of the *Tampa* and Children Overboard affairs, and at a time when there was a significant degree of public controversy over the Pacific Solution.

The portfolio was shrunk on 27 January 2006, when Indigenous Affairs was officially removed and Mal Brough became the minister for the newly created portfolio of Families and Community Services and Indigenous Affairs. Vanstone's portfolio changed to Immigration and Multicultural Affairs. She held this role for twelve months, until being removed from Cabinet in an election-year reshuffle on 30 January 2007. In her time holding the Immigration portfolio, Vanstone would regularly speak about Australia having a 'big heart' when it came to dealings with refugees. Throughout Vanstone's tenure as Immigration minister she routinely used both emotional and bureaucratic language to describe the ways in which she governed the lives of refugee and asylum-seeker children.

Vanstone interacted with the media, the public and Opposition parliamentarians with a mix of caustic humour and nonchalance. Julia Baird, in *Media Tarts*, her exploration of women politicians, describes how '[m]any journalists say they admire [Vanstone's] blunt and aggressive approach, but dislike her politics, considering her to be a moderate who sold out in her tough attacks on welfare fraud, in cutting funds in the university sector, and ... maintaining government policy on keeping asylum seekers in mandatory detention'.[9] Vanstone regularly used derogatory humour in her parliamentary appearances. One characteristic example was her response to Labor senator John Faulkner after he 'kept commenting on her size': Vanstone called him the 'King of Combover' and, according to Baird in 2004, '[s]he's still proud of the comment'.[10] When there were rumblings of discontent between Cheryl Kernot and Natasha Stott Despoja, 'Vanstone famously quipped that there was only room for one blonde in the Democrats'. After Stott Despoja expressed outrage, Vanstone retorted, 'Look, I've been attacked by the appearance police for years and you know there is nothing wrong with being blonde – otherwise you wouldn't have dyed your hair that colour.'[11]

In a committee hearing regarding changes to the process of applying for Temporary Protection Visas, Vanstone's deployment of humour indicated a lack of empathy. Discussing how the process would work, she said, 'One example that I can think of would be Mr Sisalem, who was the last man [in immigration prison] on Manus Island [the first time that the Manus Island prison was opened as an immigration detention facility]. I notice that his cat, which was apparently brought here by some charity group, has now ticked off. It would not be the only partnership that has broken up once they got where they wanted to be. The cat is just like everybody else, I suppose.'[12]

In her time as Immigration minister, Vanstone regularly asserted a desire to police Australia's borders and control the movement of people across them, and used an emotion-laden idea of the figure of the child refugee to engender public sentiment for these policies. Vanstone was intent on creating a sense of Australia as a place that both cares about refugees and protects its borders. Throughout her tenure Vanstone would return again and again to two interlinked tropes: the idea that no one wants child refugees to be in detention, and the idea that politicians and governments have difficult decisions to make – they face a crisis – and thus they routinely have to choose the lesser of two evils. Take as an example 28 October 2003. Lyn Allison, a Democrats senator who (along with other crossbench senators) would regularly use her time in the Senate to seek information about the children held in immigration detention, asked Vanstone about the ninety-five children then in detention. She inquired, 'Does the minister acknowledge the long-term mental and emotional damage these children are suffering as a result of this experience and what responsibility is your government taking for the damaged lives of these children?'[13] Vanstone concluded her lengthy reply by noting 'no-one wants to see children in detention centres. The easiest solution to this problem of course would be for people not to come in unlawfully with children, putting them at risk of being in detention centres … One of the difficult situations you face in government is that you cannot always have both things that you want. You have to choose the lesser of two evils.'[14] Vanstone's expression of empathy here – as throughout her tenure as Immigration minister – functioned to delineate the boundaries of empathy: like the borders of the nation, empathy was to be open only in certain respects, or for certain people, once weighed against other concerns.

In a 2005 reply to Democrat senator Andrew Bartlett, she again commented that '[n]o-one wants to see children in detention'. 'But,' she added, 'I do not want to separate children from their parents, either; nor do I want to say to people smugglers, "If you bring people with children they will be out and will not be detained." It is a very difficult issue.'[15] This was a sentiment that she would often voice. Similarly, she would often assert the ideas that '[m]y department takes very seriously its responsibilities to meet the fundamental needs of detainees, especially with regard to children who are in immigration detention',[16] and, 'The government has never been of the view that it is ideal to have children in detention. We have never been of that view.'[17] Such formulations help to naturalise the idea of the national borders as being in need of protection, and the harsh regulation of people's movements as inevitable. It creates the notion of a problem that is difficult to solve.

The best way to solve this crisis, Vanstone was clear, was to maintain harsh border policies. There was an emphasis on deterrence. When the Human Rights and Equal Opportunity Commission released their 2004 inquiry into children in detention, which documented instances of child abuse and demanded that all children be released from detention, Vanstone's response was, 'That's a very dangerous message to send to people-smugglers … It says to people-smugglers, "if you bring children you will be able to be out in the community very quickly", and that is a recipe for people-smugglers to put more children on these very dangerous boats and bring them to Australia.'[18]

Even when policies were changed, the rhetoric was much the same. In the 2005 committee hearings regarding the Migration Amendment (Detention Arrangements) Bill – which was primarily designed to alter the conditions under which children could be held in detention and introduce community detention for them – Vanstone asserted:

> What the government want to do is maintain strong border protection. We are very pleased that we have largely stopped people coming on boats. We hope that no more lives are lost by people taking a chance on those rickety, stinking, unsafe vessels to come in monsoon time, or at other times, and put their lives at risk. But, because we have been successful in that and we now have a smaller case load, we believe we can and should soften the individual impact of that policy, and we will.[19]

The rejection of people smugglers, and the demonisation of those who utilise them, was a constant through Vanstone's parliamentary appearances. In the committee hearings, Vanstone explained: 'If we want to talk in the compassion stakes about where my heart lies first, it is with people in refugee camps who do not have running water or power. I will always take every step I can to give them preference over people who have enough money to pay a crim, spivvy people smuggler. I am very proud to be part of a government that does that.'[20] Vanstone continued to talk about the choices that politicians are forced to make between 'policy alternatives' when 'you do not want either of them but you have to have one. Or you are forced to choose between alternatives when you want both of them but you cannot have both.' 'Government,' Vanstone said, 'is not about the luxury of writing on a whiteboard what is the ideal world ... It is not about the luxury of sitting in academia and saying, "what would be ideal?" It is about what must be done in the national interest at this time and what is fair.'[21] Vanstone here is working to affirm the government's credentials, to create a bipartisan community of politicians who care about refugees, but care about them only under particular circumstances: when they get to choose who the refugees are who will come to Australia. Politicians, Vanstone was making clear, face a struggle that only they can understand. In this parliamentary war of rhetoric, Vanstone sought to build an idea of herself, and the nation, as caring but troubled by the situation and the limited available options. She also sought to create an idea of a nation composed of people who arrive in a manner deemed suitable by the government.

In a committee response to Labor senator Joe Ludwig, Vanstone affirmed her caring credentials, disputing Ludwig's assertion that she lacked compassion. She lamented that when migrants have their claims rejected it is sad:

> That is simply because they have been through all of the processes and had all of the reviews by tribunals and judicial officers and they have been given a no. But they still desperately want to stay in Australia, so they seek ministerial intervention. To get a no from that is, of course, a very sad situation. Legally it might be quite appropriate, perhaps, but personally it is sad ... I can think of one case ... of a young child who was destined not to get the appropriate health care in his country. That health care was a transplant. I was delighted to have the opportunity to help that family.[22]

Vanstone also listed a couple of other children whose cases she intervened in to allow them to remain.

Through her parliamentary comments, and her use of her particular brand of humour, Vanstone was helping to produce a national emotional community who speak of caring about refugees, and child refugees in particular, but who also care about border protection, and care about the boats being stopped more than the children being safely and quickly resettled. She produced an idea that when the various options are weighed against each other – as though in a zero-sum game – border control remains more important. Her words do this emotional work, helping people feel as though they are part of a compassionate nation, and reassuring them that this feeling of compassion is just, even as it is employed in the service of border enforcement and the construction of ideas of who fits into the Australian settler-colonial nation. This emotional work forms part of a larger narrative numerous Immigration ministers and policymakers have seized on, routinely asserting the difficulty of their portfolio and emphasising the idea that there is a tension between the safety of the Australian nation and 'unauthorised' refugees arriving by boat. Vanstone's bluntness, as well as her occasional moments of rhetorical empathy, saw her put a unique spin on her role, but her words continued a well-worn tradition into the future: an emotional border, which sat alongside a physical border, was being perpetuated.

The Vanstonian Australian moment is part of a long, transnational history of the politics of emotion around borders that I am charting in this chapter through the figure of the Immigration minister, and in this book through the coloniality of border- and population-making more generally. Such moments are not isolated, but are transnational, border-crossing and enduring. Understood in this way, it is clear that the dilemmas and difficulties Vanstone points to are actually produced by her, by successive governments, and by international regimes, in order to further a particular emotional vocabulary and community, with a set of political goals in mind.

The creation of a sense of impossibility and crisis produces a set of emotions and processes which, as Kahnawake Mohawk anthropologist Audra Simpson described at an event at the Wheeler Centre in Melbourne in February 2016, creates an extractive economy wherein people are 'evacuated' from their histories.[23] This extractive economy is very real, with Richard Marles – then Shadow Minister for Immigration and Border Protection – asserting in a 2015 parliamentary speech that 'the most important asset that any country has is its children'.[24] As people move, they become property of the state that variously claims them or does not, but that definitely controls them. They are often not allowed to move their histories with them. But histories should move, and should be moving. The narrative could – and should – sit with and be controlled by those who move, rather than with those who control the movement. But in the meantime, Amanda Vanstone can empathise with those who face the difficulties of applying for visas because she evacuates the histories of these people, not paying attention to what brought them there.

Following Vanstone as Immigration minister, Kevin Andrews held the role for less than a year before the change of government in 2007. Kevin Rudd swept to power in December and placed Chris Evans into the role.

Chris Evans

On 29 July 2008, Senator Chris Evans, Labor Minister for Immigration and Citizenship, delivered a speech at the Australian National

University entitled 'New Directions in Detention – Restoring Integrity to Australia's Immigration System'.[25] Heralding what he declared to be a new approach in which 'the immigration system will be characterised by strong border security, firm deterrence of unauthorised arrivals, effective and robust immigration processes and respect for the rule of law and the humanity of those seeking migration outcomes', Evans followed this a year later by introducing the Migration Amendment (Immigration Detention Reform) Bill 2009 into the Senate.[26] This Bill lapsed in September 2010, but its explanatory memorandum was described to me in an interview with a former ministerial adviser as a key moment in Labor's understandings and implementation of the principle of the 'best interests of the child'.[27] The memorandum explains how the Bill amends the *Migration Act 1958* 'to support the implementation of the Government's New Directions in Detention policy', so that 'the Parliament affirms as a principle that the purpose of detaining a non-citizen is to manage the risks to the Australian community of the non-citizen entering or remaining in Australia and to resolve the non-citizen's immigration status'. Another purpose related specifically to children: it said that this Bill would 'strengthen the existing principle in section 4AA of the Act that the detention of a minor is a measure of last resort by providing that a minor, including a person reasonably suspected of being a minor, must not be detained in a detention centre established under this Act; and if a minor is to be detained, an officer must for the purposes of determining where the minor is to be detained, regard the best interests of the minor as a primary consideration'.[28] This type of legislative intervention is one example of the kind of work that Evans undertook during his time as Immigration minister.

Chris Evans was a Labor senator for Western Australia from 1993 to 2013, and Minister for Immigration and Citizenship from 3 December

2007 to 14 September 2010. I interviewed him in October 2018, when he was working at Andrew 'Twiggy' Forrest's Minderoo Foundation as a Strategic Engagement Lead for Walk Free, Forrest's organisation exploring modern slavery. It has been reported that Forrest made his money from plundering Aboriginal land through mining and has recently worked with governments to introduce the Cashless Debit Card, a mode of restricting the ways those people who are forced onto it – most of whom are First Nations peoples – can spend their money.[29]

Evans told me that being Immigration minister was 'the best job [he] ever had ... what better job for an immigrant than to allow people to come and make their lives and support them to make their lives in Australia. And so, I really enjoyed it. There was a lot of interaction with people and I got to do good things and got great satisfaction from the role.'[30]

'We're a great migrant nation,' he told me, and the Labor Party, 'once we got past the White Australia policy issues', has 'been a strong supporter of migration and humanitarian arrivals as well as skilled migration'. '[T]he policy issues were fascinating and controversial and to be frank – without being too political – the Howard government's administration of the Immigration portfolio had set a tone, culture and policy framework which I, and the Labor Party were, deeply opposed to,' he asserted. 'And a lot of the departmental officials were deeply unhappy with what had been asked of them. It was a great opportunity to come in and do what a Labor minister should do, rather than be in a portfolio where you're administering a lot of the former government's policies and there's not much policy reform. It was just a great opportunity. So, as I say, while there's a lot of pain, trauma and disappointment associated with the last period of my time in the ministry, overall it was a rewarding job.'

This period of 'pain' occurred when, due to global circumstances, 'thousands of unauthorised persons arrived by boat'. It required the majority of the Immigration department's resources and created a situation where he and those who carried out the policies received constant criticism. Evans saw this, he reiterated to me, as a period of 'trauma'. Towards the end of our interview, he told me that his time as Immigration minister is 'one of the great disappointments of my life ... just the way it fell apart and we lost control of the debate and – so as I say, it's the best job I ever had and while I loved it in many ways there's no doubt that the path that we ended up going down and where we are now as a country is terrible'.

Evans explained to me his frustration at losing control within his own party towards the end of his time as Immigration minister. In November 2009, as refugees came on boats, and Labor perceived themselves to be in the middle of a crisis, Prime Minister Kevin Rudd organised for a group of Sri Lankan refugees who had been picked up by the *Oceanic Viking* – an Australian Customs Service armed patrol vessel – to be taken from Australian waters and sent to Bintan in Indonesia. The group refused to leave the *Oceanic Viking*, leading to a month-long standoff before they were eventually forced to disembark in Indonesia. This move was one which Evans played no role in deciding: he told me that he 'was briefed after ... I was down in Bunbury at a soccer tournament with my son, a dads' weekend soccer tournament, and I'd gone for a walk and I got a call from his Chief of Staff. I was sure the decision had already been taken.' For Evans, this was the 'moment when we lost any control of the argument'. 'It just crystallised all the concerns [about Labor's approach] in a way that we'd been able to hold off beforehand. And Rudd's impetuous decision to have a brilliant intervention just saw us lead the news for a month. Coverage of the impasse was on full time, leading every *Sky News* bulletin every half hour for a month or more. So, it just cemented the view that the government can't manage this issue.' Evans told me that this was Labor's *Tampa*. I interpreted this to mean that this was a moment when a crisis was created in order to control the narrative, and doing so pitted different actors against each other. The contest over who would be in control – Prime Minister, Immigration minister, media, Opposition – was, it seemed, the key determinant.

Throughout our interview, Evans criticised what he saw as the simplification advocates do in their work for refugees and asylum seekers. In a discussion about his priorities when he first took office, he asserted: 'in fact, there were very few refugees still in, or refugee applicants still in, detention when we came to government. People always confuse the people in Villawood with asylum seekers. Well, many of them are just criminals or overstayers. They're people waiting to be deported after finishing their prison terms or what have you. The maximum security at Villawood's a very tough place, with some really unpleasant people. But you'd have the advocates out the front, demanding they be released, you know? Well, you clearly haven't met them … There were people from different ends of the immigration spectrum there, including murderers or drug dealers waiting to get deported.'

Like other Immigration ministers, Evans stressed to me that the role required 'having the guts to make the tough call' on releasing people from detention. There had been a 'default position' held by his predecessors, he said, that people should be left in detention if there was anything potentially 'dodgy' about them or their cases couldn't be easily resolved, but he 'took risks to end their indefinite detention'. This was balanced with the fact that, as he told me, 'if I let someone out with a criminal record and the next day they committed a crime in Melbourne, you know, it'd be a very short-term career as Minister for Immigration. But a large number of people were being held without charge with no way of having their case resolved. The default position had been to keep them in detention because it's easier, risk-free for the minister. The view was no-one cares about them, they're foreigners and while there's the usual suspects complaining about people in detention, that had all died away a bit.'

As Evans narrates it, there were some difficult decisions that had to be made to resolve what was otherwise indefinite detention for some.

Evans explained that for him, mandatory detention was part of a 'risk management strategy', a way of keeping track of who had arrived, 'not an unreasonable response to someone arriving without papers or visas'. He told me he believed that 'you do need a process for who you let in the country – so I don't have a problem with short-term mandatory detention'. But for him the difference was in what was to be done with them: how they would be processed, and how quickly, to avoid them being left to languish. In distinction to his predecessors, Evans told me, processing people and moving them through the system was important to him. In 2008, it was widely reported that he told Senate Estimates he was 'uncomfortable' with the degree of authority he had: 'I have formed the view that I have too much power,' he said, explaining, 'I am uncomfortable with that, not just because of concern about playing God, but also because of the lack of transparency and accountability for those decisions and the lack in some cases of any appeal rights against those decisions.'[31]

What was the extent of this discomfort, though? 'People on the left would say well, you should never have any people in detention. Well, I don't agree with that until we work out who the hell they are,'

Evans told me. 'You know, do I mean two years? No, that's clearly not acceptable. We tried to improve procedures so that we detained people for the shortest time possible subject to the checks. If you've got a Hazara family with three kids who have no health concerns, et cetera, fit a profile where you're fairly confident they'll be found to be refugees, you know, you can manage them by saying to one of the care agencies, "Can you find them a house and look after them while their refugee application is determined?"' They worked hard, he said, to 'expand community detention models. But again, that response got overrun by the numbers arriving.' Yet his aim, he was clear, was 'to take the heat out of the issue', even as he maintained his control.

But this was not always possible, even within his own office. Immigration can be a highly emotional portfolio. Evans told me a story of a woman who had previously worked in government and was a key member of his staff, who responded to Evans getting the Immigration portfolio by crying and saying, 'I can't do it. I can't do it again. I can't be doing Immigration. I can't stay.' 'When I asked "why?" she said, "Because it makes you hard." It rocked me! I thought what have I done? You know? Because she had worked in the portfolio before and this was such a strong emotional response.'

I asked him if he thought that the role had made him hard. He replied that it 'probably did make me hard about some things': 'But I was conscious of the need to fight against those reactions. You could feel yourself hardening at times of stress or difficulty – because people do game the system. They do game the system to their advantage, they want to stay. So, you'd find Afghan refugees arriving with the same story, you know? Because someone had told them that's the way you get into Australia. But the question becomes, does that mean that they do it because they're not a refugee or do they do it because they've been told that's what will work?'

Anyone from a refugee family will be familiar with these practices of playing with stories and documents. When I looked at my grandparents' naturalisation applications, held in the National Archives of Australia, the various different documents in there have multiple dates for their marriage, none of which are particularly plausible, given what my family knows of their histories separately and together. But refugees and displaced people share information in order to be able to assert themselves to government authorities in the most strategic, the most effective, ways. Governments, and border controls, can be intentionally difficult. People do the best they can to navigate them. Any of us who has filled out a tax return has thought about how they can present their year's spending in order to get the best outcome for themselves. Navigating bureaucracy is modern life. And yet. If my grandparents had used those documents to try to come to Australia in the twenty-first century, I have little doubt that they would have been imprisoned and turned away.

Alongside warnings of hardness was the advice he received from another former staffer who sent Evans a note after he took office, telling him to 'walk in their shoes'. Evans told me that he had taken this to heart: 'it was great advice' and he 'used that line the first time [he] spoke to the Department about adopting a change of philosophy. And so, they then picked that up and started using it in explaining the government's approach when briefing staff. If you walk in their shoes it gives you a whole different, more empathetic perspective while applying the official policies.' This was necessary as 'I found the technical definition of the Refugee Convention troubling and in need of modernisation. If you've got an Afghan man who left because of the violence and the war who maybe wasn't directly persecuted, but who had two daughters who were refused an education in Afghanistan, they may not be found to be refugees. But would I have left if I was him? Yes, absolutely. Technically they may not be refugees but they're people making perfectly rational decisions. It's very hard to deal with people that are making rational decisions that don't fit the Convention criteria. So if someone had told him that his way to be accepted into the country was to say the Taliban had visited his house or whatever, then he'd make from his perspective the rational decision to say the Taliban visited my house. And to be honest, the refugee assessment inside the Department was also equally poor and lacking rigour.'

Bureaucrats lacked the necessary information and were rushed for time and under-resourced, Evans said. And so their decisions were often 'not of the standard one would want'.

In our interview, Evans told me, 'If you look at our detention policy, it wasn't particularly focused on the children', or on getting children out of detention before others. 'We were able to largely make suitable arrangements for families,' he said. But he also highlighted the place of children in his thinking about refugee policy, drawing attention to the notion of these children as innocent victims in need of saving. He told me that there are 'two arguments that are sort of easy simplistic lines in this space: get children out of detention and save people from being killed on the high seas. They're both simplistic and both misrepresent the complexity of the issues but are used as if they are the only thing people need to understand.'

I asked Evans about Tony Burke's speech at the 2015 Labor National Conference – the speech in which Burke drew on his emotions about children drowning in order to argue that boat turnbacks should become Labor policy. He told me: 'I mean, I like Tony, but it was a political response driven by the imperative of the electoral politics. That National Conference wasn't great. The Liberals hide behind the mantra that they are saving people from deaths on the high seas. If you go back and look at Hansard about what they said before those deaths, they made extraordinary attacks on these people, calling them queue jumpers and making vitriolic attacks on those people seeking asylum. And then after the deaths at sea they had the perfect more middle-ground argument to make that, "We're saving these people from dying at sea." Well, there was no empathy or sympathy for them prior to that becoming the politically more compelling argument. And it's the same for children in detention in a sense, that you can be strong on getting children out of detention and therefore it's as if nothing else of the complexities of the issues really matters because that's what people focus on.

Even in considering this recognition of the politics of emotion around children, Evans was clear that he felt a certain sympathy for children that he did not hold for adults. Evans made clear that he found ministerial interventions a 'terrible' process. He told me that each minister would give priority to different types of people in their granting of approval, and applicants and their lawyers come to learn how to frame their applications. 'Your lawyer puts an application in for ministerial intervention after you've lost at all decision-making stages along the line. And the application might be only two or three pages, right? The Department clips it on a file, gives a bit of background, and throws it up to the Minister. I was getting 7000 intervention requests a year. Poorly researched, full of untested claims and sometimes individuals not even having been interviewed. Every time on the plane going home, I'd take thirty or so files. But I remember noticing that if I looked at the first file and the last one I processed, I'd got harder in my judgements as I'd worked down the pile. You know, I did a test on myself. Because it's just that by the time you'd seen thirty of them your empathy diminished. But one of the reasons for that is that the agents and lawyers all play the Minister. So, under previous Minister Andrews, basically anyone who said they're Falun Gong got in.'

Evans, though, took a 'far more rigorous approach' to granting asylum to people claiming Falun Gong membership. For him, 'what went up was successful interventions involving children. People seeking intervention who have Australian-born children. I don't think I knocked one back. I don't think so. Certainly – if I did it would have been a very young child or because of a problematic parent. But, you know, if they had been here three or four years, and they'd had one or two children born in Australia, refusal seemed like punishing the child.'

Most children in his time as Immigration minister came as part of family groups, he remembered, and the impulse was to keep families together. But there were also unaccompanied minors who came, and within that group it was so-called 'anchor children' who were a key concern for him. And '[n]early every Afghan man who arrived in Australia while I was Minister claimed to be seventeen,' Evans told me. 'And the AFP used to measure their wrists to determine their age. And that went well! But, as I say, you can be cynical and get hard about it, but everyone told them it would be advantageous to be seventeen, you know? And so, they were seventeen.' But these unaccompanied minors were 'a problem … particularly when they were allegedly seventeen-year-old Afghan boys, some of whom you knew were a lot older than seventeen. You couldn't put them into some settings, because they were young males and sexually active and putting them with children was problematic. So, there's all sorts of those management issues that people don't think about that makes managing the process very complex.'

But for Evans, what was key was having 'compassionate, risk-based policies'. He returned to this as we were concluding our interview, telling me that he 'must admit, the children's issue wasn't – I don't want to sound dismissive, but because we'd changed the philosophy of the detention, the children weren't such a big issue. Because if you're managing risk and appropriate form of detention, then you try and get the families into family accommodation so they're living as a family unit and they're not in a detention centre. We quickly decided that they weren't going into detention centres. But under the law we had to keep them in detention. This is where we stretched the definition of detention. A family might be living in a house, you know, provided in Melbourne, supported by a care organisation, but they were technically in detention. We probably stretched it beyond what would have survived a challenge in the High Court.'

Evans would not be the last Immigration minister to reclassify housing around children's imprisonment, although others have done so in order to keep people within the detention centres. In April 2016, then Immigration minister Peter Dutton claimed that no children were left in detention following the reclassification of certain sections of detention centres as 'community detention'.[32] He repeated a similar claim in June 2019.[33]

Evans was widely understood to have taken extensive action on behalf of refugees during his time in the Immigration portfolio. But Evans was not immune to arguing that border control was more important than the freedom of child refugees, despite how he and others might remember him and his actions. Evans was guided towards governmental control, exercised through risk-management discourses and concern about the state of the Australian nation. But he also presented himself as caring deeply about the refugees whose lives he controlled, as being cognisant of the positions refugees found themselves in and the kinds of ways in which they would act in their own best interests, and as being ambivalent about the emotional sway that refugee children had. Fundamentally, he was being guided by a desire to do right by Australia, to ensure no risk to Australia's security. The way that he articulates his actions, understandings and concerns perhaps exemplifies a key point: that there is no way to have complete freedom and justice for child refugees (or indeed any refugee) within the systems created by a settler-colonial state. What is done, what is possible, will always be circumscribed.

Following Evans, Chris Bowen and then Brendan O'Connor were appointed minister by Julia Gillard, with Kevin Rudd installing Tony Burke in the reshuffle when he regained the prime ministership.

Tony Burke

One of Tony Burke's final acts as Immigration minister, at 4.45pm on the Friday before the 2013 federal election, was to sign the papers to allow the release of some thirty-eight unaccompanied refugee children who were still being held in immigration prisons on mainland Australia.[34] Some children were still being held on Christmas Island, pending their later transfer to imprisonment in Nauru as a result of that government's policies of declaring that people who arrived after mid-July 2013 would never be allowed to settle in Australia (even though, as we know, many have been, in another example of the arbitrariness of Australia's immigration controls). But the released children brought 'to 409 the number of children without adult guardians released into group homes since Mr Burke was given the job in June'.[35] Burke told journalist Rick Morton that he 'was particularly concerned I would be left with about 75 children in detention, but I got them out and I am very proud of that'.[36] His pride in his achievements is, it would seem, important in his narrative of his time in office. Like other ministers across this period, Burke positions himself and his feelings at the centre of these governmental practices.

Earlier that month, a sixteen-year-old unaccompanied Somali boy was flown to Perth from the immigration detention centre on Christmas Island after he attempted suicide. The Somali community in Perth tried to reach out to him, with Hassan Egal, the president of the Somali Community Association in Western Australia, telling the ABC, 'As a community we are, traditionally we help each other, and we want to look after him after his situation gets better and give him accommodation and shelter and food, and whatever available until his case of refugee claim is under process ... His family's not here, and he's young, he's underage. We will encourage him, and we'll talk to him in the language, the food, the sense of belonging.'[37]

Burke's Immigration department refused to allow anyone from the community to visit the boy, with a spokeswoman telling the media that 'as the boy's guardian', Burke was 'maintaining a personal interest in his medical care'. She was also reported as saying that 'the focus needed to be on the boy's health and wellbeing and it was far too early to respond to requests from the community or questions about the boy's asylum claims'.[38] Here again, Burke is identified as being central to ensuring control and delivering care. In invoking the idea of being a 'father' to the Somali child, watching over his care, the government prioritises state-based relationships over communal ones. Where the community values markers of ethnic and national belonging – food, language, similarity – Burke's spokesperson deploys rhetoric that emphasises the primary importance of the individual interest of the guardian. The guardian, or the state, determines what happens to the boy.

Tony Burke sees himself as a humanitarian who suffers alongside those he cares about. Burke was Minister for Immigration, Multicultural Affairs and Citizenship from 1 July 2013 until Labor lost the 2013 election, and he finished his term on 18 September 2013. Multicultural Affairs had dropped out of the portfolio since the last Coalition minister, Kevin Andrews, had been appointed Minister for Immigration and Citizenship at the start of 2007, with Citizenship remaining grouped with Immigration during the first Rudd and the Gillard governments. It was only right at the end of this Labor term that Multicultural Affairs was again placed with Immigration.

Burke – as with other Immigration ministers – has considered the government's treatment of children a useful tactic to prevent people getting on boats. In 2013, *The Age* reported 'a defiant Tony Burke' asserting that '[t]he first group of unaccompanied minors will be sent to processing camps on Manus Island or Nauru "before long"'. Through his actions, Burke stated, he was 'taking away every incentive to get on a boat … Whoever wants to test our resolve will find out that we are serious about this and, if it takes for them to be "wheels down" on Manus Island or Nauru before they realise that we're serious, then so be it.' Burke affirmed in this moment that he was not going to be swayed by opposition from refugee advocates, or by the continued arrival of boats. 'There was more than enough capacity in PNG and on Nauru to accommodate all who tested the government's resolve,' by taking boats towards Australia to seek asylum, it was reported. This expressly included children: 'There will be more family groups in the coming days continuing to go across to Nauru and then, before long, we'll be in a situation where unaccompanied minors also find their way across to either Manus Island or Nauru.'[39]

This moving of people to Manus and Nauru was consistent with Burke's view of his humanitarian values, and indeed formed part of building a humanitarian identity. In an interview on ABC's *7.30*, Chris Uhlmann asked Burke, 'Was this what you imagined you'd be doing when you joined the Labor Party? ... That you'd be the minister responsible for the harshest asylum-seeker program that Australia's ever instituted? Is that what you signed up for when you signed up for the Labor Party?' Burke replied:

> I'll tell you what I signed up for. 'Cause one thing I won't accept is an argument that people have wanted to run that this is somehow a lurch to the right and want to see it within a left-right spectrum. The principles that I joined the Labor Party did involve making sure that you don't see the sorts of horrors that we've seen in the Indian Ocean. I haven't been minister for this portfolio for very long, but already there's been a number of people who've died on my watch and the first of them was 2.5 months old. I won't accept that there is any conflict between the principles for me joining the Labor Party and believing in a party that doesn't leave people behind and making sure that we have a policy aimed at stopping the loss of life at sea. And it's beyond that. Also, I want to see a humanitarian program that – where we choose who's coming with the United Nations, not self-selected by people smugglers. I also want to make sure that we can increase the number of refugees who we are helping.[40]

This reply does a lot of work. It puts forward Burke's humanitarian credentials while asserting that the government should have control over who comes into the country. It suggests a criminalisation of those who use people smugglers to come to Australia and uses emotive language to centre Burke's motivations – particularly as related to the 'crisis' of potential deaths of children – in the discussion. The Australian population is determined and governed through these concerns; Australia is made to seem a certain type of home for particular types of people. Through his participation in the circulation of these emotional vocabularies, Burke creates an idea of a community of people, including himself, who care about refugees and asylum seekers, and who seek to navigate a difficult situation in order to produce a good outcome. The emotional language used to describe his situation, in having to make these decisions, creates an impression of him as under pressure and having to make difficult, but necessary and ultimately humanitarian, decisions. The spectre of refugee children's lives and deaths are routinely used to heighten the emotional stakes. We saw this in his address on boat turnback policy to the 2015 Labor Party national conference too; it is worth remembering.

Thus, while Burke is known to be a Catholic, and has articulated this as 'a personal thing',[41] his understanding of himself as in control, and using that control to institute particular forms of care, is congruent with Catholic notions of undertaking benevolent, humanitarian service to those deemed needy, and also fits within larger historical strains in the thinking of Immigration ministers. Throughout his time as Immigration minister, and in the years leading up to and after that period, Burke has worked consistently to affirm that Australia has a caring spirit. The emotion around ideas of the Australian nation, and of what was best for the children under his care, were designed to produce an affective and active community.

Burke would be the last Labor Immigration minister for almost nine years, until Andrew Giles. With Tony Abbott's government taking power in 2013, Scott Morrison was appointed minister, a role he held before Peter Dutton, then David Coleman, Alan Tudge (who was acting minister while Coleman was on indefinite leave) and, finally, Alex Hawke.

Scott Morrison

On 9 November 2018, Scott Morrison gave an interview at a Lifeline event.[42] By then he was Prime Minister, but from 18 September 2013 to 23 December 2014 he had been Minister for Immigration and Border Protection. In an indicator of the political direction being undertaken by this Coalition government, the title of the portfolio had changed again: Multicultural Affairs' time with Immigration was short-lived, as the emphasis fell more explicitly on border control. Morrison told his interviewer: 'ever since I took over the job as Immigration minister many years ago, we set about the job of ensuring that there would be no children on Nauru. And that's what we've been doing ever since.'

> I: For five years.
> SM: It takes a long time. It takes a long time.
> I: Do you think about them, I mean do you think about their mental health?
> SM: Yeah look, when I was Immigration minister and when I was shadow Immigration minister - people may have observed this about me – I'm someone who likes to go, right, and speak to people. So if I make hard decisions about things, I don't do it from some room in Canberra without having personally met with and looked in the eyes of people who are affected by my decisions. I have done that on Nauru, I've done it on Manus Island. I've visited refugee camps all around the world, I've sat in

the middle of a refugee camp in Myanmar with their thousands of Rohingyans' families, but also Burmese refugees as well. I've met them and I've looked at their conditions. You know, politics is not for the faint hearted. You've got to be prepared to understand and own and carry the burden of decisions. You'll find yourself on your knees, you'll find yourself in tears, you'll find yourself wrestling with this stuff.

I: You've been on your knees in tears?

SM: Of course I have, why wouldn't I be? These aren't easy issues Michael. You've got to be prepared to go through that and expose yourself to the consequences of difficult decisions. Now, if you can't do that, do another job. Do another job. This job is not for people who can't confront this stuff and you've got to make tough calls.

Now, you don't get children off Nauru by putting more on and I – probably more than any other, perhaps a few – have to deal with the consequences and understand what happens when a young Border Force officer or a military officer has to push a child face-down from the water. I'm never going to let that happen again Michael.

I: Well, we know, but –

SM: No, you don't. This is my point, you can't deal with those two issues separately. You can't. There is no decision that you make in this space that is free of moral burden. You cannot allow yourself the leave-pass to think there is …

I: Is there a timeline when all these … I mean, certainly the public generally agrees with the border control, no argument. When it comes to the children, a lot of people don't. Is there a timeline when you might get all these children out of the detention centres?

SM: Well the number as everyone knows has been coming down dramatically. We got 8000 children out of detention in

Australia, we closed 17 detention centres. And the number... you know, we didn't send children to Manus Island, by the way. Our predecessors sent pregnant women to Manus Island. We put an end to that and when it comes to Nauru, the numbers of children have been reducing dramatically in accordance with our existing policies.

... [And to get children off] we'll continue to act in accordance with our policies and what we'll do is ensure that anything we do will also not compromise the strength of our border protection policies, which has successfully to date, for five years, five years, has ensured that people haven't got back on those boats. And I will manage both and I'll do both. But as John said, it's about being strong and compassionate, and the two are not mutually exclusive, and I think our policies and the way we have handled this have demonstrated that. There are no decisions free of moral burden.[43]

Predictably and justifiably, there was widespread outrage across social media about these comments. Father Rod Bower, an outspoken Christian minister, suggested that 'only a sociopath could pray and weep for a child on Nauru and then oppose their medical treatment in court'.[44] Sally McManus, secretary of the ACTU, asked, 'Why does he need to pray? He was the person with the power to get them out.'[45] Twitter user Peter Relph distilled the mood online when he proclaimed that 'this is the stuff of psychotic horror stories'.[46] Across all platforms, critiques popped up, focusing on Morrison's duplicity or potential sociopathy in making this set of assertions.[47]

One way to understand this moment comes from an interrogation of Morrison's Pentecostalism. Journalist James Boyce explored Morrison's

Pentecostal Christianity in *The Monthly*, arguing that 'the common [understanding] that Morrison was a hypocrite' when it comes to his treatment of detained children 'was almost certainly wrong'. 'Given how Pentecostal Christianity understands evil,' he writes, 'it is much more likely that Morrison's conviction came from the fact that he genuinely believed that the military deployment and harsh punishments for these unauthorised arrivals were the will of God.' For Morrison, Boyce says, Operation Sovereign Borders – a militarised response to preventing refugees and asylum seekers taking boats to Australia in order to claim humanitarian protection – is a war, wherein there is an attempt to defeat Satan and hasten Christ's return through the removal of non-believers.[48] A strict division into 'us' and 'them', into believer and non-believer, is core to the religious worldview of Morrison's church: the border guards are the 'us'; the refugees, including children, 'them'.[49]

But we can also think about how Morrison's words here are part of the longer trajectory of emotions produced by Immigration ministers in the late twentieth and early twenty-first century. This trajectory puts the Immigration minister's feelings at the centre of the political equation, and uses those emotions to cement the idea that border control and imprisonment are the most correct way to deal with people who are deemed 'out of place'. As Gunai/Kurnai, Gunditjmara, Wiradjuri and Yorta Yorta writer Nayuka Gorrie and white social worker Witt Church explained in *The Guardian* in 2018, 'Jail is something we take as part of the furniture in the settler state.'[50] It is part of the furniture of border control. By historicising Morrison's words here, I want to think beyond the description of him as sociopathic or duplicitous and suggest that his deployment of emotions is instead part of a communal history. Immigration ministers regularly produce a discourse that centres them as the key subjects with whom the public should empathise. This is the enduring legacy of White Australia policies: by continually producing the authority of white masculine governmental figures and approaches, it furthers racialised projects of population control, border control and the production of national emotions.

Morrison's words here point us towards the ways in which emotions around child refugees and asylum seekers are mobilised as a technique of government. Both the act of keeping children in detention and taking them out are saturated with feeling (albeit different types of feelings). That is, these children become emotionally 'sticky', to use queer theorist Sara Ahmed's term.[51] Their invocation heightens the pathos of the situation Morrison describes. This ahistorical misery – where the trouble arises from those moments Morrison declares it does, rather than (for instance) from the broader histories of the children or the reasons why they are on the boats – is then used to buttress the claims for the necessity of border control. We should note that the interviewer asserted that most people in Australia accept the idea that the borders should be controlled by the government, except in regard to children. In public discourse, as well as in the oral history interviews I conducted, a dominant narrative has emerged since the late 1990s and early 2000s as – in part – a response to the securitisation crisis the West has produced and mobilised in the post-9/11 era.

We also see in Morrison's words here the invocation of the narrative that scores of people may die at sea. Or, more precisely, that Australian citizens should not have to confront deaths at sea – in Morrison's story in 2018, the Australian citizen is incarnated as the Border Force or military officer who must pull the dead child from the sea.

There is, in Morrison's quote, a broader collision of discourses and mobilisations of emotional narratives. We see the mobilisation of concerns about three things: refugee children, the border and the difficulty of being the minister. We need to understand the importance of this final concern in order to understand properly what is at stake in Morrison's utterances, as in Vanstone's, Burke's and the others'. The problem, in short, is not Morrison. Or is not only Morrison. It is the modern settler-colonial nation-state, and all its accompanying cultures and discourses.

Morrison said, 'You've got to be prepared to understand and own and carry the burden of decisions. You'll find yourself on your knees, you'll find yourself in tears, you'll find yourself wrestling with this stuff.' This statement was the focus of a great deal of media and online commentary, and in its references to his tears and in his articulation of deeply felt emotions, there were echoes of Tony Burke's speech at the 2015 Labor National Conference.

Both of these men are Christians – of different sects, with vastly different understandings of what Christianity entails, but Christian nonetheless. This informs their politics. Their tears, the way in which they link the necessity for violent and punitive responses to people coming to Australia by boat to the emotional force of the idea of children drowning and dying at sea, seem to come as an expression, perhaps, of their Christianity: of their ideas of who should be saved, who should be rescued, who should be damned, and how. Both men imagine a border and population crisis that requires the response they usher. There is something, perhaps, Christ-like in the burden they imagine for themselves. This is not to say that a relationship with Christianity is the only way to arrive at this approach, but that for these two men, this is part of what informs their work.

And their shared vision of Christianity is potentially substantially different to other versions that exist in Australian politics. In an interview I conducted in September 2018, former Liberal politician Bruce Baird articulated a different approach to refugees and humanitarianism that his Christianity produced. Baird had held the seat of Cook before Morrison, and in fact encouraged Morrison to run for the seat. The two men know each other 'quite well', Baird told me.[52] But in response to a question about the role that Christianity played in his politics, particularly with regard to his political campaigning around refugee issues, Baird said that 'it is obviously strong in terms of this, because I felt it was a bit like the parable of the Good Samaritan. Not that I am a Samaritan. I mean, not that I am either good or am I a Samaritan. But in terms of I just think, you know, look, these people [refugees] are in genuine distress [in detention] and so I just felt that there was no way that a Christian could walk past that and just say it didn't happen. I was encouraged, also, by the fact that the Catholic bishops were quite clearly supportive and talking to people as well and getting them onside. But as a Christian, there are various things that some people take it that their role is like a moral policeman. I don't see that, as a Christian. In politics, I never saw my role like that, but rather – You know, I think symbolic of a Christian is grace and forgiveness and compassion – I think are hallmarks of that. And so, yes it had an influence, but that doesn't mean to say that the others who weren't – I mean, Petro [Georgiou] is certainly not, but all of those qualities, he has in spades. Russell [Broadbent], I am not quite sure with Russell. I could never quite pin down. He seemed to go to church, I am not quite sure where or what. It was an open question. And Judi [Moylan] – not. So, it wasn't as if we were on some mission from God in terms of it.'[53]

The three other politicians that Baird mentioned were those whom he worked with extensively to extract compromises on refugee policy from Prime Minister John Howard and Immigration minister Philip Ruddock. This meditation on Christianity and politics from Baird (and Russell Broadbent is indeed a devout Christian) is interesting for the way it opens up the speaker to a sense of possibility: there are multiple options, multiple ways of arriving at a moral response, in Baird's vision. This contrasts, it would seem, with Morrison's invocation of what is to be done. But then Baird was never Immigration minister. And for Morrison and others, particularly when it comes to child refugee policy, the path forward is articulated clearly.

Morrison has had an outsized presence in the Australian political landscape, and the 2022 federal election result was in many ways a complete repudiation of his approach from the population at large. This view was shared by some who had interacted with him in his time as Immigration minister. Gillian Triggs, former president of the Australian Human Rights Commission, remembered that '[t]he arrogance of the man' was 'breathtaking'. 'He's a most disagreeable person to deal with,' she told me, 'but I'd say I'd welcome him any day compared to [Immigration minister Peter] Dutton because Dutton won't communicate. Whereas Scott Morrison is an ego, he [also] likes the cut-and-thrust, so you can have a discussion with him. I mean, he's a bully, but I can stand up to bullies in a way. That's fine. I can stand the cut and thrust with Scott Morrison, but with Dutton, he sits there with the manspread and says, "Right, you've got 20 minutes, Gillian," listens to everything and then says, "Right, well, I've got to go now. Thank you." No debate, no discussion, no engagement, nothing. He just did what he knew he was bound to do, which is listen to me. He's the minister in charge of the Department. He had to listen to me, but that was it, nothing. No response at all on any substantive matter that I raised.'[54]

This is the mould of an Immigration minister under the Coalition governments that held office from 2013 to 2022, but in the way these men act – their confidence, their certainty that they are right, their circumscribing of what care entails – they sit within a longer and broader history of governmental hubris. Morrison's faith in punitive responses and in the provision of violence are indicative of his approach, but when he cries and expresses concern about what is to be done for the children, Morrison also uses these practices in order to assert himself. The emotion associated with children acts as a means through which to generate full governmental control.

'Australians care for refugees'?

Michael MacKellar, Liberal Minister for Immigration and Ethnic Affairs from 1975 to 1979, gave a speech at the annual staff conference and mid-year National Committee Meetings of Austcare in late 1978. In it, he articulated and celebrated an idea of the Australian nation as humanitarian and caring when it came to refugees. He told his audience:

> On your letterhead you use the words 'Australians care for refugees'. I am happy to be able to say to you that this is still very much the case ... Australia has, since the end of the Second World War, taken in upwards of half a million refugees. We have welcomed them without discrimination and without reservation. The elements of compassion and humanity which have informed the policies of all governments since 1945 have been nurtured, if not planted, by people of goodwill such as your organisation represents. Charity, the loving care of one's fellow men, is not an instinct which rises quickly to the surface of the human mind. It is naturally part of the human condition

to think first about one's own preservation, one's own welfare and the stability and comfort of one's immediate dependents ... We Australians present ourselves as a civilised, moral and often religiously-motivated society, but, despite that, as you would be so depressingly aware, the task of motivating our fellow-man into the paths of humanity and keeping him there is demanding and unending.[55]

In this speech we see the perpetuation of a narrative both nostalgic and false, a narrative that posits Australia as caring in a manner it never has been. We have seen this same pathos-laden narrative throughout this chapter, as Immigration ministers all seek to characterise themselves and the nation as invested in caring for refugees.

Looking through the lens of governmental thoughts and feelings about child refugee policy in Australia is illuminating. Witnessing how Immigration policymakers understand themselves in relation to this policy helps us to understand the guiding principles behind this policymaking: the understanding the ministers and those around them hold is that it is the minister's responsibility to control who comes to this country, what their arrival means and how they will be treated on arrival. Additionally, that to maintain this control is to maintain a set of caring, compassionate and humanitarian policy practices. While my interviews with the ministers, and the policymakers who surrounded them, also show that attitudes towards children in the 1980s are remembered as being substantially different to attitudes in the late 2000s – and we can suggest the global growth of child rights discourses since the late 1980s as an explanation for this – their reflections on how they imagine they must have responded is reflective of the pre-eminence of cultures of control and the self-belief in compassion.

What we need remember here is that such interplays between ideas of control and compassion are thoroughly settler colonial, designed to maintain white control over Australia, even as those who practise these forms of control understand themselves to be undoing White Australia. The use of the figure of the child to vouch for one's good intentions and good behaviour is a well-worn tactic of settler-colonial government.

The emotional discourses that Morrison invoked at that November 2018 event were not his alone. They were firmly located in the longer history I have sketched here, and the much longer history of settler-colonial control over Australia's borders, its techniques of government, its controlling relationship with certain types of children, and its mobilisation of practices of detention and incarceration. It is part of a longer history of conceptions of 'the white man's burden', of the idea that white governments need to control how non-white children and their families live, and of a prioritisation of the suffering that governments face when they 'must' take on this kind of control.

We can see the ministers' and former ministers' apparent dilemmas and difficulties as being self-serving, produced in order to develop an emotional vocabulary that was useful for pursuing a governmental goal: total control. The policymakers, as the primary agents of the story, create a sense of crisis, focusing on that particularly emotive figure, the refugee or asylum-seeking child, and in turn producing a set of personal and national emotions. To bring these two threads together further: when these politicians focus on their own dilemmas, or their suffering and their tears, they do so because this is precisely the narcissism of colonial whiteness on which the Australian nation-state rests. The white controller asks for sympathy in their tearful moments. This narcissism expressly evacuates the histories of the children over whom they claim to cry: commonly, there is a radical disinterest in what brought those children onto those boats. Morrison's words therefore are not an example of dehistoricised saturation of feeling – not simply the result of an individual hypocrite or sociopath – but are a political mobilisation of a history of settler-colonial feeling, one mode of producing whiteness and non-whiteness in order to limit the horizons of possibility, one means of retaining control over the lives, behaviours, fortunes and futures of child refugees and asylum seekers.

CHAPTER 6

Politicians and Political Parties

'Shame is a powerful word and a powerful emotion,' Andrew Wilkie MP told Parliament in May 2014. 'Most people have felt it at one time or another – a feeling deep inside when we know we have done something wrong. And I think we all know that the wrong that leads to shame is often a wrong done to others.'[1] Wilkie, a former lieutenant colonel in the Australian Army and a whistleblower who resigned from the Office of National Assessments 'in protest over the Iraq War', has been the independent Member for Denison (now Clark) since 2010. He was speaking in the House of Representatives on Monday 26 May 2014, introducing the Migration Amendment (Ending the Nation's Shame) Bill 2014 to Parliament.

This was a private member's Bill that Wilkie introduced to Parliament. As the explanatory memorandum made clear, it sought 'to amend the *Migration Act 1958* ... to afford specific rights to non-citizens who travel or are brought to Australia which they are currently denied under existing legislation'.[2] The Bill was also intended to ensure 'that children who are travelling with their parents are not to be separated'.[3] In his speech, Wilkie described in some detail the quality of the shame felt – as the name of the Bill makes clear – at the national level. He argued that 'millions of Australians do feel shame at the actions of this and previous governments when it comes to our country's response to asylum seekers. And moreover they feel this shame keenly, shame at actions done in their name'. He sought to persuade: 'this bill makes Australia act like the rich and civilised country that we are; a place that not only signed up to the refugee convention, but also one that believes in it. This bill would end the shame.' Australia could be righted by taking these legislative steps to change the treatment of refugees and asylum seekers, he said.

Wilkie explained that the legislation 'ends mandatory detention, ends offshore processing and ends temporary protection visas. It also gives asylum seekers full access to Medicare, Centrelink and work rights and full access to legal support and the rights of appeal.' He noted that 'we saw the pained faces of observers who tell of children in detention who have stopped speaking or who refer to themselves by number, rather than name. And surely there is no greater shame than that done to the world's children.'[4]

Given the lack of support, the bill was not considered within sufficient time (eight consecutive sitting Mondays) and on 28 October 2014 was removed from consideration by Parliament.[5] Wilkie was undeterred. In 2019 he introduced a similar bill, telling Parliament, 'We can, and must, do better … I'd remind everyone in this space that we need to stop talking about asylum seekers and refugees as a threat to national security and start recognising that Australia has a legal and moral obligation to give protection to asylum seekers, to quickly hear their claims and to provide permanent refuge if those claims are correct.'[6] This bill lapsed at the dissolution of Parliament before the federal election in 2019, and he again introduced a similar bill in February 2021 (which was also removed from consideration) and again in

August 2022.[7] In her speech seconding the 2022 version, Kylea Tink – an independent MP for North Sydney – explained, 'In 2015, as part of the We're Better Than This campaign, together with a wider group of prominent Australians from business, the arts, academia, sport and religion, I condemned the conditions in which children were being detained, particularly on the islands of Nauru and Christmas Island. We won, and 276 kids got out of detention. But due to a lack of action from successive governments, the cruelty persists.'[8]

Wilkie's – and Tink's – legislative and rhetorical approach acts to bring certain issues to the parliamentary stage. Refugee advocates use a wide range of tools to encourage public discussion and action, and for a parliamentarian, introducing a private member's bill is one such option. And in doing so, Wilkie undertakes a performance of national emotions. The 2014 Bill, and its accompanying speech and explanatory memorandum, speaks a set of ideas, rhetoric, discourses and grammars in the public arena. Wilkie drew on a history of the centrality of the treatment of refugees and asylum seekers, and immigrants more generally, to white Australian national feeling, and advanced the production and performance of that history. He highlighted the central place children have been understood to have in this emotional schema. Through this, Wilkie reinforced the twinning of two ideas, as we have already seen others doing in this book: the production of the figure of the child refugee or asylum seeker and the production of the Australian nation, through emotional discourses, or economies of emotion. We can see here what emotional work these narratives about the population group defined as 'child refugees' do in the national imagination, and what narratives of the nation do in formulating ideas about child refugees. Or, to put it another way, there is a sentiment-rich relationship between ideas of child refugees and ideas of the

Australian nation-state. As Sara Ahmed has written about Australian feelings of shame in response to the Stolen Generations, 'declarations of shame can bring "the nation" into existence as a felt community'.[9] This chapter seeks to understand the racialised dynamics of this 'felt community' and to explore the way those people we elect to represent us instantiate this community.

The words of politicians from the 1990s to the present are illuminating in this regard. The words show us how politicians think about themselves and their role, and how they think about the place of these children within Australian politics. More particularly, the words of politicians who can be broadly understood to situate their speech within a liberal politics are revealing: by looking at what they say, we can grasp what a liberal, ostensibly pro-refugee, position looks like within the context of the politics being explored in this book.

First, some context. I approached significantly more people to participate in interviews for this project than those who agreed to be interviewed, and still fewer approved the transcript of our interview. I would have liked to speak to those such as the Greens' Nick McKim and Sarah Hanson-Young, who have both held the position of Greens spokesperson for Immigration; Labor's Anthony Albanese, Tanya Plibersek and Jenny Macklin, who in the past have been active on these and related issues; and former Liberal Party MP Craig Laundy, the Assistant Minister for Multicultural Affairs in 2016. But over the course of my research, I interviewed eight current or retired politicians or people senior within a political party's hierarchies. The politicians included Labor's Andrew Giles, Anna Burke, Carmen Lawrence and Matt Thistlethwaite, and the Liberal Party's Bruce Baird and Trent Zimmerman. I also spoke to political party operatives. This chapter's discussion of their responses and ideas as they came through in the interviews therefore is not exhaustive. This is but a sampling of politicians, a snapshot of their views. But still, patterns emerged. Through their words I believe we can gain a sense of what politicians may think in this realm of policymaking. We can also see which types of politicians are open to having these conversations, putting themselves on record on these matters.

There is no doubt that immigration policy is a troublesome area. It is a portfolio in which many politicians are hesitant to work, hesitant to lead and hesitant to speak out about. There are many reasons, of course, why a politician may not want to participate in an interview about immigration policymaking, particularly given that when I was approaching potential interviewees Australia had a Coalition government, coupled with an impending election. The histories that I can write, like all histories, are necessarily circumstantial. We can only make meaning with the sources available to us, and the full range of sources is never available.

But this does not mean that sources can tell us nothing.

Understanding orientations

As I think about how Australian politicians describe themselves and their policy work regarding child refugees, like Wilkie above, I want to think about how they orient themselves. I come to this through Sara Ahmed's meditations on orientation. At the beginning of her work *Queer Phenomenology*, she asks an important question. Ahmed writes, 'What difference does it make "what" we are oriented toward?' She explains that 'orientation is a matter of how we reside in space ... of how we inhabit spaces as well as "who" or "what" we inhabit spaces with'. Orientations are a question of familiarity, of how we engage with the familiar and the unfamiliar, and how we make things familiar or unfamiliar.[10] Familiarity can also be a question of normalisation or naturalisation: what, who and which stories do we consider normal? Orientations can be understood to shape to whom we respond, and how. They illuminate the difference between, for example, looking towards justice for refugees as the purpose of policy and looking towards border control, and which people feel they are 'naturally' inclined to do. These orientations are determined by, and determine, how we live our lives, how we conceptualise the work we do and how we express our relationships to others. In this understanding, emotions are 'relational'; they are one way of situating us within a social world made up of relationships between people.[11]

Emotions, Ahmed tells us, are not static, and they do not 'reside in subjects or objects'; they are produced through 'circulation', or interaction between people.[12] As emotions circulate, they build. Through the circulation of emotions, people are brought together into shared communities. Whether we think of something as sad, or fear-inducing, or joyful, binds us to people who think similarly of it. This can be consciously articulated, but does not need to be. It is more likely that such emotions will be expressed unconsciously. But regardless, we bring others into our circle, or emotional community, by sharing our emotions. Circulation determines who we believe deserves empathy and who censure; whose histories, and particularly in this case, histories of violence and trauma, are narrated and heard, and whose are dismissed. We can understand this process in terms of what the historian Barbara Rosenwein has called 'emotional communities': the circulating emotions bring people together into a community.[13] These are communities in which 'shared vocabularies and ways of thinking … have a controlling function, a disciplining function', which push the group towards particular actions.[14] Emotions secure us to others.[15]

In this way, politicians become bonded to each other as part of an emotional community that collectively talks about a fundamentally good white Australian nation that they imagine exists. Francesco Ricatti has described this as the way in which 'white anxiety, xenophobia and racism can be emotionally "repackaged" as more palatable feelings of moral superiority', and observes that 'this tendency might also characterize progressive sections of Australian society'.[16]

Politicians' orientations

In my conversations with politicians, many told me they had experienced changes regarding who they oriented themselves towards and away from. Andrew Giles, a Labor MP and the incumbent Minister for Immigration, Citizenship and Multicultural Affairs, told me in 2018 that his perspective changed when he acted as a solicitor on record for Liberty Victoria on behalf of the refugees on the MV *Tampa*. '[This] was a really profoundly shaping experience for me and it was a challenging experience as a member of the Labor Party because there was this period of equivocation on the part of Kim Beazley before he ultimately flipped and supported the government's legislative efforts, which ended the litigation, or ended our involvement in litigation, and I think to all practical purposes ended litigation. I was disappointed by that.'[17]

This moment, he said, caused him to reflect on the role that politicians, legislation and parliamentary politics can play, and 'the limitations of do-gooding lawyers being do-gooding lawyers'. In 2013 he was elected to the House of Representatives, and has since spent significant time with Labor Immigration ministers. Being around them has meant that he now 'feel[s] much less ungenerous – I was going to say "more generous" but I prefer "less ungenerous" – to those people who have been Immigration Ministers, having sat in parliament … because I disagree with probably most of the substantive decisions that were taken by Labor [from] 2009 on. But I don't think any of them were unreasonable decisions to be made in response to the circumstances that those people found themselves in. And I think about my colleagues in the caucus who were part of government and particularly at the time when boat arrivals were high and people were dying. And I think I was too quick to judge people in terms of their electoral nervousness, less on their efforts to grapple with, really, with a matter of life and death.'

Here, he has to come to adopt the same kinds of language that they use. As he told me, 'It's something … that a policymaker has to grapple with and find better answers and, you know, I was as affected as anyone listening to Tony Burke speak at the national conference and I know that it weighs heavily on him' and on other former Labor Immigration ministers. At that national conference, Giles moved the motion opposing Labor adopting boat turnbacks as policy, and was the first speaker for the Left faction on this topic and thus against Burke's position.[18]

As a newly appointed Minister for Immigration, in June 2022 Giles moved quickly to grant the Nadesalingam family a bridging visa and then permanent residency, using the powers granted to him by the *Migration Act 1958* to intervene in this case. In February 2023, a week after Parliament reauthorised the use of the immigration prison in Nauru, Giles announced the plan to move some people who were on Temporary Protection Visas and Safe Haven Enterprise Visas onto the pathways towards permanent protection visas. But his public rhetoric conforms in some ways to the pattern of other recent Immigration ministers, in terms of its invocation of national emotions and its claims to the importance of 'strong borders'. His statement for Refugee Week, issued on 30 June 2022, read in part, 'As Minister, I am determined to make the case for a different national conversation about meeting our humanitarian commitments. For a debate anchored in compassion, in which the stories of refugees are listened to and where vulnerable human beings are afforded dignity and respect.'[19] In his statement on 5 August 2022 announcing that he was providing permanent visas for the Nadesalingam family, after outlining his 'careful consideration of the Nadesalingam family's complex and specific circumstances' and extending his best wishes to them, he went on to assert that the government would 'continue to intercept and return any unauthorised vessels seeking to reach Australia … I do not want people to die in a boat on a journey when there is a zero chance of settling in Australia.' He concluded: 'We will continue to intercept any unauthorised vessel seeking to reach Australia, and safely return those on board to their point of departure or country of origin or take them to a regional processing country.'[20] In Parliament in November 2022, in response to a question from Andrew Wilkie about the abolition of Temporary Protection Visas, Giles asserted that he was 'very proud to be a member of a government that recognises that we can be resolute in maintaining strong and secure borders whilst not abandoning our humanity'. In his answer, he leant on the rhetorical approach of ministers before him, who spoke to the complexity of the task before them and reinforced their own difficulty in managing the task, explaining, 'It's a commitment I am working towards realising together with my friend the Minister for Home Affairs … We will get this right by taking the time to get it right.'[21] It remains to be seen what kind of Immigration minister Giles will be. But what is clear is that the dominant scripts, created over a long period of time, have taken their hold and orient those who work in this policy field to hold the national, and party, line.

Throughout her parliamentary career, Carmen Lawrence always made plain her political views and sympathies. Labor's response to the *Tampa* incident marked a shift in orientation of sorts for her, as she felt strongly that the Opposition was taking the wrong tack. In the 2001 election, in her safe Labor seat of Fremantle, she 'conducted a little experiment in my own electorate'. 'Kim [Beazley] by then was closely identified with being [in] lockstep with the government on asylum-seeker policy, and I had publicly distanced myself from that position. In half the booths in my electorate I left Kim's photograph off and the other half I put it on ... And I tried to match them as precisely as possible in terms of previous votes. When Kim's face was on, we lost 2 per cent of the vote, comparatively speaking ... You might put it the other way around, that it was 2 per cent better when he wasn't on.'[22] This was a story she had never made public before, she said, but she told me seemingly to emphasise that she felt divided from her senior Labor Party colleagues on refugee policy, and that she believed there was power in being a voice of opposition within her own party. In December 2002 she resigned from the Shadow Cabinet, calling Labor's policies on refugees and asylum seekers 'brutal and inhumane'. The defiance rang through as she related this election anecdote to me.

For Bruce Baird, a former Liberal MP for the New South Wales seat of Cook, a change in orientation came from being part of the parliamentary committee conducting an inquiry into the state of the detention regime in 2003, during the Howard era of hardline anti-refugee policies. He told me that he pushed for people on the committee to take the opportunity to visit detention centres in order to talk to refugees and asylum seekers and find out what their conditions were like. He recalled that the committee visited a series of detention centres around the country, meeting with twenty-five men and twenty-five women at each centre. Sometimes children were present, with their mothers, but they were not interviewed. He found the conditions confronting: 'It was Port Hedland that somewhat shocked me because there were all these children there, and the teachers got onto us and said, 'This is terrible for the children, here. It is very traumatic being surrounded by 20-foot-high barbed wire fences, and you really have got to try to get them out of here.' And, I said, 'Well, why won't the local school take them?' and they said, 'We can't send them, and anyway, they don't want them.' Both the Catholic and the State [schools]. And then, what was worse is that we discovered that there was a detention centre within the detention centre where people, if they crossed the guards, would be put in there several days, and often their children went with them. And we just thought that was appalling. And we also discovered that they were called by numbers instead of by names. That there was one television set for the whole of the camp. That there was very little in the way of sporting equipment to keep them fit, or anything at all. No newspapers. So we actually wrote our report on the detention centre – it was very negative. We had a bad backlash in the Party Room.'[23]

This experience led Baird to take a different stance on refugees to most of his party, opposing mandatory detention. As a result, he, together with a small group, met with John Howard and Philip Ruddock, and then, he told me, after the next election he was approached by Petro Georgiou – a Liberal Party MP representing the seat of Kooyong – 'who was the one who took the initiative, said, "Bruce, we are not going to get anywhere unless we have our own private member's Bill on this, and I have been working on this," and he had somebody who was a lawyer who was working on what was needed.' Georgiou also brought in Russell Broadbent (MP for the seat of Monash) and Judi Moylan (a former MP for Pearce) to work on the private member's Bill.

And then, Baird said, 'we got together and talked about it. [Georgiou] flew to Sydney to talk to me and said, "Are you prepared to do it?" I talked to my wife. Recognised that there would be some downsides, and she said, no, she agreed that we should do it. And so, the others were committed, and so we gave notice in the party room that we were going to do it. Then, we had the bill and I can remember Sophie Mirabella calling out, "You're nothing but terrorists, political terrorists," is what her contribution was. "And you have a nice day, too, Sophie."'

Matt Thistlethwaite, who was Labor's Parliamentary Secretary for Multicultural Affairs for six months in 2013, working under Immigration ministers Brendan O'Connor and Tony Burke in the Gillard and Rudd governments, told me that in this role he 'had responsibility for looking at ministerial interventions for refugee applications for humanitarian visas, so that was a responsibility that was delegated to me by the Minister under the Act, so I had to assess the applications'. He recalled that he would get advice from the Immigration department 'about whether or not the application met the guidelines that had been published by the government': 'And one of those guidelines was the fact that we're signatories to the Convention. So we would often look at the rights of the child in a situation of perhaps – I'm just trying to think of a good example – a child with a disability, that came to Australia through the humanitarian program, had applied for asylum, might be with their parents [and] if there was evidence that the child wouldn't be able to access the same level of support in the country that they'd come from, perhaps it might be a place like remote islands of Indonesia, could be a place like Bangladesh or somewhere like that, where the level of support for kids with autism or other disabilities isn't … [available], then naturally you'd have to think okay, we're the signatory to that Convention. Am I doing the right thing by the child here? And you could use that in taking into consideration your decision on whether or not to grant a permanent visa in that category.'[24]

Here we see an orientation towards children as rights bearers and towards a notion of care involving careful consideration. The ways in which policymakers tell the story of themselves, their role and their priorities is worth analysing. Indeed, Thistlethwaite articulated to me that he sees himself as having particularly caring feelings for children, explaining that in his view 'it's human nature for people to be horrified and distraught by kids ending up in dangerous situations, because kids don't have a say in that. They don't get to determine whether or not they put their life in a risky situation. They, you know, they follow what their parents do or in some cases what someone else has sent them to do. And they're even more vulnerable in those dangerous situations, so they're the ones that if they do get thrown in the water will drown first, the kids, because they're not as strong. And that's the great tragedy of it and that's why I think kids can elicit a different emotional response from any human.'

Like some others I spoke to, Thistlethwaite leaned into the personal, familial, anecdote in order to stress his point: 'I've got four young kids myself. I see how vulnerable they are around water and how important learning to swim is. [This is] something that I'm quite passionate about that I've been working on in terms of a policy area, and yeah, when kids that come from a background that has no swimming education, no water safety education, don't grow up in a culture where they're surrounded by water, get thrown into positions like that, it'd be the ultimate terror and horror.' His background as a lifesaver comes to the fore, determining the stories that hold power for him.

Refugee children and politicians' national emotions

In December 2014, Greens senator Christine Milne, responding to the provision in the Migration and Maritime Powers Legislation Amendment (Resolving the Asylum Legacy Caseload) Bill which would 'classify children born in Australia to asylum seeker parents as unauthorised maritime arrivals', argued that these children 'are babies born in Australia on Australian soil, and they should be regarded in the same way as any other child born here and be given their citizenship – their statehood'.[25] This Bill was, Milne claimed, 'un-Australian'. 'It is a matter of shame to me,' she said, 'that this parliament will pass this legislation.'[26]

Then Opposition leader Bill Shorten narrated stories of the children who were deemed to need saving and the children who could serve as a motivating force behind action being taken. Responding to the Migration Amendment (Regional Processing Arrangements) Bill 2015 – which was designed to shore up the statutory authority of the government to implement offshore processing – Shorten touched on the 'devastating loss of life – the drownings, the perishing of vulnerable people, of children'.[27] He used the languages of humanitarianism and the power of emotion to argue for a different Australia, asserting, 'We stand here not as defenders of an inward-looking fortress where the problems of the world are never ours; instead we stand here guided by our compassion, because our compassion demands that we prevent drownings at seas, just as our compassion demands the humane treatment of all those in our care.' He continued, 'We will vote for this bill because people's safety comes first ... We will vote for this bill because we are guided by our compassion.'[28] Shorten concluded his speech by affirming his idea of the Australian nation, as expressed through citizen children:

Take what we are doing, and let us commit to a parliament which we can explain to our children we were proud to serve in, because this is the right thing to do. Let us commit to a parliament worthy of our decent, civilised, humane country, a parliament which shows us for who we truly are. The nation that we want to see in the mirror should be reflected in the parliament of Australia: compassionate, strong, generous, secure, safe and fair. We all love our country. We are all human beings who do not want to see anyone else suffer. But, because we all love our country, today let us vow to serve it better.[29]

Labor MP Michael Danby furthered the narrative of a nationally binding sentiment, claiming in 2015 that '[n]o-one likes to see children in detention'.[30] Later that year, his Labor colleague Anthony Albanese noted that 'like everyone in this House, the member for Corio [Richard Marles, then the Shadow Minister for Immigration and Border Protection] understands that no society can consider itself civilised if it does not do everything in its power to protect children ... when it comes to protecting children there should be no differences of opinion'.[31]

Labor senator Susan Lines has spoken in Parliament of taking 'a call from a refugee advocate who was in tears at the treatment of children'. 'She told me many stories,' Lines said. Such emotional anecdotes have currency in parliament.'[32] Greens representative Adam Bandt drew on his family circumstances to heighten emotion in a parliamentary speech. Responding to Coalition legislation which sought to create the possibility of returning to harm people who had been found not to be refugees, but who were known to be fleeing harm, and who therefore were owed some form of protection under international law, he explained:

> [O]ne refugee advocate told me recently that in a detention centre in Australia there is now a six-month-old baby that the doctors have started referring to as 'the baby that does not smile'; not because the family does not love it, but because the parents themselves are so full of anguish and desperation as a result of being locked up ... That is what we are doing to children now. As someone who is the extraordinarily proud father of a seven-month-old, I live for those moments when my child smiles at me, and to think that our system is breaking children – and that that is a deliberate intent of it, because it is put there as a deterrent measure – is something that shames us.[33]

Bandt noted the role that Australia has played in creating refugees through its engagement in warfare overseas, and framed the treatment of children in terms of a national debate, arguing that 'it is about creating Fortress Australia and creating a mean Australia ... we should be celebrating the fact that Australia is a land of hope for people, that Australia is a beacon of democracy, freedom and stability.' Not doing so 'makes us weaker' and so Parliament should 'instead consider what we can practically do to put in place solutions where we can take a fairer share of the burden, stop closing our door, admit we cannot have everyone coming here but work out what the happy medium is, and put in place a system that gives people hope, stops people risking their lives at sea and makes sure that we have an Australia we can all be proud of'.[34]

In the July 2019 speeches to Parliament regarding the repeal of the Medevac legislation, Andrew Giles told the House that he wanted 'to briefly share ... the human story I think best illustrates what a difference this [Medevac] regime has made and how dangerous it would be to go back'. 'The story concerns a two-year-old girl known as DIZ18,' he continued. 'DIZ18 was born in Nauru on 5 June 2016.' Giles told the story of her medical conditions, which developed in June 2018 and resulted in numerous doctors recommending she be transferred to Australia. Instead, she was sent to hospital in Papua New Guinea, after '[a] senior officer of the Australian Border Force [was] involved in the decision'. In court, the judge determined that as a result she received 'inadequate medical care', as the hospital could not provide 'the standard of care required', leading Giles to tell Parliament that 'the case of this little girl demonstrates that decisions about medical care should be taken by medical professionals': 'The Australian people are good, decent and generous. They don't want to see vulnerable, sick people in our care suffering when medical care is available to treat them. They appreciate that these circumstances are distinct from the complex policy debates in this area. This is why the parliament must not allow the Medevac legislation to be repealed.'[35] It is noteworthy how persistent both the language of nation-building and the emotions around children are, regardless of the content – or importance and utility – of the legislation being discussed.

The previous day, in a speech on immigration detention, Centre Alliance senator Stirling Griff had asked the Senate, 'In what sane universe do ministers who have children themselves turn a blind eye to the suffering of children, all in the name of an inhumane policy?'[36]

Bruce Baird told me that it was hearing stories of children when he was visiting the detention centres that particularly moved him into wanting to take action. For him, 'the standout was the image of the children there, because when we had the sessions with the asylum seekers at the various locations, it was kind of a bit of a life-changing experience.' He continued: 'The women would cry and say it is so dreadful for their children, and it is affecting them, and they would often sob and using the hijabs to, kind of, wipe their eyes and it was quite harrowing just sitting through these. And the children's reaction to it, and the men, you know, just the frustration of it all. And you just felt that the majority were genuine in wanting to escape their own situation, but then confronted with this situation in Australia which was so difficult for them. But it's the image of the children sitting there, and often they get upset. Their mum would be upset and then that would start off the children, and so on. But, you know, them just being stuck in this situation, we thought, like prisons out there in the middle of nowhere – like the Woomera one, with the big high fence of barbed wire, and so on – what does that do to the kids? Talking to some of the medicos there, the impact on the kids, and the psychiatric difficulties, and so on. So, we decided, number one, to get the children and the families out.'[37]

For anyone who has done any kind of media training, or training in how to communicate complex ideas as part of campaigning, the use of personal stories and emotional language will feel familiar. This approach is regularly used to communicate and mount a campaign, and to win an argument. There is a growing consensus of what makes good political speech, and politicians are embracing these approaches. The approach is clear, once you start looking for it. In the beginning of this book, in the opening of the prologue, you can even see me using a version of it. The pertinent question for us is: where do these forms of communication take us? Where can they take us?

Caring about refugee children

Former Labor MP for Chisholm and Speaker of the House Anna Burke, who was in Parliament from 1998 to 2016, told me in November 2017 that 'at one level it's blindingly obvious that children don't have full capacity. We want them to have full capacity to live full lives with complete agency. The only way ... is to ensure that until such time as they develop those capacities, they are protected. And that's kind of what the international Covenant says, isn't it?'[38] For Burke, children get more attention 'when they became cherishable and lovely and beautiful and darling'. Children are distinct from adults, or even teenagers: '[I]t's like your whole world's ahead of you, the possibilities are there. We are meant to be protecting those vulnerable people. You know, those vulnerable children. We don't have so much concern about the vulnerable men on Christmas Island, on Nauru and Manus who are probably slowly going mad. Well, all of them, no, literally all of them will have mental health issues. They have to. Every researcher said that, so. But you go "Poor little kid," you know, and literally we're going to damage them for life, for what? So I think it's that heartstring that pulls, my kids, a kid, you know.'

Within her electorate, the main issue that residents contacted her about was live animal exports. For Burke, though, 'I think I'm more concerned about small children, you know, just quietly.'

For politicians like Andrew Giles, caring about children can be a model for caring for others generally: 'I just think [it] seems to me to be a pretty easy question to resolve, that we should be able to look around and expand as well as the possibilities of politics, but expand what proximity means, you know, the boundaries of caring. I care about my children, I care about my friend's children. I care about the child I see fall over in front of me at the shopping centre. Obviously I don't see children falling over in shopping centres in Sydney, much less in Shanghai, but how can we create more of a sense of our responsibility in a world that's getting increasingly smaller, to people who don't have anything like the opportunities that we [have]. And, you know, part of that's obviously about having faith in a way of structuring economies that give more people – not just here – in developing countries a chance of a decent life where they can make their own decisions free of absolute poverty, whatever. Part of it's about recognising that in the medium term the world's going to have lots of people who can't live safely in their homes.'[39]

The story of a child falling is an example of a form of storytelling that Mat Tinkler feels is effective. The CEO and director of policy and international programs at Save the Children explained to me, in a discussion about the particularities of child refugees and asylum seekers, that within Save the Children 'our feeling is children are rights bearers, often they're the most vulnerable in a crisis. Therefore, their needs are huge and they need dedicated organisations that are focused on those needs. You know, their innocence, if you like, and in this context.' He gave me an example of how he draws on personal anecdote to connect with the public and with politicians: 'I went to the Melbourne Show two weeks ago with my kids, and I had a heart attack for thirty seconds when I thought I'd lost my four-year-old, because he walked straight when we walked left. Imagine if your child walks straight when you walk left in a 5000-person camp in Cox's Bazar [in Bangladesh] with no lights at night, and the risks that apply to that child. They are huge. So, that's why I think you need child-focused organisations.'[40] This form of narrative-making is strategic. Once he has visited a refugee camp overseas, he will 'usually write an op ed on my way home on the plane or something'. 'So I just try and tell a narrative, and I usually try and relate it back to experiences here, to communicate to an Australian audience. So taking my kids to the show versus a kid in a refugee camp, and that kind of thing. And I don't really – there's no process to how to choose, but usually for us, it's always about the kids, you know, it's the child perspective and trying to capture that as much as possible.' He also sometimes shares drawings or writings from children in camps.

All of these words, coming from so many different sources, work to produce an idea of the government, of the nation and of society's liberal institutions, as deeply caring. In doing so, they actually work towards obfuscating, or covering over, the punitive, violent entrenchment of national borders. As we can see, the emotions that circulate around Australia's borders are intimately linked to the emotions that circulate around the children. Ideas of the nation are built as these emotions circulate in tandem. We can see in these statements what historian Francesco Ricatti has described as 'the emotional morality of *we* Australians [being] called into question while also reaffirmed as the central focus of the asylum seeker debate'.[41]

There is a moral balancing that occurs, and through the emotional pull of this issue, many people come to feel that politicians – even if only some of them – can be trusted to make determinations about what is best. But within this trust, there is also a core 'ambivalence', as US-based legal scholar Jacqueline Bhabha has described it:

> As a society, we are stymied by a fundamental contradiction in our approach. We view the state as having a protective obligation toward vulnerable children in its role as *parens patriae*, parent of the nation; but we also expect the state to protect us from threatening, unruly, and uncontrolled outsiders, even if they are children. It is not that we have forgotten or missed the problems of migrant children. Rather they are a moving target, compelling but shifting, and we are deeply ambivalent about our responses. Our neglect of child migrants' rights is therefore a strategic

compromise that represents our unresolved ambivalence. It has enabled us to avoid the conceptual and political dilemmas raised by child migration and to sidestep the policy challenges it presents.'[42]

This balancing act was perhaps best exemplified by Trent Zimmerman, the former Liberal Member for North Sydney, who joined Parliament in 2015 and was voted out in 2022. In our interview in 2018, Zimmerman explained – echoing a sentiment he highlighted in his maiden speech in Parliament – that he is deeply committed to 'liberal values about the worth of an individual', and that 'we have an international obligation [towards refugees and asylum seekers] because the worth of any human being is no more or less than any other'. Yet 'we will', he continued, 'always be coloured by our nationalism and our nationalistic ideas. But I do think that we have an obligation to those outside our own borders, and that's why the refugee program is important.'[43]

When I asked him to describe his 'ideal' policy for child refugees that come to Australia, he responded, after a pause: 'I think it is desirable that children are put in a community setting as quickly as possible and preferably with a parent, and I think a period in detention needs to be minimised as far as practicable. I mean, I think ... basically the framework that we have over the last couple of years is a perfectly reasonable one. I mean, I think it is right to try and stop people coming here by boat and I don't think it's glib to talk about the number of people who are lost at sea when the boat smugglers were at their highest. I think it's a legitimate and serious issue. So I think having policies that deter that means that there is some consequences that in normal circumstances you accept that you otherwise mightn't. So it's sort of, it is a greater good type [of] argument. But if, as a result of those policies, we are putting people into detention, then I think we have a very serious obligation to minimise those periods for people, let alone children.'

This slippage from child refugee policy to people arriving on boats is revealing of where child refugees and asylum seekers sit within the current Australian political imagination. It is, Zimmerman makes plain, impossible to remember these children without also thinking of 'the boats'. The priority of 'best interests of the child' sits secondary to the priorities of the maintenance of the Australian border. Indeed, Zimmerman had earlier told me that 'I think that we can be proud as a nation of the role that we've played in resettling refugees over the last, well, in the post–Second World War period, and we've provided sanctuary to some 900,000 people. And I think having a significant part of the permanent migration intake as part of our resettlement program is important. It's obviously – the numbers have gone up by 5000 over the last couple of years. I think that that's broadly about right. I mean, it's always one of those difficult things where you set the boundary, but I do think there has to be a boundary.'

There has been a general agreement, enunciated in this interview by Zimmerman, but repeated in almost every other interview I have conducted and almost every speech made in Parliament about child refugees, that there needs to be a limitation on who comes to Australia. Concerns about boat arrivals, often expressed through emotional rhetoric, serve as a way of discussing the imagined benevolence of the Australian state, even as those in charge face the difficulty of supposedly not knowing how to act. Public servants, politicians and political operatives all emphasise that it is near impossible to balance children's needs and rights with the understood right of the state to decide how to construct and then manage its border.

Anna Burke is now a member of the Administrative Appeals Tribunal, and thus responsible for hearing immigration appeals. She was one interviewee who contacted me, after I gave my business card to Andrew Giles, who offered to pass it on to her. When we met, I asked her about the timing of her emailing me – some months after he passed on my details, and as the detention centre in Manus Island was being closed down. Burke reflected on her reasoning as she spoke to me: '[Giles] gave me your card, and I've been sitting on it. I was somewhere. I had – to be brutally honest – three very large Comcare matters that fell over, so it was like, sure ... and then I had to deport somebody, so my conscience was pricked in my new role, which is, on the other end of the scale, which is, really, really hard regardless of what the *Herald Sun* says.'[44]

In this scenario, Burke describes herself as both the very instantiation of the border and as pained by this role. For Burke, participating in my research project, helping to describe the ways that policies are made for child refugees and to critique the policies that she has witnessed, could perhaps (it would seem) serve as a form of salve for her difficulty of enforcing border policies.

Rescuing the children

We can see these discourses, narratives and feelings coalescing and climaxing at certain moments. In February 2016, following a case brought by a Bangladeshi asylum seeker who had been imprisoned in Nauru before being brought to Australia for medical treatment, the Australian High Court ruled as legal the detention in Nauru of asylum seekers who had travelled towards Australia by boat.[45] Media and public discussions of this case focused on whether a larger group of 267 asylum seekers who had been brought from detention in Nauru to

Australia for medical treatment could remain in Australia. Following the judgement, Immigration minister Peter Dutton made clear that he intended to send them all back to detention in Nauru. Of the 267 people who were to be removed because of the judgement, 39 were children and a further 33 were babies born in Australia. As the judgement was handed down and in its aftermath, it was these children and babies who were the focus of public discussion.[46]

On 2 February, the day before the High Court handed down their ruling, *The Age* and *The Sydney Morning Herald*, the two newspapers in major Australian cities then owned by Fairfax, published a front-page spread with pictures of the faces of twelve of the babies subject to this ruling. The accompanying article began:

> Samuel arrived into the world chubby; a miniature wrestler who, eight months on, has just produced his eighth tooth. Born at the Royal Darwin Hospital, his parents had him baptised as soon as they could and earmarked him for great things.
>
> The dream is that their boy will become an Australian doctor or lawyer, but Samuel is unlikely to realise it. He is one of 37 babies the Turnbull government wants to put on a plane, as early as next week, and send to Nauru's offshore processing centre.[47]

These same photos were used by GetUp, a largely online campaigning group describing itself as 'an independent, grassroots, community advocacy organisation that seeks to build a more progressive Australia and hold politicians to account'.[48] GetUp, together with the Human Rights Law Centre, launched an online campaign using the photos and the accompanying words: 'These are photos of babies [Prime Minister] Malcolm Turnbull wants to send to Nauru. We say, Let

Them Stay.'[49] ChilOut (Children Out of Detention) – an activist and advocacy group focused on child refugees and asylum seekers – issued a statement on the day of the judgement, noting that they had 'spoken to children in detention in Australia who are slated to be transferred to Nauru and they consistently tell us they are living with daily fear and anxiety about being sent there'.[50]

In the days after the ruling, various state premiers – along with large numbers of the general public – called for all the asylum seekers to be allowed to remain in Australia, particularly those children born in Australia. These were children who, in a sense, had already joined the Australian community. Queensland Premier Annastacia Palaszczuk was quoted in the media as having 'joined calls urging the Prime Minister not to send Australian-born asylum seeker children back to offshore detention centres'. She pledged to call Prime Minister Malcolm Turnbull to detail the effects of offshore detention on children, adding: 'It's about time we put politics to one side.'[51]

Victorian Premier Daniel Andrews released a Facebook post with a photo, taken from behind, of himself and two children at Melbourne Zoo:

> I can't show you their faces, but I can tell you a bit about these two beautiful kids who I took to the Melbourne Zoo.
>
> They're ordinary Victorians in almost every way. They go to their local primary school; they laugh, they learn, they play.
>
> But one thing is very different: any day now, these two boys will be deported to Nauru and will stay there indefinitely.
>
> Dozens more children face the same fate.
>
> Please, Prime Minister: it doesn't have to be like this.
>
> […]

Perhaps they don't really know what might be happening to them. Perhaps they don't yet understand.

But they love this place. And they certainly loved their trip to the zoo.

They loved seeing the baby animals in their sanctuary, safe and sound.

I wish I could have shown you their faces at that moment. You wouldn't believe how much they smiled.[52]

Later that month, a community picket was set up outside Brisbane's Lady Cilento Children's Hospital, as threats were made to remove a baby and her mother. Baby Asha (a pseudonym) became a touchpoint for those arguing that the government should move those seeking asylum into community detention, rather than sending them back to Nauru.[53]

These campaigns focusing on the children, it should be clear from these quotes, were deliberately highly emotive. Advocates circulated images of smiling babies, sometimes alongside baby animals, and referred to their 'chubbiness', emphasising that they are just like every other Australian child and that the loss they would face by being removed to Nauru was great, to produce a discourse around asylum seeker and refugee policy that was saturated with affect: with feelings of sadness and despair, but also of the potential for hope. There was a mobilisation and production of a set of emotional ideas surrounding asylum-seeker and refugee children that foregrounded the notion that they required saving, in order to try to influence government policy. Australia, here, could be the saviour. But only if it oriented itself towards its imagined best self. Through these campaigns, these children came to be constructed in the political imagination as 1) innocent victims requiring state aid; 2) ordinary, everyday children; and 3) highly vulnerable. Alongside this, a community of dissenters was brought together through their shared vision of themselves as advocates for these vulnerable children, (re)defining Australia as a source of aid.

Some of the politicians I spoke to saw this campaigning as highly effective. Giles talked about how we care more about 'sick babies' because they elicit the most sympathy.[54] While he supported the view that 'children by reason of their particular vulnerability should be afforded particular support and protection', he struggled with 'how it can be okay to subject an adult woman or man to' the conditions of the detention centres. But 'kids are easy', within the discussions in the caucus. Their emotional salience is strong. Anna Burke told me that in her view, 'it becomes more real when it's a child': 'The last image out of the Vietnam War is that child running but all of the hundreds of other people who were napalmed and killed but it's that … child, you know. It's the poignancy of it that, you know, they are vulnerable, we're there to protect them. And we're not, and our government should be.'[55] Similarly, Carmen Lawrence told me that campaigns like this are a good idea as they are 'trying to keep the light on'. 'The alternative is to say nothing. I think shining the light on what's happening is necessary – I'm full of admiration for the people who continue to do that day in, day out,' she said.[56]

After a week of protests, Baby Asha and her family were placed into community detention, an Australian-based but still highly regulated and punitive form of imprisonment.[57] Other children, and other adults, continued to be sent to detention in Nauru, where some still languish in dire conditions.

Later that same year, in July, ABC's *Four Corners* broadcast an episode detailing the brutal mistreatment and torture of Aboriginal children in Don Dale Prison in the Northern Territory. It was titled

'Australia's Shame' and it was horrifying viewing.[58] Immediate outrage sparked around the country. It was a moment of national feeling. Partly to dampen this public outrage, the Turnbull government announced a royal commission the very next day. It was welcomed by many but did not replace the need for a deeper, broader conversation about the work needed to bring about structural change to deal with the underlying problem of colonisation and its ongoing effects. First Nations scholars and communities continue these conversations though, pointing out into the present the ways that imprisonment is used by the settler-colonial government to try to capture Aboriginal children. This jailing is part of the same process as the stealing of children. National discussions, as well as national emotions and national campaigns, about Aboriginal children and refugee children continue to swirl, as imprisonment continues to be used – relatedly but differently – for both. This is part of ongoing government attempts to control and contain these children.

Listening to child refugees

Refugee children can and do also advocate for themselves. If we look towards the children we can find persuasive instances of public advocacy – for instance, the words of a seventeen-year-old asylum seeker held in detention on Christmas Island, who submitted four poems to the 2014 Australian Human Rights Commission's National Inquiry into Children in Immigration Detention. Drawing on history, emotion, critical analysis and political claims, one of the poems, 'Dear Bird Send My Message' read, in part:

> Dear bird send my message.
> Send an image of my eyes- to Abbott-
> where tears are rolling like a river,

send my heart full of sorrow,
send my mind full of thoughts,
send him images of why I came.

Dear bird send my message.
Send my emotions to Morrison
who is enjoying my pain,
who does not think that I am a human being like him,
who thinks that i am just a number the waste of population.[59]

Undertaking a similar political and emotional project was the Free the Children Nauru Facebook page, launched by children and adults on 2 November 2015 in order for the children to communicate with children outside the detention centre, as well as with their supporters. On this page, children posted a range of political assertions with the stated aim: 'The asylum seeker and refugee children doomed on Nauru speak out and share their dreams and hopes with other children around the world.' On 18 November, one child posted that they were unsure what to tell their audience and had been advised by their teachers to share 'facts and geography' about Nauru, and encouraged to 'find humour in everything'. For a brief moment that humour was sustained, before the author turned to the desperation of the situation: 'We are very tired and now they are building new accommodation and we think they want to tell you that it is good now. But it's not good because all of Nauru is like a gaol. All of the children's are busy writing and finding things to show you that will make you happy, buut know our hard life too. Thank you.'[60]

Another post, on 27 November, described the ways that security guards would act, told followers about the new camp being built and mentioned the families being separated. The author wrote: 'Border force doesn't call us when we get touched badly in school, but they worry about who write facebook page. We are refugee now but no difference. They said we have to get out of mouldy tent tomorrow and family separate like we animals. I really breaking now into pieces I can't really hold on anymore I m too tired.'[61] Refugee and asylum-seeker children's voices are thus deeply powerful and a threat to the established political order. As I read and understand their words, it would appear that they are working to challenge normative ideas of what speech a child is capable of, and to cross borders to bring very different communities together through their speech acts, which appear to call for liberation, *rather than saving*.

In this way, it seems to me, the emotional discourses circulated by the children are vastly different to those issued by the parliamentarians: there are fundamentally different vocabularies at play. While both are intended to serve as calls to action for those brought into the consumption and circulation of the emotions, the children demand action in solidarity, while the parliamentarians' emotional language is used in the service of producing a shared knowledge of Australia as a nation of saviours. The children seem to speak in a bleaker emotional language, refusing the logic of 'caring' that the politicians produce, and demanding an engagement with the people of Australia, as distinct from the Australian nation-state. They are displaying the force of their survival: they are to be worked with, not pitied or seen as a source of another's shame. This is, perhaps, the power of emotional truth-telling in the face of the political use of emotions to govern and control. It is a speaking back to those emotional discourses that rest on a paternalistic nation-building.

For refugee children are constantly trying to talk to politicians. In an article about a theatre performance put on by refugee children, the journalist wrote that one of the children, Bassam, 'said he hoped politicians enjoy the show, but the young refugees in the performance also hope decision-makers learn a few lessons as well': '"In Australia, there's a lot of refugee things going on and I think that after we tell our stories, they take something from it, maybe they help more with refugees," Fereshteh Mirzaei said.'[62]

'White Saviours'

Graham Little noted in his 1999 book *The Public Emotions*: 'Political leaders must, of course, represent our interests, our traditions, our ideas and our policies. But we also need them to express and consolidate what we feel.'[63] But who is this 'we'? Who politicians orient themselves towards, how they narrate their political impulses, does tremendous work in determining the policy they will produce. As they tell themselves and those around them stories – stories of themselves, of the children they govern, of the nation they imagine – they produce a collection of what is termed 'policy settings' that determine the horizons of possibility. Some politicians think carefully about who they attach to and what this will mean for the futures they produce. Others are less careful, more inclined to fit the circumstances into what they already know. But overwhelmingly, whichever approach they take on this spectrum, they are guided by a belief in an Australia they can control.

Politicians' ideas of themselves as arbiters of the nation and its emotions – particularly in relation to the assumed wellbeing of children – is an expression of Australia's settler-colonial sentiment. Writing in 2012, author and critic Teju Cole described what he termed 'the White Savior Industrial Complex' as being 'not about justice' but instead 'about having a big emotional experience that validates privilege'.[64] While Cole was writing about the United States – which is also of course a settler colony – there is something of this logic in the emotional calls to the shape of the Australian nation I have described. The imagined Australian nation is part of this 'white saviour' project. Gamilaroi writer Luke Pearson has written about Tony Abbott's work in 2018 as Prime Minister's Special Envoy on Indigenous Affairs, noting that his recommendations speak of a 'notion of the white saviour coming to the rescue of the lowly "savage", because the way of the whitefulla is so superior that any level of mistreatment is seen as better than any form of Indigenous existence that operates outside of its direct control'.[65] This is the attitude of governments and politicians. And so we see this recur with attitudes towards refugees and the Australian nation. But we need to disrupt it.

CHAPTER 7

Public Servants

In 2016, the Secretary of the Department of Immigration and Border Protection issued a statement responding to the 'Let Them Stay' campaign, which called for children and their families who had been brought from Nauru to Australia for medical treatment to be allowed to stay. Asserting that 'No child will be returned to a place of harm', Michael Pezzullo refuted the expert advice from paediatricians, medical experts and 'the department's very own medical adviser' that immigration prison is medically harmful for all children. Pezzullo asserted that some children were being removed from detention, but experts pointed out that it was not safe for any child to be in there at all: all children needed to stay in Australia. But Pezzullo continued to prioritise his own sources.[1]

The public service plays a crucial role in shaping, creating and enacting policy, but too often policy is understood to be the purview of politicians only. There is a vast history of the public service and its vital role in shaping policy that is yet to be written.[2]

This chapter contains a tale of three public servants – three men who have held senior positions across the public service and within the Immigration department. Two of the men are relatively well known to the public, one much less so. But all three have had a tremendous impact on the shape of child refugee and asylum-seeker policy. John Menadue was Secretary of the Department of Immigration and Ethnic Affairs in the 1980s; Wayne Gibbons worked in various parts of the Department across the 1970s to 1990s; and Michael Pezzullo has been Secretary of the Department of Immigration and Border Protection since October 2014. I interviewed Menadue and Gibbons, while Pezzullo declined an interview.

John Menadue

John Menadue AO was born in South Australia in the 1930s and has had a fulsome and storied career. When Gough Whitlam was the Leader of the Opposition in the 1960s, Menadue was his private secretary. After that, Menadue worked as general manager at News Limited in Sydney, before serving as Secretary of the Department of Prime Minister and Cabinet from 1974 to 1976, working for both Whitlam and Malcolm Fraser. He was the seventh Australian ambassador to Japan, and in 1980 Fraser appointed him Secretary of the Department of Immigration and Ethnic Affairs. Later, he was Secretary of the Department of Trade, CEO of Qantas and a director of Telstra. He has chaired various health reviews and was made an Officer of the Order of Australia in 1985 for public service.[3] Menadue has written an autobiography, *Things You Learn Along the Way*, and maintains a policy journal called *Pearls and Irritations*, where he regularly contributes to the public conversation and provides a space for liberal perspectives on government and policy.[4]

Given that it takes time for policy changes announced by government to wend their way through the minutiae of the bureaucracy of public service, during his period as secretary Menadue helped dismantle some of the remaining formal bureaucratic aspects – and 'changed attitudes' – of the White Australia policy. And even though he no longer holds a public position, he continues to advocate vocally for refugee and asylum-seeker policies shaped by white liberalism. In February 2017, for instance, Menadue co-wrote an article in *The Guardian* with Frank Brennan, Tim Costello and Robert Manne, which argued that, while 'proven refugees' 'languishing' in detention need to have their claims for permanent resettlement granted, the general population needs to accept the position emanating from both major political parties – that people coming to Australia by boat to seek asylum will be stopped and turned around 'if that can be done safely, transparently, and legally'.[5] In this, he follows the same path as many other policymakers: he balances discourses of concern with exploring the need for measures that are punitive, ethically unjust and against the spirit (and perhaps the letter) of international law.

Menadue was the ambassador to Japan when he got a phone call from Prime Minister Malcolm Fraser offering him the role of the Secretary of the Department of Immigration. When we met in Sydney in September 2017, he told me that Fraser said to him, 'What did you want to do when you come back to Australia?' 'I said, "I want to come back and bury White Australia." And he said, "You're on." As quick as that.'[6] This desire to 'bury White Australia' came from spending time at university with 'three Malaysian students' – which 'really was a shock', having come from a country town populated, he remembered, exclusively with white people – and his stint in Japan, where he found Australia subject to regular criticism because of the White Australia policy. Menadue told me that 'we're all conditioned by a culture in the society in which we live and it's when we're confronted with something different, people that are different, that you think hell, maybe I need to rethink. And that's a painful process very often. You don't learn in comfort zones. That's my experience. You learn when you're challenged, which is a bit worrying at times. Some people react to that by just retreating completely, and others say, "Well, maybe there is something there I need to think about."'

For Menadue, Japan was a chance to learn from others, to be surrounded by those with different perspectives on the world. The process produced new emotions and connections. And so from the beginning of his time in the Immigration department, he told me, he worked to dismantle the focus on migration from England, encouraging the public servants under his charge not just to advertise migration to Australia to people in the United Kingdom, but to actively consider looking further afield, in line with the 'non-discriminatory policy' that was now in place. But throughout our interview, Menadue emphasised the important role that 'fear of the foreigner' has played in immigration programs in Australia. This fear, he said, bonded together, and bonds together still (at the time we spoke, 2017), workers in the Immigration department: it is one of the emotions that orients them to each other, creating an emotional community, a shared way of feeling.

Menadue told me that he believed the broad immigration and refugee programs that formed part of the dismantling of official White Australia approaches and the installation of policies of multiculturalism 'changed Australia for the better'. 'It was a case of nation-building on a pretty heroic scale. Maybe we pushed it too fast and too hard, maybe, but looking back, it was successful. So I think it was that element of a sense of nation-building and the ending of White Australia which gave the satisfaction' of the job. He described to me the parameters and limitations of what he considers 'successful multiculturalism':

'It depends on broad adherence to particular basic and agreed structures and attitudes in terms of the structures, the parliament, rule of law, separation of powers, beyond that into the English language – if you like the British system, which I think most people will agree is (apart from the monarchy) not a bad sort of system … And that diversity brings strength and challenges, but diversity for its own sake is not to be supported. Diversity is fine if it contributes to a greater good, but in diversity, child marriage, polygamy, genital mutilation, whatever, isn't in my view a diversity that improves Australia. That's a value judgement I would make. And I have a view on the burqa, for example, which I think it's contrary to multiculturalism because it does divide unnecessarily and in my view public space should be secular and neutral whether you're Catholic, Jewish, Muslim or whatever. It's not a view which the left endorses. They state a politically correct view, "oh, that doesn't matter," but I think it does matter, to then building a stable, strong multicultural society.'[7]

In this lengthy answer, we get a sense of where Menadue appears to position himself – who he sees himself aligned with and in community with, and who he expresses disagreement with. To many of us, this quotation will imply that Menadue likes a form of diversity that does not contain *too much* difference. He aligns himself with the idea that government can and should control the make-up of the Australian populace. In a series of 2015 writings with two other former public servants from the Immigration department, Menadue makes clear that refugee, humanitarian and settlement policy can be viewed primarily through the prism of the Australian state: what effects policies will have, what the state can and should do, and what policymakers should do to best control the borders and the people who cross them.[8] This is an example of what psychologist Danielle Every has described as 'liberal binaries' being used in political discourse 'to establish an exclusionary humanitarianism as obvious, natural and right'.[9]

Menadue told me that he thinks there is a deep-seated fear in Australia about asylum seekers arriving on boats, and that Australians will never be comfortable with people making their own way without prior authorisation to Australia via sea. That is why, he suggested – like numerous others I have interviewed – the boats need to be controlled. At the same time, he believes 'our refugee flow' should be increased, through a vital 'spirit of generosity' and 'for humanitarian reasons': 'We've behaved disgracefully on that in recent years, but also refugees are just such superb settlers. I think we have a self-interest in the sort of get-up-and-go of refugees. They choose, they self-select themselves. Better than a migration officer ever could select them. They're the people who are prepared to abandon everything. Everything, being physically apart from family, for a new life. And they don't sit around and make a judgement whether we'll go or not. "Well, we're going." And that's why they're so good as small business entrepreneurs, hard work. I'd choose a refugee any day over a migrant for that reason.'

But, he continued, 'The selective high schools are just dominated by migrants and particularly refugee children. Just – I think too much – it frightens some Australians but it's just that commitment of parents. I think they do cram schools and so on, which I worry a bit about, but it's a bit overdone, I think, but it's just recognition of how those refugee families are determined to make a new life. Remarkable people.' He later told me that recognising the importance of 'caring for the stranger' is an important driver in refugee policy as 'who knows, we might be a stranger ourself one day'. But the important principle in the making of 'good policy' is the understanding that 'these strangers are usually such superb settlers. The odd Jewish family's done well.' Disconcertingly, Menadue and I shared a chuckle at that comment – my chuckle almost certainly from awkwardness. Here was a moment when he attempted – perhaps successfully – to incorporate me into the 'we' of the governing white Australian nation. But, he reiterated, he thinks those two things – caring for a stranger and the contribution migrants make – are the two important considerations in policymaking.

For Menadue in this interview, as for many others, people are useful if they contribute, if they add something that the government sees as valuable. Migrants and refugees are not, we could say, considered primarily in terms of their claims for justice but rather as fitting into a binary of productive and unproductive, 'deserving' and 'undeserving'.[10] The Melbourne-based refugee organisation RISE argues that such views of refugees are 'misconceptions' that play a role in escalating 'existing xenophobia' in the community because they suggest that people need to contribute in particular ways to be considered worthy of being part of the community.[11] Such sentiments aid in the exclusion of refugees: they orient bureaucrats towards a state with an instrumental view of its population, rather than towards refugee or migrant justice and freedom. What could it look like, I felt myself wondering, if the reverse were true?

In the interview I asked Menadue what he remembered about his work with children in particular. He told me that he had little memory of interacting with children, but he had a sense of himself and of his department as having acted when asked to by the UN. Like others who worked in the public service in this policy area in the 1970s and 1980s, he had only a 'vague' memory of this work. But his first explanation of the place of children in policy discussions was articulated through the lens of the problematic language of people as 'anchors'. Menadue told me that 'a feature of any refugee flow, almost any one, is that they send teenage boys out, sort of their anchors. Get them through because they're usually pretty resilient. You don't have to commit the whole family and so if you can get them through the process into a new country then they're the anchor to bring the rest, which is understandable. People don't like it. And then that creates particular problems of how do you handle young children. And these are children. In many cases they're thirteen, fourteen, fifteen. But there's a political reason for them doing it. And so they're not helpless little kids. There's a plan there by their parents and others, so I think sometimes people like Frank Brennan and others, they're talking about these kids in special protection, and they say, "Oh, you can't treat them as refugees. You've just got to give them entry." Well, if you do that, you'll have more anchors coming. So I'm a bit hard-headed on that one. But they've still got to be treated decently and the best way to treat them is to put them with their parents if you possibly can. But they don't want that, of course.'

Menadue's distinction between the 'anchors' and 'people [who] don't like it' is telling. He is evidently addressing a non-refugee audience with this framing, imagining refugees as individuals to be governed, rather than to be addressed directly. 'People' here are counterpoised to the refugees and asylum seekers who are either on the move or whose family members are on the move. This is a common rhetorical approach, and one it is important to draw attention to, to make clear the way the phrasing serves to build a sense of an emotional community.

The concept of children as 'anchors' was not Menadue's alone. Michael MacKellar, the Liberal minister for Immigration and Ethnic Affairs from December 1975 to December 1979, issued a press release in November 1978, claiming:

> In an attempt to circumvent immigration policy a growing number of visitors are having children in Australia in the belief that having an Australian-born child will guarantee them resident status ... Not only were the number of instances on the increase, but it appeared that some of the people had been actively encouraged to adopt this practice ... Such people will not receive preferential treatment by virtue only of having a child born in Australia ... It is just another of the wide range of tactics that are continually used to circumvent entry rules.[12]

We will return to this idea.

One of the last questions I asked Menadue was about the role of emotions in Immigration policymaking. He told me: 'Emotion is fear of the foreigner. Fear of the stranger. A person that's different and what do you know about them? I think it's a natural sort of human reaction in it – the worry about the person that's different. But I often think also, in addition to that sort of fear of a foreigner, there is also a decency in everyone that they will respond to a person in need. As Abraham Lincoln described, the better angels of our nature.' Emphasising the complexity for policymakers, he continued, 'I think it's a mistake to think that it's all just black and white. I'm sceptical of foreigners. I hope I've got a generosity as well, but that struggle goes on in everyone and it goes on in every country. But it's got to be managed.'

Thinking historically, we can understand that these 'fears' are social rather than natural – they are learned, developed, coerced and controlled by governments and societies. They are not natural, but the project of naturalisation is a deeply political one: it is political work to make something natural, to describe and define it as naturally occurring. 'Fear of the stranger' or 'the foreigner' is not simply innate in everyone:

it is learned, developed by ideologies and projects of racism, xenophobia and nationalism, and then routinely spoken of as hegemonic. There is a process of naturalisation, and that process is ongoing, continually creating some people as 'other'.

But the words spoken here, and the discourses of which they are part, are a product of the time in which we recorded this interview as much as the time in which Menadue held power as secretary of the department. His mention of the burqa and its place within Australian multiculturalism was certainly reflective of the discussion of the day: in the weeks previous it had been a topic of debate among the political classes, with various right-wing politicians and newspapers openly calling for Muslim women to be banned from wearing it.[13] In this way, oral history interviews bring together past and present, wending time together. They are a reflection of a continuing process of thinking and creating stories and understandings. And as such, they offer us an insight into how policymakers continue to grapple with their beliefs and their work, and in that way an opportunity to understand them within a continuing historical present.

Wayne Gibbons

Wayne Gibbons is a former public servant who spent most of his working life working on high-profile reforms. While most of us have probably never heard of him, he has played an important role in shaping decades of public policy in Australia.

In the 1970s, he was private secretary to Al Grassby and Clyde Cameron (both Ministers for Immigration in the Whitlam government) and Michael MacKellar (in the Fraser government), before working as the coordinator of the Australian Indo-Chinese Refugee Resettlement Program from 1978 to 1980, when he was based in Southeast Asia.[14]

In the early 1990s he was Deputy Secretary of the Department of Immigration and Multicultural Affairs under Minister Gerry Hand, and played an important role in developing the government's new policy of mandatorily detaining people who took boats to Australia to seek asylum without having prior authorisation. He was moved from that department in 1993 'after a legal attack in the Federal Court in Melbourne claiming institutional department bias against Cambodian boat-people'.[15] He then worked in the Department of Employment, Education and Training, which was eventually renamed the Department of Employment and Workplace Relations. There, in 2002, as Deputy Secretary of Employment, Gibbons was responsible for turning the Commonwealth Employment Service into the Job Network – that is, he was involved in privatising that aspect of the Australian welfare state.[16] This meant he 'had to implement a government decision to retrench 6000 people and outsource all employment services'.[17] We can see the ongoing effects of this policy in the current-day Centrelink.

Gibbons was then appointed CEO of the Aboriginal and Torres Strait Islander Commission (ATSIC), a position he held from 2002 to 2004. ATSIC had been a platform for Indigenous self-determination, before Gibbons moved its functions into the government-controlled Aboriginal and Torres Strait Islander Services (ATSIS) and coordinated the abolition of ATSIC, which became official in May 2005.[18] He then headed up the Office of Indigenous Policy Coordination, and while in that role he authorised Greg Andrews, a senior public servant at the Office of the Information and Privacy Commissioner, to appear on *Lateline* in June 2016. Filmed in shadow and with his voice disguised, Andrews was described as 'an anonymous youth worker' in his television interview – which he was not. *New Matilda* notes it was 'a description Andrews maintains – and the ABC admits – was concocted by the

[sic] *Lateline*'. Andrews falsely alleged that there was a paedophile in Mutitjulu – an Aboriginal community in Central Australia – who was trading sex for petrol.[19] This interview was used as part of the basis for the Northern Territory Intervention, which Gibbons has been called 'one of the brains behind'.[20] Many feel the Intervention, and its violent repressive treatment of First Nations peoples, continues into the present, in an entrenched and expanded form. Through Gibbons' work – as through the work of other people who have worked as public servants or as ministers in the relevant portfolios – we see a very clear example of the intersection between refugee policy and Aboriginal policy in the colonial government.

I met Gibbons at his home in Canberra in November 2017. He was a good storyteller, sharing with me numerous tales from his time as a public servant. Gibbons explained that he began working in the Immigration department in 1969, 'on the day Armstrong stood on the moon'. When he began, he told me, the department was divided into policy for people from Europe, policy for people from Britain, a 'non-European policy', in which, 'to put it pretty crudely and simply, we were there to basically say no, unless they were exceptional people', as well as 'a mixed-race area, which were looking for people who looked white but were not European'. 'They were the graduations in those days and it reflected the public attitudes that were very strong in the post-war period, through the fifties, [and it] started to weaken a bit in the sixties but still very much, you know, you were risking your political survival as a politician if you pushed too hard on that front,' he said.

After working for various Immigration ministers and heading up the refugee program in Southeast Asia, Gibbons told me he returned to Australia, working first in Melbourne and then in Sydney, and finally in 'Canberra in a policy role as a First Assistant Secretary'. He told me he 'had two focuses: one [was] on modernising the Department's whole approach to people management, electronic visas, electronic inwards and outwards, so you could reconcile who's coming in and who's coming out, you could keep Bureau of Census and Stats up-to-date on that critical part of population growth, all of that, linked it to the airlines so that as you checked in in New York or London or wherever, you got your clearance before you boarded, [that] sort of thing. But the other thing was trying to change the organisational culture of the department. We were at that point probably, when was it, almost a decade past the Grassby revolution or Whitlam–Grassby revolution, followed by the Fraser multicultural policy initiatives, which were even more significant and, I thought at least, a more genuinely sympathetic approach to multicultural immigration by any Prime Minister. The Department really wasn't well organised for all this. It still had many vestiges of the old approach, so I convinced the Secretary to give me hold of the whole redevelopment policy task.'

Gibbons, like Menadue, narrates himself as having brought positive policy changes around multiculturalism to the Immigration department. Understanding himself as a reformer, as someone who took charge and was in control, was key to Gibbons' approach to public policy. This continued later in his career, both in Immigration and Aboriginal Affairs. Gibbons told me that Philip Ruddock, then the Coalition's Minister for Immigration and Multicultural and Indigenous Affairs, 'rang me up one day and said, "Look, the Government has to do something about ATSIC. It's spending vast amounts of money with limited outcomes for Indigenous peoples. Would you take it on?" And I, really it's one of the areas I'd never turned my mind to. I knew nothing about Indigenous culture. Knew everything about Cambodians, Vietnamese, Japanese, Chinese, et cetera, et cetera.

By the way, my wife's Japanese. But I knew very little. And I don't like the Outback, desert and all that much. It's alien to me. So my heart sank … [But] I took it on.'

In his narrative of this project, Gibbons told me that one key issue was 'the amount of misuse of public moneys', but more significantly, 'child abuse and women abuse is the thing that gave me nightmares after I started to travel into these places and saw it and eventually convinced both sides of politics that it had been a terrible mistake, and so it was abolished. ATSIC was abolished. And I also conceived the idea of an intervention.' He told me he disagreed with Mal Brough, then the Minister for Families, Community Services and Indigenous Affairs, about sending the army into Aboriginal communities as part of the Intervention (something the Coalition would go on to do), but he said, 'there were communities where, before you could even contemplate saving children, you had to go in and take control, stop handing over all the money as cash, provide food, provide care, and you had to invest in stabilising the environment long enough for normality to return and for children to start living without fear, et cetera, et cetera'. Here we see clearly the sentiment of child rescue, and the belief in white masculine government as knowing how best to control and govern Aboriginal lives, that was also carried into the governing of refugee lives.

When Gibbons worked under Gerry Hand, he saw Hand becoming 'very anxious about illegal migration'. 'He was taking a lot of stick from members of his own party because of the concerns growing in the electorates about people getting on planes, getting visitor visas, coming here and staying, and so I was involved in working with him on a policy response to that, which was the foundation of denial of entry to the community. So detention, if you like.'

'Mandatory detention?' I clarified.

'I'll come back to that point because that is not as simple as it sounds,' Gibbons replied.

When we returned to it later in our discussion, he told me that Hand's intention had been to 'deny the product that's being marketed by people smugglers' by 'preventing illegal immigrants living in the community, where they would often enlist the support of local citizens to help them stay'. Gibbons explained that 'the idea was we will not allow visitors who overstay their visas to remain in the community. We'll pull them out of the community, so they will find it harder to solicit local support.' Out of sight, out of mind, disconnected, *emotionally removed*. In doing so, he said, they were trying to send a message both to 'marketers' of 'a back door to Australia as a place of settlement', and to Australians who might be concerned about 'large numbers of overstayers': in both cases, it was designed to show the Australian government as being in control.[21]

For Gibbons, international human rights law was inappropriately applied in Australia. As he told me, 'following the introduction of Administrative Law we started to have judges – and there were a few who were very activist on the immigration front – reach into various international agreements like the Convention on Refugees and try to import those principles into Australian law, notwithstanding they're only treaties and they're not part of our domestic law. So Hand saw all this as the ship of state being veered off course in this area which should be controlled by the government of the day.' We see in this the same narrative put forward by former Immigration minister Nick Bolkus when I interviewed him; he told me about lawyers intervening in deportation proceedings whenever they could. It continues to the present day through the dismissal of the responsibility in the

Convention on the Rights of the Child to prioritise the best interests of the child: lawyers intervening on behalf of people making asylum claims are seen as a disruption to the proper functioning of the state and its borders. The same hostile approach can be seen in so many of the more recent government approaches to refugees, including the cruel handling of refugees brought to Australia from Manus Island and Nauru to receive medical treatment under the Medevac legislation. Rather than being treated, they were held for long periods of time in immigration detention, where their health further suffered.

But Gibbons identified this approach as starting earlier, particularly under Robert Ray, who was Minister for Immigration from September 1988 to April 1990. Gibbons explained that the Immigration department was determined that politicians would retain control over who could come to Australia and how. It was a situation where 'we just couldn't let the courts keep determining immigration policy in the absence of any legislation, so the decision was taken to codify immigration law'. It was decided to begin by 'shutting the door' as a first principle, and using regulations to open it at certain times or for particular 'classes of people'. How this opening occurs has changed over time, leading, as Gibbons noted, to copious amendments to the *Migration Act*. But that control, and the importance of ministerial discretion, has been retained as key. And this set of changes, in Gibbons' view, was one of the 'great revolutionary reforms during my time in Immigration'.

Notions of control ran throughout Gibbons' narrative of policymaking. As we discussed the first boatloads with Vietnamese refugees arriving in Australia's north – boats that he went to Darwin to meet – he told me that 'the one thing that came through it all is you'll never succeed in immigration on any front if you lose public support': 'And what was it about the Australian public that was important to retain that support? The thing was, they had to be convinced that they were in control, that they're in control of the agenda. If they think it's out of their control, or it's being foisted on them, the door closes very quickly.' The motif of government control over the 'doors' recurred throughout Gibbons' account.

When he was based in Kuala Lumpur, Guam and Vietnam, in his role as coordinator of the Australian Indo-Chinese Refugee Resettlement Program, Gibbons explained that he worked alongside officials from countries such as Canada, the United States, France and some other European countries, to select refugees for resettlement. While the refugees would have some say in their preferred destination – particularly if they spoke a relevant language or had family already in a country – it was the role of the officials, by and large, to determine where people would live. Australia, in Gibbons' memory, 'favour[ed] families over single males'. This was for 'policy reasons': 'We wanted people who could be settled easily. The judgement was it was easier to take the whole family.' Using similar language to Menadue, Gibbons saw these refugees as entrepreneurial, as expert settlers, as taking on life in a way that other refugees were being imagined as not doing.

He told me, 'I felt absolutely convinced while on those islands, Pulau Bidong, Pulau Tengah, et cetera, that the people we were taking were going to be successful as settlers. Their energy, their ability to cope, to improvise, et cetera, was on full display. When you take 20,000 people and put them on an uninhabited island that looks like Mt Taylor sticking in the ocean, no bigger than Mt Taylor … forest, rainforest down to the beach. Nothing there, a three-hour boat trip to the nearest fishing port. Refugees arriving by the hundreds every day … But these people within days of arrival had built their own accommodation using trees they cut down, rice sacks as cover.

They denuded the whole island within six months. Although I went back a few years ago and the rainforest has recovered. There's a resort on the island now.

'But it wasn't just that. They paid attention to important facilities. They built a jetty. They built toilets over the ocean, hundreds of yards offshore, that sort of thing. They had commerce on the island: there were people making rice cakes and all sorts of customary food and selling it in a little market on the beach. They were full of enterprise, you could feel their human spirit that told you these people aren't going to sit in a camp in Australia waiting for social security. They're going to get on and do something.'

Here ideas of deserving and undeserving, of competent and incompetent, of successful and deficient, come to the fore. These refugees were different, Gibbons told me, from those who came from South America, who were not as independent. And he wondered how this was all passed down generationally: 'Were the children of Vietnamese refugees going to inherit an Australian approach, as it has evolved, which has become more focused on, more reliant on, intervention and government than being self-reliant, or have they inherited the culture of their upbringing?' Through this questioning, the concern was placed on Australia's population and how it would be shaped through this act of nation-building. In Gibbons' narrative, this 'was the defining moment in the move to bury White Australia, 'cause it did'. 'And that convinced me at the time that we did it the right way because public support for it was maintained all the way through, so we were blessed by having a group of people who were adaptable, determined, innovative, who didn't become after arrival in Australia a burden, if you like, that turned Australians against them. They did well,' he told me.

For Gibbons, this control over who comes and how they come is so important that he believes 'the left of politics made a serious mistake. They were interested in keeping public support for immigration. They should've supported measures to quickly close ... down the boats. But by championing that more recent stream of boat people, they alienated many people who were important to the future of immigration, and then I – although I don't work anymore and mix with the people who work in this area much, I'm a keen walker and every month I go walking with a group of former colleagues and it's recently grown as younger ones have retired. And they remark on the whole cultural change in the administration of immigration. It's now a police border force whereas when I worked in it, it was a nation-building people movement organisation. Our whole approach was not about the border per se. That was just part of the mechanism to facilitate the smooth running of everything. It was about where do we get people, how do we settle them, how do we avoid ghettoes, problems, you know – it was really an organisation about building the nation. It's a term I don't like, but Grassby used it ad nauseam, "the family of the nation", you know. It was about maintaining that.'

When he described efforts to stop Vietnamese refugees coming to Australia by boat, Gibbons told me, 'They'd all been determined to be prima facie refugees, they were all going to be resettled. There was no justification in allowing them to take the risk, and so our instructions were: stop them.' Here, as elsewhere in this book, we see a policymaker making decisions for refugees and asylum seekers about which risks exist, which are justifiable, and which are simply lessons that need to be taught. The responsibility for decision-making is routinely understood to be held by the white men who are in control in Australia.

During Gibbons' time in the Immigration department, there was not a great deal of discussion of children as a distinct group – as I found with other public servants from this era.[22] But like Menadue, Gibbons drew my attention to unaccompanied children, as well as to children who came as 'anchors' for their families but came with another family group and 'lied about who their parents were'. This was a problem, he said, as 'you need to know. You need to know': 'One of the basic principles about people selection is you've got to get your facts clear before you can make judgements. If you make judgements without doing that, the consequences down the line can be quite extreme.' This knowledge was important to prevent allegations or cases of kidnapping or abuse, but for him, the principle of the 'best interests of the child' was too flimsy to be of any real use. As he stated, 'if you go back to the fifties, what was considered the best interests of the child then would be abhorrent to contemporary advocates … When you look back over history you've got to keep in mind you can't judge it all by today's values. What did the community support?'

During the interview, Gibbons told me a story of being in Malaysia, sitting in a hotel eating breakfast along with other migration officers from around the world, when a boat crashed onto the beach. They ran out to help. One woman who Gibbons pulled from the water was deceased: he felt it in her body as he lifted her up.

Later in the interview I returned to this, asking him: 'That experience of being on the beach and seeing a boat break up and holding people's bodies, does that affect your approach to working in Immigration?' He told me, '[I]t affected me fairly strongly because you can't confront tragedy like that. It's like when you suddenly confront an accident, two cars collide, someone's seriously injured. It's a traumatic experience. This was more serious than that and it happened suddenly.' But, he said, 'we weren't responsible' for what happened: it was the organisers of the boat who packed people in, as well as the situation in their homeland that caused the passengers to board the boat, that were responsible, in his narrative.

He then continued, 'What did traumatise me and leave me scarred was some of the things I saw in Indigenous communities, you know, and our naivety as a community in believing some people who are at the heart of the problem.' He told me about some communities he visited in the Northern Territory, and what he was told and felt that he saw. Here Gibbons emotionally linked creating policy for refugees and for Indigenous people, narrating them both as projects of what I would identify as colonial control. The project of control, of being subjected to white emotions, remains. This is the 'white masculine possessive' that Aileen Moreton-Robinson writes of, which is so central to the shaping of this nation.[23]

And so we must understand this governing as deeply colonial. Expertise and control is routinely understood to be held by the white men who dominate policymaking, and who rely on the sentimentalising of children imagined to be suffering, innocent and powerless.

Michael Pezzullo

In June 2017, I emailed a former senior public servant who had worked for a long time in the Immigration department, requesting an interview for my research for this project. The public servant had retired in 2016, alongside numerous others, at a time when the Immigration department changed under the leadership of Secretary Michael Pezzullo and the Coalition government's Minister for Immigration and Border Protection, and then Minister for Home Affairs, Peter Dutton.[24] There was a shift at this time towards a more military- and security-based approach to governing immigration, including Australia's 'humanitarian intake', and away from viewing settlement and integration support programs as a fundamental part of the work of the department.[25] As Wayne Gibbons told it to me, there has been a 'transformation of the department from an organisation focused on settling people into the Australian community as part of a national population-building strategy to a border police, uniforms and guns, you know, that sort of culture. The great tragedy in the way it's been done is that the executive, probably encouraged by ministers ... made a bad choice by taking the Customs element – the borders, the uniforms, the guns etc – and building the department around them and letting go staff who were sympathetic to population building, to immigration settlement services. Anyone with skills to do with the immigration and settlement services are no longer wanted. It's not about nation-building anymore.'

A public servant with whom I was emailing 'respectfully' declined to participate in an interview, telling me, 'I am presently on vacation in the Greek islands ... the first decent break in many years ... and I have spent much time reflecting on my career of nearly 40 years in the federal public service. I have decided that I do not want to re-live any of that period when I was dealing with refugee issues. I left that period of my career with my marriage barely intact and with a severe impact on my physical and emotional well-being.'

'I appreciate,' they continued, 'that Australia's refugee policies and programs are fertile ground for researchers, the broader academic and legal fraternity and journalists. However, no one has given a nanosecond of thought as to the impact on the thousands of decent, hard working public servants who have been in the frontline of developing and delivering government policies and programs in this field.' When later granting me permission to quote them, they clarified that they 'would not want to be represented as a public servant who did not agree with the government policy I was charged with implementing. The point I tried to make in my previous response is that government policy in this field is challenging, difficult to implement and emotionally charged … and that it takes its toll on those who have the responsibility of implementation.'[26]

In this brief email correspondence, this respondent pointed to the ways that different emotional connections and attachments are made – to our jobs, to the ideas we produce in them, to the labour we undertake, to the people with whom we interact. Our work takes a toll, they asserted. This is a theme that echoes throughout this book. Policymakers engage emotionally with their jobs, and this orients their approaches to what they consider to be important. The toll is brought about by the structures and histories that create the conditions within which they work.

While this former public servant was not just talking about working under the direction of Michael Pezzullo, many have complained about the turn that the department has taken under his leadership.

Pezzullo became Secretary of the Department of Home Affairs when the portfolio was created on 20 December 2017. This was a role that morphed from his previous position of Secretary of the Department of Immigration and Border Protection, to which he was appointed on 13 October 2014. Previously, he had been COO and then CEO of the Australian Customs and Border Protection Service, and before that he held the role of Deputy Secretary Strategy in the Department of Defence. Indeed, Defence was where his public service career began, in 1987. Between the end of his initial appointment in Defence in 1992 and his return in 2002, he primarily held roles in Labor offices: first on the staff of Gareth Evans, the then Foreign minister, and next five years as deputy chief of staff to Kim Beazley while he was Leader of the Opposition.[27] Pezzullo drafted Beazley's response to the *Tampa* incident, devising then the idea of a Department of Home Affairs.[28] But before all that, Pezzullo studied history at the University of Sydney. According to an interview he conducted with journalist Peter Mares, he was a keen war historian and would have continued down the path of academia had his honours supervisor, Richard Bosworth, not discouraged him, 'telling him it offered few jobs and poor career prospects. Instead, he encouraged Pezzullo to consider a more secure future in government service'.[29] When I contacted him for an interview, his executive assistant declined on his behalf, noting that the First Assistant Secretary Strategic Research and Communication would talk with me instead.[30] Despite multiple follow-ups, that interview never eventuated.

In his public statements, Pezzullo routinely expresses concern for child refugees and asylum seekers in a manner similar to numerous other policymakers we have encountered in this book: narrating a general concern for their welfare, balanced with a determination that their perceived vulnerability should not be exploited by those he deemed to have nefarious aims. In 2015, he reiterated familiar narratives of Australian virtuousness, telling a Senate Estimates hearing focused on the treatment of refugees and asylum seekers in Australian detention centres in Nauru and Papua New Guinea (which spent considerable time discussing the children among that group) that 'each and every one of my staff in the department work diligently, conscientiously':

> As part of our general commitment to public service values but also the values of the department, we undertake our roles conscientiously and with diligence. And at a more fundamental

level, at a level of humanity, we all understand the circumstances as parents or members of families, as the case may be – everyone has got a sibling, a parent or a child in one way or another. Our officers would apply normal Australian compassion and decency, as we would expect in any organised service or agency of the government.[31]

At another hearing in 2015, this one predominantly focused on the Australian Human Rights Commission's *The Forgotten Children* report, Pezzullo told Senate Estimates: 'I would suggest very strongly to this committee that [his officers] did not forget any children. There were no forgotten children in that sense. All of us, whether we are parents or not parents, understand the sanctity of protecting children. I think all of us would understand the clear imperative to do so.' He further asserted that 'certainly speaking on behalf of my officers now – I have been secretary since October – but when this problem was at its peak, because I saw it from the Customs side, there were very diligent, conscientious and very passionate and committed Australians who were doing their very best to indeed not forget children.'[32] Passionate and committed Australians: the story of Australian generosity has been firmly entrenched.

But of course this contrasts strongly with the experiences of at least some of the children. The group of children detained in Nauru who formed a Facebook page called 'Free the Children Nauru' wrote on 11 November 2015: 'When we see people like our page and say something in coment we want to scream our happiness because we know you and you know us. We want to say we love you! It is also amazing to see people that did not know us be so kind and know that we hear. Might because we not forgotten childrens. We hope we not forgotten child's.'[33] It also contrasts with the submissions that refugee children made to the Human Rights Commission's two inquiries into children in detention, first in 2004 and then again in 2014.

In a long series of questions at Senate Estimates on 8 February 2016, where they discussed the imprisoning of children in Nauru, Pezzullo told the senators that 'it is the government's policy that it will do whatever possible within the ambit of the policy to get children out of detention'. But, he continued, 'the question of having any children in detention of course is a factual matter that needs to be determined on each case. If you had a standard policy … that no child would ever go into detention irrespective of how they got here, that would just open the door for many more to arrive.'[34] In these words we hear the echo of many others we have encountered in this book, explaining why children 'need' to be detained: because to say that they do not would encourage other children to make their way to Australia. It has become the standard rationale, and it is part of a story that governmental institutions tell about their right to control other people's decisions. This kind of controlling approach has been noted by journalist Kirsten Drysdale as being key to Pezzullo's character.[35] Pezzullo, like Gibbons and Menadue, is a reformer. Reformers actively take control.

A similar line was repeated in Senate Estimates on 21 October 2019, in testimony regarding the Medevac legislation, which was then in force. Pezzullo and his colleagues argued that the application of the legislation meant that people who in the future may be detained in either location could access its provisions. This was a problem, in their imagining, regarding children who may be born: they were concerned that refugees who were pregnant might make their way to Nauru or Manus Island in order to access the Medevac provisions. Pezzullo told the hearing that while you cannot put boundaries around eligiblity, 'we don't want to give away how you hack the system ... if you are a smuggler, you might be thinking about the sorts of demography you might try to penetrate our defences with, knowing that, if you could hook it to future births, you could get the whole family in. We are very concerned about that.'[36] His colleague Pip de Veau – an Assistant Secretary, Legal Division and General Counsel – asserted that 'the added complication is that, once a child born in the future becomes a relevant transitory person on the recommendation of doctors to be brought here for assessment [under the legislation], the rest of the family unit provisions also kick in, so the entire family would be brought'.[37] Here is a 2019 version of the 'anchor child' concern.

It is this approach – seeing children as a threat that needs to be controlled and contained – that appears to be most common during Pezzullo's time working in border control. Journalist James Button wrote of Pezzullo that when he took over he 'took a cleaver to the structures, culture and identity of the old immigration department'.[38] Drysdale noted that Pezzullo 'describe[d] those who worked for the former Department of Immigration as "care bears"', and that he enforced the wearing of 'militaristic Border Force uniforms' in the department, including 'the chinos-and-polo-shirt coders who sit in a basement all day and have no interaction with the public'. There was a cultural push to refer to individuals by formal titles in office discussions, and more and more staff undertook weapons training. While there has been a new government since mid-2022, it does not seem like the cultures of these departments have changed: Border Force and Home Affairs are widely understood to now be draconian, highly regimented places, where Pezzullo remains in charge and where a focus on punitive control dominates.[39]

This focus came through in a speech that Pezzullo gave to the Australian Strategic Policy Institute in December 2014, where he asserted that 'sovereign decision-making within the state, and a global order of sovereign states: these are the core elements of the modern international system'. In this speech, Pezzullo set out his theory of borders, asking his listeners to 'see borders as the connection points of a globally connected world. In other words, global travel and trade, labour mobility, and the migration and movement of peoples are best mediated and managed by connected border systems'. Pezzullo believes deeply in borders in a world that is both globalised and based around state sovereignty. As he told his audience, 'the border is a strategic national asset', a mode of maintaining control and extracting positive value. He believes that 'we should see the border as a *space* where sovereign states control the *flow* of people and goods in to and out of their dominion'.

This was a speech that articulated a belief in the vitality of the state and the need for strong borders that can withstand 'threats' to sovereignty. In a passage devoted to warcraft and securitisation, Pezzullo proclaimed the greatness of Australia's 'maritime border zone', asserting that 'the ocean around us is the crown jewel of our border protection system, and we must do everything reasonable within law, resources and government policy to ensure that this remains the case'.[40] What a remarkably colonial way to think about that watery, oceanic, dynamic space! How different from historian Samia Khatun's description of the Indian Ocean 'as a site of epistemic struggle ... something akin to an immense reservoir of knowledges' that can be understood better through the storytelling practices and insights of South Asia.[41]

In his speech, Pezzullo drew heavily on his own credentials as the child of migrants, as well as on Australia's history of 'nation-building' through its migration program. Returning to the familiar theme of a desire to be compassionate and having that compassion thwarted by 'bad refugees', Pezzullo told his audience that

> if we reframe the departmental mission in the terms that I have described in this address, namely mediating the tension between globalisation and sovereignty by managing secure and connected borders, we will be better placed to give the government of the day space in which to deal with those in need of genuine assistance, through our humanitarian and refugee programmes. It is hard to be compassionate if you are dealing with overwhelming and immediate pressures on your borders.

He concluded with a rebuke to people smugglers as a group who 'treat vulnerable people as commodities, and do so with a reckless disregard for human life', and reiterated the importance of 'ensur[ing] our sovereignty in a globalised world' through 'well managed and secure borders'.[42] But this is part of a long history, as James Button noted: 'Settler societies get to curate their populations much more than others do, and Australia, a huge island in a wide sea, has been free to pursue this advantage more aggressively than just about any other nation.' Under Pezzullo, he argued, that curation has been guided more by 'arrogant gods' than by caring 'angels'.[43]

Here, then, we have a perfectly encapsulated call to history and future, through the terms offered by discourses of statecraft, nation-building, care and control. This idea of control is central to Pezzullo's understanding of his task. It is perhaps what makes him the person most suitable for his role at this moment in time. A deep belief in defence and security thinking, a faith in government and policymakers to determine people's future, and a desire for authoritarian leadership – all while also articulating a patronising vision of 'care' for those understood to be lesser and lacking – can be considered the most concise articulation of the shape of Australian child refugee policy in the present day. This is cruel care distilled. It is notable that Pezzullo has retained his position under the Albanese government, even as other department secretaries did not when Labor came to power: does this indicate that the Albanese government, and Immigration minister Andrew Giles, are set to maintain the previous government's hardline approach to people at the borders? It would seem so, at least in the immediate term.

And so by looking at the work of these three public servants, we gain an idea of the different ways that all the aspects and branches of policymaking come together to produce the policies and politics that we, as the public, see. While Menadue, Gibbons and Pezzullo might see themselves as working in different ways from one another, and might have different motivations bringing them to their task, the result echoes in its similarities across the decades. We can see the strands of control, of heightened emotion, of the call to authority, and of the belief that white government knows what is best and acts with benevolent care, even as the measures that are created can at times produce great harm for those people who are subjected to them.

Conclusion

In 2016 – as I was conducting research for what would become this book – I had a free week between studying in the archives at the United Nations library and elsewhere in Geneva, and attending a conference in Glasgow. And so I got on a plane and flew to Poland, to visit the lands that my family had been expelled from in the 1940s. Standing at the site which Polish ID documents say once contained the apartment building my grandfather and his parents and brothers had lived in during the 1930s (which is now a carpark), I said kaddish, the Jewish prayer for the dead.

Kaddish is meant to be said in front of a group of people, because they need to respond. You need to be heard when you say kaddish, your mourning and grief held and echoed back by a community. But something felt fitting about being alone, in front of this carpark, across the road from buildings that had been graffitied with 'Zyd' ('Jew') and Magen Davids (the Jewish Star of David) and swastikas (which need no explanation). I said the prayer and took a selfie, conscious that I was taking more selfies while in Poland than I normally do. Perhaps my camera was testifying to my presence. It could demonstrate the continuation of our family and our lives. It could prove, perhaps, that we could return. That by becoming refugees, some of us – not nearly all, but some – had lived.

I have carried this history with me in the writing of this book. Every author, every policymaker, indeed every person, carries a set of histories with them as they move through the world. These histories are individual, familial, communal, structural. They are formed by moments we can control and moments we cannot. They are created through violence and love, resistance and distress. Histories of ancestors being made into refugees, of the decisions they were forced to make to ensure their survival, and the life they created for themselves and their descendants in a new land, are embedded in every page. Similarly, an understanding that violence can be intransigent, brutal, humiliating and fierce imbues each page.

Alongside this is the knowledge that communities and peoples working together can bring about change. It is possible to fight against cruelty, led by those most in its path – for they know the way out.

In this book I have charted the work of many who have created or upheld violence, as well as those who believe they are helping overcome it. I have not traced the stories of those subjected to this violence because this is not my task to undertake. The people I spoke to and the archives I examined – by and large – reflect the perspectives of those who control, not those who are controlled.

I discuss 'discourses' and 'narratives' because while words and slogans are taken up by individuals, they are also broader than individuals. Any of us can participate in them. Most of us do, at some point. As someone who is simultaneously a member of a minority religion and community and a coloniser, I am keenly aware of the possibilities created by living within the systems I live in, and the limitations it imposes. I am always learning; I can always learn more.

This is not a complete history: there is much else to be said. The history of Australian child refugee and asylum-seeker policy is lengthy and complex, and it requires further research. Is this book a first step in a new direction? Who knows the right way to write a history? Is there indeed ever a right way?

Something I have been struck by as I have undertaken this research is that most people will rarely describe themselves as racist, as violent or as uncaring. Although that seems an obvious thing to say, I am interested in how this comes to be. What are the histories that make people want to claim for themselves a benevolent identity, a sense of their work as good and themselves as caring? It is those histories this book has examined, looking at the ways the interplay of narratives of care, control and cruelty have shaped Australian child refugee policy into the modern era. I have told a story of structures and of individuals; of the ways that policymakers – like all of us – are shaped by personal histories and by the communal, collective histories of the nation. I have thought about the human work of making policy, of how through policymaking worlds are made. Violence is enacted. And we learn that 'good intentions', that 'meaning well', is insufficient, and indeed irrelevant. When policymakers speak of or gesture towards populations of child refugees as mere groups to be governed or moved by, we need to unpack these formulations.[1] Through this we learn the importance of feeling, but also that feeling is not enough. The actions that those feelings lead us to are political. Not all actions taken in response to distress or empathy produce good results. As we have seen, 'feelings' have too often led policymakers to dwell on themselves. What would happen if those feelings instead led to greater openness, to less consideration of policymakers' pains and difficulties?

As a policymaker, a historian or a reader of these histories, our task is not to refuse emotional engagement but rather to seek to bring emotions to the forefront, turn them against themselves, find

Cruel Care

ways to dismantle the divides that are being created between people through the use and naturalisation of emotional discourses – of fear, alienation, discomfort and patronising benevolence towards particular acts or people. We need to understand how Australian history is being sentimentalised and endeavour to rethink this nationalist approach, which reiterates a dangerous imaginary that Australia has been kind and gentle. This colonial country is founded on violence and exclusion, on cruel care and control. Aboriginal sovereignties persist. We need to keep this knowledge at the forefront of the way that we understand our histories and create our futures. It is not beside the point or tangential. The task before us is not to better manage the borders or the population: it is to disrupt this whole system that relies on these management practices.

For we see how cruel care persists into the present. In the dying hours of the Morrison government, on Election Day 2022, Scott Morrison instructed Border Force to release details of the interception of a boat carrying Tamil asylum seekers from Sri Lanka towards Australia.[2] News of this interception – which seemingly went against Morrison's long-held position that his government and the immigration bureaucracy did not comment on 'on-water matters', as it was famously phrased – was broadcast and text messages were sent to voters in key battleground seats. Seats the Liberal Party hoped to retain.

They were unsuccessful. The Albanese government was sworn in on the Monday.

And by the Tuesday, those passengers on the boat were sent back to Sri Lanka, to an uncertain but almost surely violent future.[3] A few weeks later, the new Home Affairs minister, Clare O'Neil, visited Sri Lanka to reinforce the message that the governments of the two countries would work together to prevent fishing vessels being used to carry refugees. Australia was funding the installation of tracking devices on more than 4000 Sri Lankan fishing boats, it was reported.[4]

Throughout that first week of the Albanese government, there was talk of the Nadesalingam family and whether they would finally get to go 'home to Bilo'. Granting them a visa that would enable them to do so had been a Labor election promise. And so on Friday 27 May, Jim Chalmers tweeted a photo of himself in his office captioned, 'Speaking with the Murugappan family about my decision today as interim Home Affairs Minister to enable them to return #HometoBilo, the big-hearted QLD town which has embraced them so warmly #auspol'.[5]

In response, Twitter feeds streamed with Australians tweeting that they were overcome with joyful emotion. Amid this dwelling on their own reactions, some refugees instead tweeted of the need to give all refugees permanent visas and true freedom.[6] The contrast between the discourses could not have been more stark. And it was heightened further when the family were given permanent residency in August 2022. Behrouz Boochani tweeted, 'Congratulations to this beautiful family, but lets say everything in Aus is about white saviour culture. The very public return of this family is a paradoxical and challenging story. Specially when we remember that there are still more 100s refugees remaining in Port Moresby&Nauru.'[7]

This one week in the Australian government's treatment of refugees thus encapsulated the child politics that is at stake in this book. I have little doubt that a key reason why the Nadesalingam family was so embraced – why so many Australians invested emotionally in them – was because the family included two small children, and because a group of predominantly white Queenslanders spoke up about the contribution that this Tamil family had made to the broader community. But had that family been on the boat that tried to arrive on Australia's shores on Election Day, they would have been sent back without us ever knowing their names. This is not a contradiction: in its arbitrariness, its use of emotions, and its reinforcing of government control, it is an approach that sits at the heart of what constitutes Australia's treatment of refugees.

Acknowledgements

The responsibilities of writing this history have sat heavily with me. These are difficult histories to engage with. In writing them I have responsibilities to the people I interviewed and those who I encountered in the archives. I have responsibilities to the children whose lives have been affected by these policies, and to all refugees and asylum seekers. And I also have obligations to the Country I live on.

I live on the unceded sovereign Country of the Wurundjeri people of the Kulin Nation, and this book was written there as well as on the Country of the Ngunnawal and Ngambri peoples. Being on this Kulin Country brings certain responsibilities, primarily – in my understanding, as I have heard from Welcomes to Country by Boon Wurrung elder N'arweet Carolyn Briggs and by Senior Wurundjeri Elder Joy Wandin Murphy – a responsibility to act with 'purpose' and with respect for the lands, waters, animals and people. It entails remembering that I am lucky to be here, and that I benefit immeasurably from being hosted by the Kulin Nation. Informed by work by writers such as Gamilaraay mari Jared M. Field (Spearim), I remember that I am trying to be in enduring respectful relations with the Kulin Nation, and that this requires continual work on my part.[1] This knowledge infuses the history this book tells and the political perspectives I bring to its telling. Alongside the fact that I am the granddaughter of Jewish

Acknowledgements

Holocaust survivors – someone from a migrant family who survived genocide and migration, and from a marginalised religious and ethnic group – my position as a coloniser shapes my approach to understanding and writing history. In writing about the ways that migrants to Australia remember their migratory and settlement histories, cultural studies academic Joseph Pugliese has shown 'there can be no "innocence" about the violent colonial history of this country'.[2] Migrants are part of it. I am part of it.

This book is, then, influenced by the places where it was written and the relationships with the many others that I have formed or continued as I have worked on it. Thinking this through in order to write these acknowledgements has been a wonderful and overwhelming task. I have been working on this project since December 2014 and I am indebted to many people.

I am grateful to Joy Damousi for appointing me as a Postdoctoral Research Fellow on her ARC Laureate Research Fellowship project and thereby providing me with the opportunity to undertake this research. I am thankful as well for the intellectual community she created through this project, and to the other members of the Laureate team: Mary Tomsic, Rachel Stevens, Niro Kandasamy, Sarah Green and Anh Nguyen. Thank you all for helping me develop, think through and improve my work.

That project was located in the University of Melbourne's School of Historical and Philosophical Studies, my work home for a very long time. Conversations and engagements with many people there, most particularly Samia Khatun, Alessandro Antonello, Hannah Loney and Katherine Ellinghaus, as well as support from Katherine McGregor and Andrew May – and the brilliant professional staff, particularly June McBeth – sustained me. I'm thankful to have been able to be

Acknowledgements

in the department at the same time as some fabulous postgrads, in particular Genevieve Fitzgerald, Dave Henry and Beth Marsden. At the university we formed a peer mentoring group for a few years, and regular conversations and ongoing solidarities there were invaluable: I thank Elise Klein, Rachel Hughes, Mary Tomsic, Meighen Katz and Julie Fedor. And I'm grateful to Annalisa Giudici and Kate Fullagar for my time spent working with them on book reviews at *Australian Historical Studies*.

I am deeply appreciative of everyone who participated in an interview for this research. This work could not have been done without their generous participation and willingness to share information and insights. Many interviewees will find their words in these pages – for those who I have not quoted directly, I assure you that your words were invaluable in helping me understand the history I was investigating. I want to thank Bernard Unkles for giving me early advice on the public service.

Archivists and librarians working across institutions around the world opened up a world of knowledge for me. I thank those at the United Nations library and archives in Geneva, the United Nations archives in New York, the National Archives of Australia (in both Canberra and Melbourne), the National Library of Australia, the State Library of NSW, and the Special Collections and Interlibrary Loans services at the library at the University of Melbourne.

My three months spent as a Visiting Fellow at the Humanities Research Centre at the ANU was a true gift, enabling me to knuckle down and focus on my writing, as well as to engage in invaluable conversations. I thank the HRC for their financial support for this project, and I thank Will Christie, Kylie Message, Penny Brew, Melissa Lovell, Jennifer Rutherford, Cynthia Chris, Arlene Stein and everyone

Acknowledgements

else who was there over that time, for their welcome and collegiality – as well as Ellen Smith for being a fellowship friend in Canberra.

I was privileged to give talks and contribute writing across the years of doing this research and I am so grateful to everyone who invited me, commented on my work, wrote with me and helped me think this project through. My sincere thanks to Alexandra Dellios, Agnieszka Sobocinska, Catherine Kevin, Christina Twomey, Charlotte Greenhalgh, Clare Corbould, Katherine Ellinghaus, Adil Hasan Khan, Hazem Alnamla, Ann Genovese, Sarah Pinto, Ryan Gustafsson, Jon Piccini, Madelaine Chiam, Alison Duxbury, Ben Silverstein, Ashley Barnwell, Signe Ravn, Benjamin Thomas White, Savitri Taylor, Jodie Boyd, Klaus Neumann, Rachel Ida Buff, Kate Ogg, Nishadh Rego, Emily Foley, Margaret Allen, Jane Haggis, Carly McLaughlin, Marc Mierowsky, Karen Block, Marilena Indelicato, Sara Dehm, Max Kaiser, Claire Loughnan, Anna Szorenyi and Philomena Murray. I am grateful to Matthew Klugman, Erica Millar, Ben Silverstein, Frank Bongiorno and Sian Vate for reading chapters for me once this work was in book form. Thanks as well to the audiences and peer reviewers who asked incisive questions and gave me helpful tips, and to the many academics who supported me and my work along the way, particularly Peter Gattrell, John Docker, Ann Curthoys, Alison Phipps, Catherine Kevin, Zora Simic and Kalissa Alexeyeff. Supportive comments from Patrick Wolfe and Tracey Banivanua Mar early in this project have stayed with me, and I remain indebted to them both.

I have indeed been incredibly lucky to be surrounded by some who represent the best of academic generosity and friendship. It was a slog to get this book to publication and I absolutely would not have got there without the sage, big-hearted and glorious wisdom and hard work of Matthew Klugman. I also have him to thank for coming up with the

Acknowledgements

perfect title, *Cruel Care*. Conversations and messages with Sarah Pinto got me through some difficult times. Katherine Ellinghaus's friendship and help over a very long period is something I am always grateful for. Generous support from Robert Reynolds has been invaluable in helping me navigate academic life.

When I was in between jobs and needed work, there were some people who came to the rescue, and I am truly thankful to them: Robert Reynolds, Leigh Boucher, Michelle Arrow, Una McIlvenna, Claire Loughnan, Katherine Ellinghaus, Adil Hasan Khan, Carolyn Holbrook, Erica Millar, Julia Dehm, Lynette Russell and Sara Dehm. And I've also had the opportunity to work on other rewarding projects over the course of writing this book. Thank you to David Slucki, Karla Elliott, Rebecca Forgasz, Karen Block, Sarah Strauven, Michael Green, André Dao, Claire Smiddy and Charlene Edwards.

In 2021 I was fortunate to land at the Peter McMullin Centre on Statelessness, where I have completed this book. Working there has proved to be a truly enriching experience. I thank Michelle Foster, Adil Hasan Khan, Philippa Gerrard, Deirdre Brennan, Thomas McGee, Sumedha Choudhury, Andrea Immanuel, Bongkot Napaumporn, Jade Roberts, Katie Robertson, Susan Kneebone and Amelia Walters, as well as Amanda Porter, Piers Gooding, Ann Genovese and Sundhya Pahuja, wonderful colleagues and friends at the Melbourne Law School.

I thank the Australian Research Council through ARC Laureate Research Fellowship Project [FL140100049], 'Child Refugees and Australian Internationalism from 1920 to the Present', for their support for the research and writing of this book, and through ARC Discovery Project [DP210100929], 'Understanding Statelessness in Australian Law and Practice', for support for writing and editing this book, as

Acknowledgements

well as the Peter McMullin Centre on Statelessness for their support for its publication.

I was so pleased when Monash University Publishing agreed to publish this book. Working with them to bring it to life has been a dream. I thank Julia Carlomagno for all her work to make the book happen, Ian See for his terrific proofreading, and everyone else at the press – Sam van der Plank, Les Thomas, Sarah Cannon and Joanne Mullins – for their efforts in turning my words into an actual book and helping to promote it.

Kristine Jover's friendship and support – in person and in the DMs – is incomparable. You're the best. I remain always thankful for the continuing conversations and love from Sian Vate. And really, over the course of writing this book so many friends have enriched my life immeasurably. Just the biggest thanks to Imogen Jubb, Mischa Barr, Paris Gadsden, Julia Dehm, Adil Hasan Khan, Joan Nestle, Di Otto, Ilise Cohen, Sahar Vardi, Rosa Manoim, Vlada Bilyak, Moriel Rothman-Zecher, Nader Ruhayel, Jacqui Brenner, Kelly Laing, David Slucki, Helen Slucki, Esther Singer, Sivan Barak, Max Kaiser, Yoel Caspi, Sonya Goldberg, Liam Neame, Jessica Morrison, Nasser Mashni and Noura Mansour.

I don't know what I would do without the generosity and sharp mind of Erica Millar. Claire McLisky has been a beautiful friend and co-thinker. I will always be grateful to be thinking, working and fighting alongside Crystal McKinnon. Thank you all, deeply.

My family are incredibly important in my life. Sara, thank you for your wonderful friendship and support, and for dealing with my emergency last-minute fact-checking. Ben, thank you for endless conversations, the precision of your thinking, your big clever mind, and your generosity and care (in the best sense of the word). I'm so

Acknowledgements

incredibly glad we're in this work and this world together. Mum and Dad, thank you for your love, and for setting me on the right path into the world. Leo, thank you for the chats, the laughs, and for making sure I always have a bed in Sydney. Edith, thank you for your smiles and hugs. The two of you: thank you for having me as your tante, I love it.

In 2016, as a result of research that Krystyna Duszniak helped us with, my family learned some more about our relatives who had been murdered during the Holocaust. About those who didn't survive long enough to become refugees. The memory of one in particular – Zalman Stawski – has been front of mind for me. He was my grandfather's brother, and he was married and had two sons before the war. He, his wife (Fraidel/Frania) and their sons (Aaron and Moshe), were all murdered. I often find myself wondering what he would have been like as a great-uncle if he had lived. I dedicate this book to his memory, and to the memory of everyone who has faced the brutal, heartbreaking cruelty of state violence.

This book is derived in part from an article published in *The History of the Family*, 2017, copyright Taylor & Francis, www.tandfonline.com /10.1080/1081602X.2016.1265572, and from an article published in *History Australia*, 2020, copyright Taylor & Francis, www.tandfonline.com/10.1080/14490854.2020.1840287. It also contains material that has appeared in various publications: '"I am responsible": histories of the intersection of the guardianship of unaccompanied child refugees and the Australian border', *Cultural Studies Review* 22, no. 2, pp. 65–89 (Creative Commons licence); '"Best interests of the child": Australian refugee policy and the (im)possibilities of international solidarity', *Human Rights Review* 22, no. 4, 2021, pp. 389–405; '"His happy-go-lucky attitude is infectious": Australian imaginings of unaccompanied child refugees, 1970s–1980s', in Jordana Silverstein

Acknowledgements

and Rachel Stevens (eds), *Refugee Journeys: Histories of Resettlement, Representation and Resistance*, ANU Press, Canberra, 2021, pp. 71–88 (Creative Commons Attribution – NonCommercial – NoDerivs 2.0 Australia licence); '"Because we all love our country": refugee and asylum-seeking children, Australian policy-makers, and the building of national sentiment', *Australian Journal of Politics and History* 65, no. 4, 2019, pp. 532–48; and '"I'm skeptical of foreigners": making space for discomfort in an oral history interview', *Oral History Australia*, no. 41, 2019, pp. 12–21.

Notes

CPD = Commonwealth Parliamentary Debates
NAA = National Archives of Australia
NLA = National Library of Australia

Introduction
1   Doherty, 2018.
2   Dehm and Vogl, 2019.
3   Taylor, 2021.
4   'Dawn to Dusk Vigil – Home to Bilo, Sydney', *Time for a Home*, https://web.archive.org/web/20210306235150/www.timeforahome.com.au/events/dawn-to-dusk-vigil-home-to-bilo-sydney
5   Karp, 2022.
6   Gillespie, 2022.
7   Doherty, 2016b; Holt, 2019.
8   Human Rights and Equal Opportunity Commission Report, 'Chapter 24: Juvenile Justice', April 1997; Donovan, 2013; Farnsworth, 2016.
9   Allam, 2022.
10 Gibson, 2022.
11 Watego, 2021, pp. xii, 8–9.
12 Jessee, 2011, pp. 287–307.
13 Malkki, 1996, pp. 377–404.

Chapter 1
1   Pugliese, 2015, pp. 88, 95.
2   McKinnon, 2020, pp. 691–92.
3   Smith, 2022.
4   Wolfe, 2006, pp. 387–409.
5   McKinnon, 'Indigenous music as a space of resistance', in Banivanua Mar and Edmonds (eds), 2010, p. 256.

Notes

6 Banivanua Mar, 2016.
7 Silverstein, 2022, pp. 566, 583.
8 'John Howard's 2001 election policy speech', 28 October 2001, uploaded to YouTube 22 February 2013 by Malcolm Farnsworth. Transcript available at: https://electionspeeches.moadoph.gov.au/speeches/2001-john-howard
9 Hage, 1998.
10 Snoek, 2019.
11 Prince and Lester, 2022.
12 'About Deathscapes,' *Deathscapes*, https://webarchive.nla.gov.au/awa/20201103065140/http://pandora.nla.gov.au/pan/173410/20201103-1648/www.deathscapes.org/about-project/index.html
13 Gibson, 2007; Gibbons, 2014; Kingston, 1993, p. 3. See also 'ATSIC's disappearing act: 1300 staff to 20', *Sydney Morning Herald*, 25 April 2003.
14 Jacobs, 1990, pp. 35–45, 54. I am grateful to Victoria Haskins for telling me about this history at the 2018 International Australian Studies Association (InASA) conference.
15 A.O. Neville, Commonwealth of Australia, 'Aboriginal welfare: initial conference of Commonwealth and State Aboriginal authorities, Canberra 21–23 April 1937', L.F. Johnston, CGP, Canberra, 1937, p. 11.
16 Baird, 2008, p. 291.
17 Watego, 2016; Perera, 2004; Birch, 2021.
18 Klaus Neumann, 'Oblivious to the obvious? Australian asylum-seeker policies and the use of the past', in Neumann and Tavan (eds), 2009, p. 60.
19 Moreton-Robinson, 2004.
20 McKinnon, 2018, p. 198.
21 Boochani, 2018, p. 158.
22 Submissions no. 60, no. 62 and no. 93, Australian Human Rights Commission, 2014.
23 Bennoun and Kelly, 1981, p. 3. See also Evenhuis, 2013, p. 537.
24 Basham and the Australian Churches Refugee Taskforce, 2014. For a foundational history of childhood, see Ariès, 1962.
25 Sandberg, 2015, p. 223.
26 Gordon and Peleg, 2019.
27 Personal communication with Laura MacColl, Executive & Research Assistant to the National Children's Commissioner, Australian Human Rights Commission, 9 March 2018.
28 Sheldon, 2016, p. 4.
29 Interview with Liana Buchanan, Melbourne, 8 August 2018.
30 Interview with Oliver White, Sydney, 18 April 2018.
31 United Nations Convention and Protocol Relating to the Status of Refugees (1951), 2010, www.unhcr.org/en-au/3b66c2aa10
32 Damousi, 2018, pp. 211–26.

Notes

33 Damousi, 2020, p. 713.
34 Erica Meiners argues that racialisation means that some people do not have access to childhood. See Meiners, 2016.
35 Ticktin, 2017, p. 583.
36 Mathias Cormann, 'Questions Without Notice', 5 December 2019, Senate, CPD, p. 5286.
37 Amanda Stoker, 'Bills – Migration Amendment (Repairing Medical Transfers) Bill 2019 – Second Reading', 2 December 2019, Senate, CPD, p. 4769; Fiona Martin, 'Matters of Public Importance – Morrison Government', 25 February 2020, House of Representatives, CPD, p. 1635.
38 Scott Morrison, 'Questions Without Notice – Asylum Seekers', 4 December 2019, House of Representatives, CPD, p. 6981.
39 Andrew Giles, 'Bills – Migration Amendment (Repairing Medical Transfers) Bill 2019 – Second Reading', 23 July 2019, House of Representatives, CPD, p. 759; Josh Wilson, 'Bills – Migration Amendment (Repairing Medical Transfers) Bill 2019 – Second Reading', 24 July 2019, House of Representatives, CPD, p. 944.
40 Talbot and Newhouse, 2019, pp. 85–90.
41 For example, Vasefi, 2022; Vasefi, 2021.
42 'The fall of Saigon, 1975', NAA Fact sheet 243, National Archives of Australia, www.naa.gov.au/sites/default/files/2020-05/fs-243-the-fall-of-saigon-1975.pdf
43 'Historical migration statistics', Department of Home Affairs, Commonwealth of Australia, 1 April 2019, https://data.gov.au/data/dataset/historical-migration-statistics
44 Phillips and Spinks, 2013.
45 'Visa statistics: immigration detention', Department of Home Affairs, Commonwealth of Australia, www.homeaffairs.gov.au/research-and-statistics/statistics/visa-statistics/live/immigration-detention
46 Anthea Vogl, 'What is a bogus document? Refugees, race and identity documents in Australian migration law', in Biber, Luker and Vaughan (eds), 2022, pp. 94–111.
47 Laughland, 2014.
48 Doherty, 2015.
49 Refugee Council of Australia, 'Statistics on people in detention in Australia', 9 July 2021, www.refugeecouncil.org.au/detention-australia-statistics/4/
50 Human Rights Law Centre, 2023.
51 Karp, 2022.
52 Neumann, 'Oblivious to the obvious?', in Neumann and Tavan (eds), 2009, p. 47.

Chapter 2

1 The full transcript is available at 'Interview with Ray Hadley, radio 2GB–4BC', 14 February 2019, https://minister.homeaffairs.gov.au/peterdutton/Pages/int-ray-had.aspx

Notes

2 Moreno-Lax, 2017; Crock, 2011, pp. 33–53.
3 Yaxley, 2015.
4 Burke, speech, 2015.
5 Galloway, 2022.
6 Giles, speech, 2015.
7 See, for example, Sharon Pickering and Melissa Phillips, 'Houston report on asylum seekers: did the panel listen to the experts?', *The Conversation*, 16 August 2012.
8 Boochani, 2019; Doherty, 2022.
9 Gleeson, 2016, pp. 46–47. Testimony by Greg Lake on p. 47. Lake provides similar testimony in a 2016 interview with journalist Michael Green in Behind the Wire and the Wheeler Centre, 'The Messenger: #5: A Safer Place', 13 March 2017.
10 Ibid., pp. 46–47.
11 Peterie, 2017, pp. 361, 362.
12 Damousi, 2018, p. 217.
13 Office of the United Nations High Commissioner for Refugees, 1994, pp. 5–6.
14 Tobin, 2015, p. 171.
15 United Nations High Commissioner for Refugees, 1987, pp. 4–5.
16 Pobjoy, 2017, p. 196; United Nations Treaty Collection, '11. Convention on the Rights of the Child', https://treaties.un.org/pages/ViewDetails.aspx?src=IND&mtdsg_no=IV-11&chapter=4&clang=_en
17 Bhabha, 2006, p. 1528.
18 See *Migration Act 1958*, Section 4AA, www5.austlii.edu.au/au/legis/cth/consol_act/ma1958118/s4aa.html
19 Musgrove and Swain, 2010, p. 37.
20 Liddell, 2010, p. 30.
21 Higonnet, 2006, pp. 1565–66.
22 Janet Meurant, Welfare Services, 'File Note', 5 February 1985, NAA: A446, 1985/75379.
23 Cabinet Submission JH02/0117 – 2002–2003 Humanitarian Program – Decisions JH02/0117/CAB, pp. 8–9, NAA: 14370, JH2002/117.
24 Attachment B, Cabinet Submission JH02/0117 – 2002–2003 Humanitarian Program – Decisions JH02/0117/CAB, pp. 13–17, NAA: 14370, JH2002/117.
25 'Migration and Maritime Powers Legislation Amendment (Resolving the Asylum Legacy Caseload) Bill 2014 Explanatory Memorandum', Parliament of the Commonwealth of Australia, 2014, p. 5.
26 Interview with Chris Evans, Perth, 4 October 2018.
27 Interview with former ministerial adviser, 5 September 2017.
28 Interview with Mat Tinkler, Melbourne, 6 October 2017.
29 Whyte, 2018.
30 Interview with Mat Tinkler, Melbourne, 6 October 2017.

Notes

31 Interview with Gillian Triggs, Melbourne, 28 March 2018.
32 Taylor, 2015; Shaw, 2019, pp. ix–127.
33 Department of Foreign Affairs Outward Cablegram, 4 April 1975, NAA: A1209, 1975/657, 'Adoption of Vietnamese orphans – Uplift flights – Cables'.
34 Information on *Operation Babylift* from Shaw, 2019, pp. 194, 199–205.
35 Taylor, 2015.
36 Higgins, 2017, pp. 1–6.
37 Neumann, 2015, pp. 245–89.
38 Ibid., 286–87. For further exploration of this period of policymaking, see Higgins, 2017.
39 Zulfacar, 1988.
40 Plant, 1988, p. 36.
41 Lloyd, 1983, p. 2.
42 Ibid., p. 7–8.
43 Ibid., p. 17 and p. 12.
44 Patrick Shaw and Dighton Burbidge, 'Report of the Australian Delegation to the Conference on the Status of Refugees Held at Geneva from the 2nd July to 25th July, 1951', NAA: A1838, 855/11/11 PART 3, pp. 8, 12.
45 Plant, 1988, pp. 37, 39–40, 42, 44.
46 'Refugee Children', Report of the Working Party Convened by the Standing Committee on Social Welfare Administrators, Presented to the Autumn Conference of Social Welfare Administrators, April 1984.
47 Human Rights and Equal Opportunity Commission, HREOC Report No. 25.
48 Levett, 2008.
49 Human Rights and Equal Opportunity Commission, HREOC Report No. 25.
50 McSherry and Dastyari, 2007, p. 265.
51 'Border Protection Bill 2001: Explanatory Memorandum', Parliament of the Commonwealth of Australia, 2001, p. 1.
52 Trask, 2021.
53 Arne Rinnan quoted in Pascoe, 2021.
54 This brief history taken from Reilly, 2017.
55 Homan, 2001, p. 8.
56 Baird, 2008, p. 292.
57 'Senate Select Committee on the Scrafton Evidence', Chapter 2, 9 December 2004, Senate, Parliament of Australia. See also David Marr and Marian Wilkinson, *Dark Victory*, Allen & Unwin, Crows Nest, 2003.
58 Baird, 2008, p. 302; Trioli, 2012.
59 John Howard, 2GB radio interview, 8 October 2001, cited in Goodnow, with Lohman and Marfleet, 2008, p. 135.
60 Perera, 2009, particularly pp. 1–14.

Notes

61 Editorial, *Sydney Morning Herald*, 10 October 2001, p. 16.
62 For coverage see, for instance, Tony Kevin, 'Twisting tale of dog that didn't bark', *The Canberra Times*, 23 March 2002, p. 4.
63 Bolt, 2003, p. 16.
64 Fickling, 2003; Baker, 2018; Topsfield, 2006.
65 See, for instance, 'Fed: Refugees rescued after damaging boat – govt', *AAP General News Wire*, Sydney, 23 February 2007, p. 1.
66 Burke, 2007, p. 20.
67 Major General Craig Furini, AM, CSC, Commander, Joint Agency Task Force Operation Sovereign Borders, 'Migration Legislation Amendment (Regional Processing Cohort) Bill', 22 August 2019, Department of Home Affairs, Legal and Constitutional Affairs Legislation Committee, CPD, 22 August 2019, p. 35.
68 Joe Hockey, 'Budget: Questions Without Notice', 4 June 2014, House of Representatives, CPD, p. 5535. *The Messenger* podcast used this soundbite to demonstrate the operations of border control and the emotions at work (and their affective work) in parliamentary debates. See Behind the Wire and the Wheeler Centre, 2017, op. cit.
69 Hasham, 2015, p. 4.
70 Davidson, 2015.
71 Interview with Anna Burke, Melbourne, 9 November 2017.
72 Faulkner, 2019, p. 2.
73 Ticktin, 2017, p. 579.
74 Sheldon, 2016, p. 3.
75 Krakouer, 2019.
76 Watego, 2018.
77 Baird, 2008, p. 295.
78 Damousi, 2018, p. 225.
79 Malkki, 1996, p. 388.
80 On this understanding of the colonial discourse, see Samah Sabawi's comments in 'Jewish community forum on BDS – hosted by AJDS', 10 March 2019 , https://soundcloud.com/ajds-1/ajds-jewish-community-forum-on-bds
81 Ricatti, 2016, p. 487.
82 Ticktin, 2016, p. 256.
83 Ibid., p. 268.

Chapter 3

1 Interview with senior figure within the Labor Party, Canberra, 12 September 2017.
2 Butler, 2022.
3 Boris Johnson, 'This cap on bankers' bonuses is like a dead cat – pure distraction', *The Telegraph*, 3 March 2013, quoted in O'Malley, 2017.

Notes

4 'Border Protection Bill 2001: Explanatory Memorandum', Parliament of the Commonwealth of Australia, 2001, p. 1.
5 Kim Beazley, 'Border Protection Bill 2001: Second Reading Speech', 29 August 2001, House of Representatives, CPD, pp. 30570–72.
6 John Faulkner, 'Border Protection Bill 2001: Second Reading Speech', 29 August 2001, Senate, CPD, p. 26971.
7 Jupp, 2007, p. 135.
8 Interview with former ministerial adviser, 5 September 2017.
9 Button, 2018. Emphasis added.
10 See for instance Larissa Behrendt, 'The emergency we had to have', in Altman and Hinkson, 2007, pp. 15–20.
11 McQuire, 2019.
12 See Pugliese, 2019, p. 461, where Pugliese raises the question of what is being reiterated, or cited, in our politics.
13 'Opposition Leader Peter Dutton', *Insiders*, ABC, 19 June 2022.
14 White, 2019.
15 Klein, 2007, inner cover, also p. 6.
16 Ibid., p. 6.
17 Ibid. pp. 9, 21.
18 Ticktin, 2016, p. 262.
19 Brian Massumi, 'The future birth of the affective fact: the political ontology of threat', in Gregg and Seigworth, 2010, p. 54.
20 Laura Sell, 'Q&A with Brian Massumi', Duke University Press, 19 August 2015.
21 Edelman, 2004; Meiners, 2016.
22 'Every boat is the first boat,' *Deathscapes*, https://webarchive.nla.gov.au/awa/20201103065140/http://pandora.nla.gov.au/pan/173410/20201103-1648/www.deathscapes.org/case-studies/every-boat-is-the-first-boat/index.html
23 'Christmas Island survivor slams rescue operation', *ABC News*, 27 July 2011.
24 Interview with former ministerial adviser, 5 September 2017.
25 Interview with Matt Thistlethwaite, Sydney, 21 March 2018. Subsequent quotations also from this interview.
26 For refugee accounts of hunger strikes and self-harming while in detention – and the political meaning behind such actions – see, for instance, Lucy Fiske, 'Human rights and refugee protest against immigration detention: refugees' struggles for recognition as human', *Refuge* 32, no. 1, 2016, pp. 18–27.
27 Farrell, Evershed and Davidson, 2016.
28 Interview with former ministerial adviser, 5 September 2017.
29 Rosenwein, 2006.
30 Elliott and Gunasekera, 2015, p. 19.
31 Interview with Elizabeth Elliott, Sydney, 28 November 2018.

Notes

32 Ahmed, 2006.
33 M.J.R. MacKellar, Minister for Immigration and Ethnic Affairs, 'Immigrants or refugees', paper delivered at the Australian Institute of International Affairs Seminar, 19 August 1978, NLA: MS 5000, Box 496, p. 21.
34 Ahmed, 2011, p. 240.
35 Tingle, 2012, p. 11.
36 'Federal Court judge to hear "Baby Ferouz" case', *Brisbane Times*, 16 June 2014.
37 This description of what happened, along with the direct quotes, is based on the details contained in Robertson, 2014.
38 Christine Milne, 'Migration and Maritime Powers Legislation Amendment (Resolving the Asylum Legacy Caseload) Bill, Second Reading Speech', 4 December 2014, Senate, CPD, p. 10275.
39 Farrell, 5 December 2014.
40 Medhora, 2014.
41 Gordon, 2014.
42 Sarah Hanson-Young, 'Migration and Maritime Powers Legislation Amendment (Resolving the Asylum Legacy Caseload) Bill 2014', Committee Speech, 4 December 2014, Senate, CPD, p. 10331 and Medhora, 2014.
43 Medhora, 2014.
44 Ricky Muir, 'Bills – Migration and Maritime Powers Legislation Amendment (Resolving the Asylum Legacy Caseload) Bill 2014 – Second Reading Speech', 4 December 2014, Senate, CPD, pp. 10307–08.
45 Ibid., p. 10307.
46 Farrell, 18 December 2014.
47 Ricky Muir, 'Bills – Migration Amendment (Protection and Other Measures) Bill 2014, Second Reading Speech', 16 March 2015, Senate, CPD, p. 1464.
48 Amanda Vanstone, 'Speech: Migration Amendment (Detention Arrangements) Bill 2005, In Committee', 23 June 2005, Senate, CPD, p. 70.
49 Ibid., p. 150.

Chapter 4

1 'No. 94 – Name withheld – Unaccompanied child detained in Nauru OPC', Australian Human Rights Commission National Inquiry into Children in Detention, 2014.
2 Perera and Pugliese, 2012, p. 89.
3 Giannacopoulos, 2020, p. 1086.
4 Hyndman, 2000, p. xx.
5 'Protection for children from overseas', *The Argus*, 3 July 1946, p. 28.
6 Taylor, 2006, p. 186.
7 'Protection for children from overseas', p. 28.

Notes

8   'Guardian of all child migrants', *The Argus*, 9 July 1946, p. 3; Arthur Calwell, 'House of Representatives: Immigration (Guardianship of Children) Bill 1946: Second Reading Speech', CPD, 31 July 1946, p. 3370.
9   Taylor, 2006, p. 186.
10 Bhabha and Crock, 2007, p. 31.
11 Australian Senate Community Affairs References Committee, *Lost innocents: Righting the record: Report on child migration*, Senate Community Affairs References Committee Secretariat, Canberra, 2001; Department of Social Services, 'Apology to the Forgotten Australians and Former Child Migrants', www.dss.gov.au/our-responsibilities/families-and-children/programs-services/apology-to-the-forgotten-australians-and-former-child-migrants
12 Neumann, 2015, p. 71.
13 Arthur Calwell, 'House of Representatives: Immigration Speech', CPD, 9 August 1946, p. 4206.
14 Arthur Calwell, 'House of Representatives: Immigration Speech', CPD, 22 November 1946, p. 502.
15 Thomas White, 'House of Representatives: Immigration (Guardianship of Children) Bill 1946: Second Reading Speech', CPD, 8 August 1946, pp. 4089–90.
16 Arthur Calwell, 'House of Representatives, Immigration (Guardianship of Children) Bill 1948: Second Reading Speech, Procedural Text', CPD, 5 October 1948, p. 1121.
17 'Care of child immigrants', *West Australian*, 19 November 1948, p. 5.
18 Copy of order by the Minister of State for Immigration, 30 August 1950, NAA: A432, 1950/1613.
19 'Aircraft sought to fly refugees from Hungary', *Canberra Times*, 14 November 1956, p. 2.
20 Neumann, 2015b, p. 71.
21 'Immigration (Guardianship of Children) Amendment Bill 1993: Explanatory Memorandum', Parliament of the Commonwealth of Australia, 1993, p. 4; and 'Same-Sex Relationships (Equal Treatment in Commonwealth Laws–General Law Reform) Bill 2008: Explanatory Memorandum,' Parliament of the Commonwealth of Australia, 2008, pp. 131–54.
22 'Migration Legislation Amendment (Regional Processing and Other Measures) Bill 2012: Explanatory Memorandum', Parliament of the Commonwealth of Australia, 2012, p. 1.
23 'Migration and Maritime Powers Legislation Amendment (Resolving the Asylum Legacy Caseload) Bill 2014: Explanatory Memorandum,' Parliament of the Commonwealth of Australia, 2014, pp. 40–41.
24 *Migration Legislation Amendment (Regional Processing and Other Measures) Act 2012*, www.comlaw.gov.au/Details/C2012A00113
25 Question from Kim Carr, 'Senate Committee Inquiry: Regional Processing Centre in Nauru: Commonwealth government's responsibilities relating to the management of the Nauru Regional Processing Centre', CPD, 20 July 2015, p. 23.

Notes

26 Office of the United Nations High Commissioner for Refugees, *Refugee Children: Guidelines on Protection and Care*, United Nations High Commissioner for Refugees, Geneva, Switzerland, 1994, pp. 20–23.

27 'Migration and Maritime Powers Legislation Amendment', p. 5.

28 Harold Holt, 'House of Representatives: Immigration (Guardianship of Children) Bill 1952, Second Reading Speech', CPD, 4 June 1952, p. 1376.

29 See, for example, John Wheeldon, 'The Senate: Question, Vietnamese Orphans, Speech', CPD, 9 April 1975, p. 844. It should also be noted that age of majority laws in Australia are state-based, rather than federal, in contradistinction to the age-based definition offered by this Act.

30 Scott and Swain, 2002, p. 10.

31 Coper, 1976, pp. 351–52.

32 *R v Director General of Social Welfare (Vic); Ex parte Henry* [1975] HCA 62, [3] (Stephen J.).

33 Coper, 1976, p. 352.

34 Bagaric, Boyd, Dimopoulos, Tongue and Vrachnas, 2006, pp. 179–80.

35 Crock and Berg, 2011, pp. 42–48, 54–61.

36 *R v Director General of Social Welfare (Vic); Ex parte Henry* [1975] HCA 62, [3] (Gibbs J.).

37 *R v* Director *General of Social Welfare (Vic); Ex parte Henry* [1975] HCA 62, [7] (Stephen J.). Similarly, Justice Mason wrote in his judgement, 'The immigration power is not confined to regulation of the physical entry of an immigrant into Australia; it may be exercised so as to apply to him at least until he becomes a member of the Australian community.' *R v Director General of Social Welfare (Vic); Ex parte Henry* [1975] HCA 62, [7] (Mason J.).

38 *R v Director General of Social Welfare (Vic); Ex parte Henry* [1975] HCA 62, [8] (Stephen J.).

39 *R v Director General of Social Welfare (Vic); Ex parte Henry* [1975] HCA 62, [12] (Mason J.). Emphasis added.

40 *R v Director General of Social Welfare (Vic); Ex parte Henry* [1975] HCA 62, [10] (Murphy J.).

41 *R v Director General of Social Welfare (Vic); Ex parte Henry* [1975] HCA 62, [11] (Stephen J.).

42 Arthur Calwell, 'House of Representatives: Immigration (Guardianship of Children) Bill 1946: Second Reading Speech', CPD, 31 July 1946, p. 3369.

43 See, for instance, 'Young migrants: minister as guardian', *West Australian*, 2 August 1946, p. 10; and Arthur Calwell, 'House of Representatives, Immigration (Guardianship of Children) Bill 1948: Second Reading Speech, Procedural Text', CPD, 5 October 1948, p. 1121.

44 John Spicer, 'The Senate: Immigration (Guardianship of Children) Bill 1952, Second Reading Procedural Text', CPD, 5 June 1952, p. 1454.

45 Robert Clothier, 'The Senate: Immigration (Guardianship of Children) Bill 1948, Second Reading Speech', CPD, 25 November 1948, p. 3506.

Notes

46 Edelman, 2004, p. 11.
47 Persian, 2015, p. 93.
48 John McEwen, 'House of Representatives: Immigration (Guardianship of Children) Bill 1948, Second Reading Speech', CPD, 18 November 1948, p. 3205–06.
49 'Shaftesbury Homes operations hinge on state government recognition', *Longreach Leader*, 23 September 1949, p. 19.
50 Harold Holt, 'House of Representatives: Nationality and Citizenship Bill 1953, Second Reading Speech', CPD, 1 December 1953, p. 734.
51 'Adoption Plan: British child migrants', *Sydney Morning Herald*, 12 June 1948, p. 2.
52 'Orphans from Germany: may be adopted here', *Sydney Morning Herald*, 14 December 1948, p. 1.
53 Enid Lyons, 'House of Representatives: Immigration (Guardianship of Children) Bill 1948: Second Reading Speech', CPD, 18 November 1948, p. 3203.
54 Ibid., p. 3204.
55 Annabelle Rankin, 'The Senate: Immigration (Guardianship of Children) Bill 1948, Second Reading Speech', CPD, 25 November 1948, p. 3506.
56 John Ignatius Armstrong, 'The Senate: Immigration (Guardianship of Children) Bill 1948, Second Reading Speech', CPD, 25 November 1948, p. 3506.
57 Crock, 2011, pp. 33–53.
58 *R v Director General of Social Welfare (Vic); Ex parte Henry* [1975] HCA 62, [11] (Stephen J.).
59 *R v Director General of Social Welfare (Vic); Ex parte Henry* [1975] HCA 62, [17] (Murphy J.).
60 *R v Director General of Social Welfare (Vic); Ex parte Henry* [1975] HCA 62, [5] (Jacobs J.).
61 NAA: B925, V1978/60922 Part 3: 'Isolated refugee children'.
62 Zulfacar, 1984, p. 6; Zulfacar, 1992, pp. 78–81.
63 Confidential report by the A/Director Regional Services, Ivan Beringer, addressed to the Deputy Director-General, dated 30 July 1976, NAA: B925, V1978/60922 PART 1.
64 The cost-sharing agreement is available in NAA: A14039, 2520: Cabinet Memorandum 2520 – Immigration and Ethnic Affairs – 1985–1986 Budget – new policy proposal – cost-sharing program for care of refugee minors – Decisions 5059/ ER (Amended) and 5667. Additionally, there is correspondence, briefings and planning for this change in arrangements (previously, it had just been the federal government in control; this move shifted the funding. Delegation of guardianship responsibilities to state authorities had already occurred in 1972. See NAA: A446, 84/79151).
65 Interview with Ian Macphee, Melbourne, 3 August 2017.
66 Mr Alan Noel Thornton, Joint Select Committee on Australia's Immigration Detention Network hearing, CPD, 6 September 2011, p. 6.

Notes

67 Greg Kelly, Joint Select Committee on Australia's Immigration Detention Network hearing, CPD, 5 October 2011, pp. 99–100.
68 Australian Human Rights Commission National Inquiry into Children in Immigration Detention, 2014.
69 Zwi and Mares, 2015, pp. 659, 660.
70 Julia Gillard, 'Ministerial Statements – Managing Migration', House of Representatives, CPD, 3 December 2002, pp. 9469–70.
71 'Refugee Children', Report of the Working Party Convened by the Standing Committee on Social Welfare Administrators, Presented to the Autumn Conference of Social Welfare Administrators, April 1984, p. 26.
72 Julia Gillard, 'Migration Legislation Amendment Bill (No. 1) 2002 – Consideration in Detail', House of Representatives, CPD, 12 December 2002, p. 10407.
73 Crock, 2005, pp. 128–29.
74 Chris Evans, *Standing Committee on Legal and Constitutional Affairs – Immigration and Citizenship Portfolio – Department of Immigration and Citizenship*, Senate Estimates Committee, CPD, 21 October 2008.
75 Sarah Hanson-Young, 'Motion – Convention on the Rights of the Child', Senate, CPD, 14 March 2012.
76 Penny Wong, *Committees – Environment and Communications References Committee, Australia's Immigration Detention Network Committee – Government Response to Report*, CPD, 29 November 2012.
77 Sarah Hanson-Young, 'Second Reading Speech – Guardian for Unaccompanied Children Bill 2014', Senate, CPD, 16 July 2014.
78 Interview with Gillian Triggs, Melbourne, 28 March 2018.
79 'Submission No. 42 – Name withheld – Child who lived in immigration detention previously', Australian Human Rights Commission National Inquiry into Children in Detention, 2014, p. 7.
80 'Submission No. 92 – name withheld – Unaccompanied child detained in Nauru OPC', ibid., pp. 1–3.
81 'Submission No. 21(A) – Name withheld – Unaccompanied child asylum seeker', ibid., pp. 3–4.
82 Millar, 2015.
83 'Evacuees paint glowing picture of Australia', *Australian Women's Weekly*, 2 February 1946, p. 9.
84 Haebich, 2008, pp. 92–93.
85 'Father Calwell', *Courier-Mail*, 15 September 1948, p. 1.
86 Neil O'Sullivan, 'Senate: Immigration (Guardianship of Children) Bill 1948, Second Reading Speech', CPD, 25 November 1948, p. 3505.
87 Leslie Haylen and Arthur Calwell, 'House of Representatives: Immigration (Guardianship of Children) Bill 1948: Second Reading Speech', CPD, 18 November 1948, p. 3204.

Notes

88 Robert Clothier, 'The Senate: Immigration (Guardianship of Children) Bill 1948, Second Reading Speech', CPD, 25 November 1948, p. 3506.

89 Leslie Haylen, 'House of Representatives: Immigration (Guardianship of Children) Bill 1948: Second Reading Speech', CPD, 18 November 1948, p. 3204.

90 Neil O'Sullivan, 'Senate: Immigration (Guardianship of Children) Bill 1948, Second Reading Speech', CPD, 25 November 1948, p. 3505.

91 Robert Clothier, 'The Senate: Immigration (Guardianship of Children) Bill 1948, Second Reading Speech', ibid., p. 3506.

92 Annabelle Rankin, 'The Senate: Immigration (Guardianship of Children) Bill 1948, Second Reading Speech', ibid.

93 Haebich, 2008, p. 97.

94 For a description of amendments, see Chris Bowen, 'Migration Legislation Amendment (Offshore Processing and Other Measures) Bill 2011 – Second Reading Speech', House of Representatives, CPD, 21 September 2011.

95 Ibid.

96 A Working Party on the Problems of Unattached Refugee Children was formed in 1978 in order to try to deal with some of these problems. It contained representatives from all states, as well as the Commonwealth. See NAA: B925, V1978/60922 PART 1 and PART 2.

97 Sara Wills, 'Between the hostel and the detention centre: possible trajectories of migrant pain and shame in Australia', in Logan and Reeves (eds), 2008, p. 268. Quote from Glenda Sluga is from Wills, emphasis in Wills.

98 Swain, 2008, p. 201.

99 Kevin and Agutter, 2017, p. 557.

100 Stoler, 2009.

101 Mamdani, 2012, p. 2.

102 There are many of these cables in NAA: B925, V1978/60922 PART 4.

103 'Timorese Children', no date, NAA: B925, V1978/60922 PART 1.

104 Victoria Undurraga, Settlement Officer, Midway Centre, to Ms Margaret McCready, Executive Officer, Settlement Unit, 21 December 1979, NAA: B925, V1978/60922 PART 3.

105 Assistant Director, Settlement Services Section, 'Report on Timorese Refugees: "Isolated Children"', 14 April 1976, NAA: B925, V1978/60922 PART 1.

106 J. Zaia, Welfare Officer, Migrant Services, 'Reports on Timorese Without Parents (Midway)', 7 July 1976, NAA: B925, V1978/60922 PART 1. The report begins by noting, 'These reports are only factual – they will be followed up with recommendations and suggestions for the children's future.'

107 NAA: B925, V1978/60922 PART 2.

108 'Progress Report on Welfare of Isolated Timorese Children at Enterprise Hostel', 9 April 1976, NAA: B925, V1978/60922 PART 1.

Notes

109 No author, 'Report on child', NAA: B925, V1978/60922 PART 1. To try to ensure anonymity, I have removed all names (which are provided in the original documents).
110 F. Wositzky, Report on child, NAA: B925, V1978/60922 PART 1.
111 J. Zaia, Welfare Officer, Migrant Services, 'Reports on Timorese Without Parents (Midway)', 7 July 1976, NAA: B925, V1978/60922 PART 1.
112 In the NAA's RecordSearch database, the file is noted as being 'Open with exception' for reasons under 33(1)(g): 'would unreasonably disclose information about the personal affairs of a person'. See 'Glossary (A–Z)', National Archives of Australia, www.naa.gov.au/help-your-research/using-collection/access-records-under-archives-act/why-we-refuse-access
113 F. Wositzky, Welfare Officer, Enterprise Hostel, no date, NAA: B925, V1978/60922 PART 1.
114 K. Richardson, Migrant Coordinator, and K. Gough, Principal, Springvale Primary School, 15 July 1976, NAA: B925, V1978/60922 PART 1.
115 Deputy Director General, Victorian Resettlement Co-Ordinating Committee, Confidential Note: 'Unattached refugee children still in Victoria', 30 July 1976, NAA: B925, V1978/60922 PART 1.
116 Deputy Director General, Victorian Resettlement Co-Ordinating Committee, Confidential Note: 'Policy Framework', 30 July 1976, NAA: V1978/60922 PART 1.

Chapter 5

1 Mehdi Ali, as told to Osborne, 2022.
2 All references to the interview with Ian Macphee and quotes from Macphee come from our interview in Melbourne on 3 August 2017.
3 Interview with Derek Volker, Canberra, 13 September 2017.
4 Interview with John Menadue, Sydney, 11 September 2017.
5 Ian Macphee, 'Refugee policy: ministerial statement', House of Representatives, CPD, 16 March 1982, p. 991.
6 Interview with Nick Bolkus, Adelaide, 27 June 2018. All quotes from our interview are from this interview.
7 Nick Bolkus, 'Matters of Urgency: Immigration: Asylum Seekers', Senate, CPD, 26 August 2002, p. 3704.
8 Enloe, 1990, 29ff.
9 Baird, 2004, pp. 238–39.
10 Ibid., p. 237.
11 Ibid., p. 239.
12 Amanda Vanstone, 'Speech: Migration Amendment (Detention Arrangements) Bill 2005, In Committee', Senate, CPD, 23 June 2005, p. 136.
13 Lyn Allison, 'Questions without Notice: Immigration: Children', Senate, CPD, 28 October 2003, p. 16978.

Notes

14 Amanda Vanstone, ibid., p. 16979.
15 Amanda Vanstone, 'Questions without Notice: Treatment of Detainees', Senate, CPD, 10 May 2005, p. 34.
16 Amanda Vanstone, 'Questions on Notice: Immigration: Detainees', Senate, CPD, 1 April 2004, p. 22719.
17 Amanda Vanstone, 'Speech: Migration Amendment (Detention Arrangements) Bill 2005, In Committee', Senate, CPD, 23 June 2005, p. 75.
18 Morris, 2004, p. 2.
19 Amanda Vanstone, 'Speech: Migration Amendment (Detention Arrangements) Bill 2005, In Committee', Senate, CPD, 23 June 2005, p. 70.
20 Ibid., p. 150.
21 Ibid.
22 Ibid., p. 200.
23 Audra Simpson, Wheeler Centre talk, 22 February 2016, www.wheelercentre.com/events/audra-simpson/
24 Richard Marles, 'Second Reading Speech, Migration Amendment (Mandatory Report) Bill 2015', House of Representatives, CPD, 12 October 2015, p. 10699.
25 Evans, 2008.
26 Migration Amendment (Immigration Detention Reform) Bill 2009, www.aph.gov.au/Parliamentary_Business/Bills_Legislation/Bills_Search_Results/Result?bId=s720.
27 Interview with former ministerial adviser, 5 September 2017.
28 'Migration Amendment (Immigration Detention Reform) Bill 2009: Explanatory Memorandum', Parliament of the Commonwealth of Australia, 2009, p. 1.
29 See, for instance, Brad Thompson and Peter Ker, 'Forrest links mining royalties to Indigenous misery', *Australian Financial Review*, 1 September 2021; Sally Whyte, 'A brief history of Twiggy Forrest's obsession with cashless welfare', *Crikey*, 17 August 2017; Minderoo, 'Cashless Debit Card FAQS', www.minderoo.org/cashless-debit-card/faqs/
30 Interview with Chris Evans, Perth, 4 October 2018. All quotes from the interview with Chris Evans are from this same interview.
31 Metherell, 2008.
32 Doherty, 2016b.
33 Holt, 2019.
34 Morton, 2013.
35 Ibid.
36 Ibid.
37 Gribbin, 2013.
38 Perptich, 2013, p. 3.
39 Gordon, 2013.
40 Uhlmann, 2013.

Notes

41 Beech, 2017.
42 Elton-Pym, 2018. Lifeline is a 'crisis support suicide prevention' Australian organisation; see www.lifeline.org.au/
43 'Q&A, Lifeline Australia Luncheon', 9 November 2018, Transcript ID: 41943, https://pmtranscripts.pmc.gov.au/release/transcript-41943
44 Fr Rod Bower, Twitter, 9 November 2018.
45 Sally McManus, Twitter, 9 November 2018.
46 Peter Relph, Twitter, 10 November 2018.
47 See, for instance a search on twitter: https://twitter.com/search?q=morrison%20pray%20cry&src=typd
48 Boyce, 2019.
49 Ibid.
50 Gorrie and Church, 2018.
51 Ahmed, 2004a, p. 120.
52 Interview with Bruce Baird, Sydney, 24 September 2018.
53 Ibid.
54 Interview with Gillian Triggs, Melbourne, 28 March 2018.
55 M.J.R. MacKellar, Minister for Immigration and Ethnic Affairs, Address to the Annual Staff Conference and Mid-Year National Committee Meetings of Austcare, 26 November 1978, NLA: MS 5000, Box 499, pp. 2–3.

Chapter 6

1 Andrew Wilkie, 'Migration Amendment (Ending the Nation's Shame) Bill 2014 – Second Reading Speech', House of Representatives, CPD, 26 May 2014, p. 4031.
2 See 'Migration Amendment (Ending the Nation's Shame) Bill 2014: Explanatory Memorandum', Parliament of the Commonwealth of Australia, 2014.
3 Wilkie, 'Second Reading Speech', p. 4032.
4 Ibid., p. 4031.
5 This came under Standing Order 42, 'The Clerk shall remove from the Notice Paper items of private Members' business and orders of the day relating to committee and delegation reports which have not been called on for eight consecutive sitting Mondays.' See House of Representatives Standing Orders, Parliament of Australia, 2017.
6 Andrew Wilkie, 'Refugee Protection Bill 2019 – Second Reading Speech', 21 October 2019, House of Representatives, CPD, pp. 4674, 4675.
7 Andrew Wilkie, 'Ending Indefinite and Arbitrary Immigration Detention Bill 2021 – Second Reading Speech', 22 February 2021, House of Representatives, CPD, pp. 1384–85; Andrew Wilkie, 'Ending Indefinite and Arbitrary Immigration Detention Bill 2022 – Second Reading Speech', 1 August 2022, House of Representatives, CPD, pp. 258–59.

Notes

8   Kylea Tink, 'Ending Indefinite and Arbitrary Immigration Detention Bill 2022 – Second Reading Speech', 1 August 2022, House of Representatives, CPD, p. 259.
9   Ahmed, 2004b, p. 101.
10   Ahmed, 2006, pp. 1, 7.
11   Harding, 2010, p. 34.
12   Ahmed, 2004b, p. 8.
13   Rosenwein, 2006, pp. 24–27.
14   Ibid., p. 25.
15   Ahmed, 2004b, p. 11.
16   Ricatti, 2016, p. 479.
17   Interview with Andrew Giles, Melbourne, 29 January 2018. Subsequent quotations also from this interview.
18   Yaxley, 2015; Giles, 2015.
19   Andrew Giles, 'Celebrating World Refugee Week', 30 June 2022, posted on Twitter.
20   Andrew Giles, 'Immigration status resolution for the Nadesalingam family', 5 August 2022.
21   Andrew Giles, 'Questions Without Notice – Asylum Seekers', House of Representatives, CPD, 9 November 2022, p. 2688.
22   Interview with Carmen Lawrence, Perth, 3 October 2018.
23   Interview with Bruce Baird, Sydney, 24 September 2018. Subsequent quotation also from this interview.
24   Interview with Matt Thistlethwaite, Sydney, 21 March 2018.
25   Christine Milne, 'Migration and Maritime Powers Legislation Amendment (Resolving the Asylum Legacy Caseload) Bill 2014 – Second Reading Speech', Senate, CPD, 4 December 2014, p. 10275.
26   Ibid., p. 10277.
27   Bill Shorten, 'Migration Amendments (Regional Processing Arrangements) Bill 2015 – Second Reading Speech', House of Representatives, CPD, 24 June 2015, p. 7491.
28   Ibid., p. 7492.
29   Ibid., p. 7494.
30   Michael Danby, 'Petition – Asylum Seekers, Mirabel Foundation – Speech', House of Representatives, CPD, 4 March 2015, p. 2106.
31   Anthony Albanese, 'Migration Amendment (Mandatory Reporting) Bill 2015 – Second Reading Speech', House of Representatives, CPD, 23 November 2015, p. 13394.
32   Susan Lines, 'Migration Amendment (Regional Processing Arrangements) Bill 2015 – Second Reading Speech', Senate, CPD, 25 June 2016, p. 4570.
33   Adam Bandt, 'Migration Amendment (Complementary Protection and Other Measures) Bill 2015 – Second Reading Speech', House of Representatives, CPD, 2 February 2016, p. 83.

Notes

34 Ibid., pp. 84, 85.
35 Andrew Giles, 'Bills – Migration Amendment (Repairing Medical Transfers) Bill 2019 – Second Reading', House of Representatives, CDP, 23 July 2019, pp. 758–59.
36 Stirling Griff, 'Matters of Public Importance – Immigration Detention', Senate, CPD, 22 July 2019, p. 430.
37 Interview with Bruce Baird, Sydney, 24 September 2018.
38 Interview with Anna Burke, Melbourne, 9 November 2017.
39 Interview with Andrew Giles, Melbourne, 29 January 2018.
40 Interview with Mat Tinkler, Melbourne, 6 October 2017.
41 Ricatti, 2016, p. 484.
42 Bhabha, 2014, p. 11.
43 Interview with Trent Zimmerman, Sydney, 4 June 2018. Subsequent quotations also from this interview.
44 Interview with Anna Burke, Melbourne, 9 November 2017.
45 *Plaintiff M68/2015 v Minister for Immigration and Border Protection* [2016] HCA 1. Judgement handed down 3 February 2016 and available at http://eresources.hcourt.gov.au/showCase/2016/HCA/1
46 See, for instance, Nicole Hasham, 'High Court finds offshore detention lawful', *The Sydney Morning Herald*, 3 February 2016; Elizabeth Byrne and Stephanie Anderson, 'High Court throws out challenge to Nauru offshore immigration detention; Malcolm Turnbull vows people smugglers will not prevail', *ABC News*, 8 February 2016.
47 Gordon, McKenzie and Baker, 2016.
48 'About GetUp!', www.getup.org.au/about
49 Human Rights Law Centre, Twitter, 3 February 2016.
50 ChilOut Revived, Facebook, 3 February 2016.
51 AAP, 2016.
52 Daniel Andrews, Facebook, 8 February 2016.
53 Ireland, Snow and Branco, 2016.
54 Interview with Andrew Giles, Melbourne, 29 June 2018.
55 Interview with Anna Burke, Melbourne, 9 November 2017.
56 Interview with Carmen Lawrence, Perth, 3 October 2018.
57 Doherty, 2016a.
58 Meldrum-Hanna, 2016.
59 'Dear Bird Send My Message', from 'Submission No. 20 – Name withheld – 17 year old asylum seeker', Australian Human Rights Commission National Inquiry into Children in Detention, 2014, p. 4.
60 Free the Children NAURU, Facebook, 18 November 2015. All posts quoted here verbatim.

Notes

61   Ibid., 27 November 2015.
62   Bolger, 2019.
63   Little, 1999, p. 15.
64   Cole, 2012.
65   Pearson, 2018.

Chapter 7

1   Jackson, 2016.
2   For work on this already undertaken see, for instance, Tingle, 2012, pp. 1–65; Laura Tingle, 'Political amnesia: how we forgot how to govern', *Quarterly Essay* 60, 2015, pp. 1–86; James Walter and Carolyn Holbrook, 'Policy narratives in historical transition: a case study in contemporary history', *Australian Historical Studies*, 49, no. 2, 2018, pp. 221–36; Carolyn Holbrook, 'Redesigning collaborative governance for refugee settlement services', *Australian Journal of Political Science* 55, no. 1, 2020, pp. 86–97.
3   This biographical information is taken from https://johnmenadue.com/precis/
4   John Menadue, *Things You Learn Along the Way*, David Lovell Publishing, Melbourne, 1999; John Menadue, *Pearls and Irritations*, https://johnmenadue.com
5   Brennan, Costello, Manne and Menadue, 2017.
6   Interview with John Menadue, Sydney, 11 September 2017. All further quotations from Menadue are from this interview.
7   For more of Menadue's thoughts on Australian multiculturalism, see John Menadue, 'Australian multiculturalism: successes, problems and risks', in Kramer (ed.), 2003, pp. 79–91.
8   See Peter Hughes, Arja Keski-Nummi and John Menadue, 'Immigration policy and administration', pp. 181–92; Peter Hughes, Arja Keski-Nummi and John Menadue, 'Refugee policy', pp. 193–99; and Peter Hughes, Arja Keski-Nummi and John Menadue, 'Settlement policy and services', pp. 201–06, all in Menadue and Keating (eds), 2015.
9   Every, 2008, pp. 211–12.
10   Peterie, 2017, pp. 351–52.
11   RISE (Refugees, Survivors and Ex-Detainees), 'RISE Submission to the Joint Standing Committee on Migration's Inquiry into Multiculturalism in Australia', 5 May 2011, pp. 3–4.
12   M.J.R. MacKellar, Minister for Immigration and Ethnic Affairs, 'Press release: Increasing Attempts to Circumvent Immigration Controls', 13 November 1978, NLA: MS 5000, Box 499.
13   For coverage see, for instance, Michelle Grattan, 'Tony Abbott: consider burqa ban in places "dedicated to Australian values"', *The Conversation*, 6 September 2017; Natasha Bita, 'Should Australia ban the burqa?', *The Daily Telegraph*, 9 September 2017; Amy Remeikis, 'One Nation leader Pauline Hanson wears burqa in Senate question time stunt', *The Sydney Morning Herald*, 17 August 2017.

Notes

14 Gibbons, 2014.
15 Gibbons' role in developing mandatory detention and move from the department in Kingston, 1993, p. 3.
16 Bushell, 2002.
17 Interview with Wayne Gibbons, Canberra, 14 November 2017. Unless otherwise stated, all further quotations from Gibbons are from this interview.
18 'Losing self-control', *The Sydney Morning Herald*, 1 May 2003.
19 Graham, 2014; and 'Public servant a no-show at hearing', *The Sydney Morning Herald*, 3 November 2006.
20 Gibson, 2007.
21 Email communication with Wayne Gibbons, 20 January 2020.
22 Interview with senior policy adviser, Melbourne, 13 October 2017; interview with Derek Volker, Canberra, 13 September 2017.
23 Moreton-Robinson, 2015, pp. 3–8.
24 This has been widely documented. See, for example, Button, 2018. For another reflection by someone who formerly worked in the department see, for instance, Shaun Hanns, 'I left the immigration department to speak out', *The Monthly*, November 2018. On the general upheavals in the Australian federal public service around this time, see, for instance, Jack Waterford, 'Forget the "disruption" fad, why not just "better" government and public service?' *The Sydney Morning Herald*, 15 December 2017; Noel Towell, 'Department faces biggest APS executive exodus in three decades', *The Sydney Morning Herald*, 23 July 2015; Noel Towell, 'New border force hires after high-profile exits', *The Canberra Times*, 27 February 2015, p. 5.
25 McKenzie-Murray, 2015; Tranter, 2016.
26 Email correspondence with former public servant, 30 June 2017 and 17 July 2017.
27 This biographical information is taken from 'Who we are: Michael Pezzullo', Department of Home Affairs, 29 March 2019.
28 Drysdale, 2019.
29 Mares, 2017.
30 Email correspondence with Emily Slatter, Executive Assistant to the Secretary, Department of Home Affairs, 7 September 2018.
31 Michael Pezzullo, 'Senate Estimates: Legal and Constitutional Affairs Legislation Committee', CPD, 26 May 2015, p. 84.
32 Ibid., 23 February 2015, p. 89.
33 Free the Children NAURU, Facebook post, 11 November 2015.
34 Michael Pezzullo, 'Senate Estimates: Legal and Constitutional Affairs Legislation Committee', CPD, 8 February 2016, p. 21.
35 Drysdale, 2019.
36 Michael Pezzullo, 'Senate Estimates: Legal and Constitutional Affairs Legislation Committee', CPD, 21 October 2019, pp. 91–92.
37 Pip de Veau, ibid., p. 92.

Notes

38 Button, 2018.
39 Drysdale, 2019.
40 Michael Pezzullo, 'Sovereignty in an age of global interdependency: the role of borders', speech given at Australian Strategic Policy Institute, Canberra, 19 November 2014. Emphasis in the original.
41 Khatun, 2018, p. 21.
42 Michael Pezzullo, op. cit., 2014.
43 Button, 2018.

Conclusion
1 Malkki, 1996, pp. 377–404.
2 Greene, 2022.
3 Murray, 2022.
4 Hurst, 2022.
5 Jim Chalmers, Twitter, 27 May 2022.
6 Farhad Bandesh, Twitter, 27 May 2022.
7 Behrouz Boochani, Twitter, 5 August 2022. Also reported in the media, such as in Millie Roberts, 'Biloela family permanent residency is a massive win, but now the government needs to help others', *Junkee*, 8 August 2022.

Acknowledgements
1 Field, 2021.
2 Pugliese, 2002, p. 9.

Bibliography

AAP, 'Queensland ready to take asylum seeker children, says Premier', *The Courier-Mail*, 7 February 2016.

Ahmed, Sara, 'Affective economies', *Social Text* 22, no. 2, Summer 2004a.

———, *The Cultural Politics of Emotion*, Edinburgh University Press, Edinburgh, 2004b.

———, *Queer Phenomenology: Orientations, Objects, Others*, Duke University Press, Durham, 2006.

———, 'Willful parts: problem characters or the problem of character', *New Literary History* 42, no. 2, Spring 2011.

Allam, Lorena, 'Half of Australia's youth detainees are Indigenous children, research finds', *The Guardian*, 1 April 2022.

Altman, Jon, and Hinkson, Melinda, *Coercive Reconciliation: Stabilise, Normalise, Exit Aboriginal Australia*, Arena, Melbourne, 2007.

Ariès, Philippe, *Centuries of Childhood: A Social History of Family Life*, Knopf, New York, 1962.

Australian Human Rights Commission, *The Forgotten Children: National Inquiry into Children in Immigration Detention 2014*, https://humanrights.gov.au/our-work/asylum-seekers-and-refugees/publications/forgotten-children-national-inquiry-children

Bagaric, Mirko; Boyd, Kim; Dimopoulos, Penny; Tongue, Sue; and Vrachnas, John, *Migration and Refugee Law in Australia: Cases and Commentary*, Cambridge University Press, Cambridge, 2006.

Baird, Barbara, 'Child politics, feminist analyses', *Australian Feminist Studies* 23, no. 57, 2008.

Baird, Julia, *Media Tarts: How the Australian Press Frames Female Politicians*, Scribe, Melbourne, 2004.

Bibliography

Baker, Nick, 'Asylum seeker family receive $100,000 over mistreatment in Australian detention', *SBS News*, 12 December 2018.

Banivanua Mar, Tracey, *Decolonisation and the Pacific: Indigenous Globalisation and the Ends of Empire*, Cambridge University Press, Cambridge, 2016.

Banivanua Mar, Tracey and Edmonds, Penny (eds), *Making Settler Colonial Space: Perspectives on Race, Place and Identity*, Palgrave Macmillan, Basingstoke, 2010.

Basham, Jennifer and the Australian Churches Refugee Taskforce, *Protecting the Lonely Children: Recommendations to the Australian Government and the UN Committee on the Rights of the Child with Respect to Unaccompanied Children who Seek Asylum and Refuge in Australia*, 2014, https://bettercarenetwork.org/library/particular-threats-to-childrens-care-and-protection/children-and-migration/protecting-the-lonely-children-recommendations-to-the-australian-government-and-the-un-committee-on

Beech, Alexandra, 'Keeping the faith: Tony Burke on equality, childhood unionism and mid-week jam sessions', *ABC News*, 5 May 2017.

Bennoun, Robert and Kelly, Paula, *Indo-Chinese Youth: An Assessment of the Situation of Unaccompanied and Isolated Indo-Chinese Refugee Minors*, Indo-China Refugee Association of Victoria, Melbourne, 1981.

Bhabha, Jacqueline, 'The child – what sort of human?', *PMLA* 121, no. 5, 2006.

——, *Child Migration & Human Rights in a Global Age*, Princeton University Press, Princeton, 2014.

Bhabha, Jacqueline and Crock, Mary, *Seeking Asylum Alone, A Comparative Study: A Comparative Study of Laws, Policy and Practice in Australia, the UK and the US*, Themis Press, Leichhardt, 2007.

Biber, Katherine; Luker, Trish; and Vaughan, Priya Devii (eds), *Law's Documents: Authority, Materiality, Aesthetics*, Routledge, London, 2022.

Birch, Tony, 'Aboriginal communities and nations to decide who is and who is not a member of their sovereign country', *IndigenousX*, 12 August 2021.

Bolger, Rosemary, 'Refugee children hope Parliament House performance inspires better understanding', *SBS News*, 20 February 2019.

Bolt, Andrew, 'Time to ditch lessons in hate', *Sunday Herald Sun*, 7 December 2003.

Boochani, Behrouz, *No Friend but the Mountains: Writing from Manus Prison*, Picador, Sydney, 2018.

Bibliography

———, '"The boats are coming" is one of the greatest lies told to the Australian people', *The Guardian*, 2 July 2019.

Boyce, James, 'The Devil and Scott Morrison', *The Monthly*, 1 February 2019.

Brennan, Frank; Costello, Tim; Manne, Robert; and Menadue, John, 'We can stop the boats and also act decently, fairly and transparently', *The Guardian*, 14 February 2017.

Burke, Tony, 'PM can't seek refuge in lies and ignorance', *The Daily Telegraph*, 25 April 2007.

———, 'Speech to the Australian Labor Party's National Conference – Saturday, 25 July 2015', www.tonyburke.com.au/speechestranscripts/2015/7/27/speech-to-the-australian-labor-partys-national-conference-saturday-25-july-2015.

Bushell, Sue, 'Employment deployment', *CIO from IDG*, 25 November 2002.

Butler, Josh, 'The nerve centres: inside the Coalition and Labor election campaign headquarters', *The Guardian*, 11 April 2022.

Button, James, 'Dutton's dark victory', *The Monthly*, February 2018.

Cole, Teju, 'The White-Savior Industrial Complex', *The Atlantic*, 21 March 2012.

Coper, Michael, 'The reach of the Commonwealth's immigration power: judicial exegesis unbridled', *The Australian Law Journal* 50, no. 7, 1976.

Crock, Mary, 'Lonely refuge: judicial responses to separated children seeking refugee protection in Australia', *Law in Context* 22, no. 2, 2005.

———, 'Of relative rights and putative children: rethinking the critical framework for the protection of refugee children and youth', *Australian International Law Journal* 18, no. 1, January 2011.

Crock, Mary and Berg, Laurie, *Immigration, Refugees and Forced Migration: Law, Policy and Practice in Australia*, Federation Press, Annandale, 2011.

Damousi, Joy, 'The campaign for Japanese-Australian children to enter Australia, 1957–1968: a history of post-war humanitarianism', *Australian Journal of Politics and History* 64, no. 2, 2018.

———, 'Child sponsorship, development and aid: PLAN and UNICEF in Australia, 1945–1975', *History Australia* 17, no. 4, 2020.

Davidson, Helen, 'Hospital doctors protest to demand release of children from detention', *The Guardian*, 11 October 2015.

Bibliography

Dehm, Sara and Vogl, Anthea, 'Refugee rejection is more complex than a soundbite: why Tamil family should stay', *The Age*, 5 September 2019.

Doherty, Ben, 'Manus Island: refugee assaulted by guard and told to find his own medicine', *The Guardian*, 14 September 2015.

———, 'Baby Asha discharged from hospital into community detention', *The Guardian*, 22 February 2016a.

———, 'Asylum seeker children still in detention despite claims all have been released', *The Guardian*, 2 April 2016b.

———, '"Hardly anyone is getting off": despite Labor's promises, refugees needing urgent medical care remain on Nauru', *The Guardian*, 18 December 2022.

———, 'Small town rallies after asylum seeker family carried off in dawn raid', *The Guardian*, 12 March 2018.

Donovan, Samantha, 'Victoria Police settles racial profiling case', *ABC PM*, 18 February 2013.

Drysdale, Kirsten, 'How you become Australia's most powerful bureaucrat', *Crikey*, 11 July 2019.

Edelman, Lee, *No Future: Queer Theory and the Death Drive*, Duke University Press, Durham, 2004.

Elliott, Professor Elizabeth and Gunasekera, Dr Hasantha, *The Health and Well-being of Children in Immigration Detention: Report to the Australian Human Rights Commission Monitoring Visit to Wickham Point Detention Centre, Darwin, NT*, 16–18 October 2015.

Elton-Pym, James, 'Scott Morrison prayed and cried "on his knees" for asylum seekers', *SBS News*, 9 November 2018.

Enloe, Cynthia, 'Womenandchildren: making feminist sense of the Persian Gulf Crisis', *Village Voice*, 25 September 1990.

Evans, Chris, 'New directions in detention: restoring integrity to Australia's immigration system', speech given at Australian National University, 29 July 2008, http://pandora.nla.gov.au/pan/67564/20100913-1000/www.minister.immi.gov.au/media/speeches/2008/ce080729.html.

Evenhuis, Mark, 'Child-proofing asylum: separated children and refugee decision making in Australia', *International Journal of Refugee Law*, 25 October 2013.

Every, Danielle, 'A reasonable, practical and moderate humanitarianism: the co-option of humanitarianism in the Australian asylum seeker debates', *Journal of Refugee Studies* 21, no. 2, 2008.

Bibliography

Farnsworth, Sarah, 'Young South Sudanese "constantly stopped" by police, as community grapples with Apex stigma', *ABC News*, 4 December 2016.

Farrell, Paul, 'Ricky Muir vote reinstates TPVs and hands Coalition hollow asylum victory', *The Guardian*, 5 December 2014.

———, 'Some babies born to asylum seekers in Australia may be allowed to stay', *The Guardian*, 18 December 2014.

Farrell, Paul; Evershed, Nick; and Davidson, Helen, 'The Nauru files: cache of 2,000 leaked reports reveal scale of abuse of children in Australian offshore detention', *The Guardian*, 10 August 2016.

Faulkner, Joanne, 'Ghosts of eugenics past: "childhood" as a target for whitening race in the United States and Canada', *Critical Race and Whiteness Studies Journal – First Glimpse*, 2019.

Fickling, David, 'Child asylum seeker sues Australian government for mental trauma in Woomera', *The Guardian*, 28 October 2003.

Field, Jared, 'On "Our African roots": A First Nations response', *IndigenousX*, 19 October 2021.

Galloway, Anthony, 'Border protection in spotlight after Albanese said he favours boat turnbacks over offshore detention', *The Sydney Morning Herald*, 14 April 2022.

Gardner, Katy, 'Transnational migration and the study of children: an introduction', *Journal of Ethnic and Migration Studies* 38, no. 6, 2012.

Giannacopoulos, Maria, 'Without love there can be law but no justice', *Globalizations* 17, no. 7, 2020.

Gibbons, Wayne, 'The boats were not sabotaged', *Pearls and Irritations*, 21 March 2014.

Gibson, Jano, 'FOI documents show the NT is breaching its own independent monitoring policy at Don Dale Youth Detention Centre', *ABC News*, 24 August 2022.

Gibson, Joel, 'One of the brains behind the NT intervention retires', *The Sydney Morning Herald*, 28 November 2007.

Giles, Andrew, 'Speech to ALP National Conference on Boat Turnbacks', 25 July 2015, www.andrewgiles.com.au/media-centre/opinion-pieces-speeches-transcripts/speech-to-alp-national-conference-on-boat-turnbacks/

Gillespie, Eden, 'Nadesalingam family feel "peace" after being granted permanent residency in Australia', *The Guardian*, 5 August 2022.

Bibliography

Gleeson, Madeline, *Offshore: Behind the Wire on Manus and Nauru*, NewSouth, Randwick, 2016.

Goodnow, Katherine, with Lohman, Jack and Marfleet, Philip, *Museums, the Media and Refugees: Stories of Crisis, Control and Compassion*, Berghahn Books, New York, 2008.

Gordon, Faith and Peleg, Noam, '"The Australian government is not listening": how our country is failing to protect its children', *The Conversation*, 8 October 2019.

Gordon, Michael, 'People sent offshore will include children', *The Age*, 22 August 2013.

——, 'Ricky Muir's anguish on asylum vote', *The Sydney Morning Herald*, 5 December 2014.

Gordon, Michael; McKenzie, Nick and Baker, Richard, 'The faces of the babies Australia wants to send back to "hell" on Nauru', *The Sydney Morning Herald*, 2 February 2016.

Gorrie, Nayuka and Church, Witt, 'We need to abolish prisons to disrupt a society built on inequality', *The Guardian*, 26 November 2018.

Graham, Chris, 'ABC *Lateline*'s "fake youth worker" wins plum Abbott govt job', *New Matilda*, 2 July 2014.

Greene, Andrew, 'Scott Morrison instructed Border Force to reveal election day asylum boat arrival', *ABC News*, 27 May 2022.

Gregg, Melissa and Seigworth, Gregory J. (eds), *The Affect Theory Reader*, Duke University Press, Durham, 2010.

Gribbin, Caitlyn, 'Somali community in Australia seeks access to boy in detention', *PM*, ABC Radio, 2 September 2013.

Haebich, Anna, *Spinning the Dream: Assimilation in Australia 1950–1970*, Fremantle Press, North Fremantle, 2008.

Hage, Ghassan, *White Nation: Fantasies of White Supremacy in a Multicultural Society*, Pluto Press, Annandale, 1998.

Harding, Jenny, 'Talk about care: emotions, culture and oral history', *Oral History* 38, no. 2, Autumn 2010.

Hasham, Nicole, 'Faith irrelevant to immigration policy: Shorten: Religion priority idea slammed', *The Canberra Times* 9 September 2015.

Higgins, Claire, *Asylum by Boat: Origins of Australia's Refugee Policy*, UNSW Press, Sydney, 2017.

Bibliography

Higonnet, Margaret R., 'Child witnesses: the cases of World War I and Darfur', *PMLA* 121, no. 5, 2006.

Holt, Rebekah, 'Peter Dutton is repeating false claims there are no children in detention', *Crikey*, 18 June 2019.

Homan, Stewart, 'PM has shown leadership', Letter to the Editor, *The Canberra Times*, 10 September 2001.

Human Rights and Equal Opportunity Commission, *Bringing them Home – Report of the National Inquiry into the Separation of Aboriginal and Torres Strait Islander Children from Their Families*, April 1997.

——, *Report of an Inquiry into a Complaint by Mr Mohammed Badraie on Behalf of His Son Shayan Regarding Acts or Practices of the Commonwealth of Australia (The Department of Immigration, Multicultural and Indigenous Affairs): HREOC Report No. 25*, 2002.

Human Rights Law Centre, 'Permanent residency extended to temporary protection visa holders, but thousands still left in limbo after a decade', 13 February 2023.

Hurst, Daniel, 'Australia funds GPS trackers on Sri Lankan fishing boats, partially to deter people smugglers', *The Guardian*, 22 June 2022.

Hyndman, Jennifer, *Managing Displacement: Refugees and the Politics of Humanitarianism*, University of Minnesota Press, Minneapolis, 2000.

Ireland, Judith; Snow, Deborah; and Branco, Jorge, 'Asylum seeker row: Baby Asha can stay in Australia, for now', *The Sydney Morning Herald*, 22 February 2016.

Jacobs, Pat, *Mister Neville: A Biography*, Fremantle Arts Centre Press, Fremantle, 1990.

Jackson, Allison, 'How one wrong word made Australia's migration agency look like Holocaust deniers', *The World*, 9 March 2016.

Jessee, Erin, 'The limits of oral history: ethics and methodology amid highly politicizes research settings', *The Oral History Review* 38, no. 2, Summer/Fall 2011.

Jupp, James, *From White Australia to Woomera: The Story of Australian Immigration*, second edition, Cambridge University Press, Port Melbourne, 2007.

Karp, Paul, 'Biloela Tamil family wins challenge to decision barring them from reapplying for bridging visas', *The Guardian*, 24 January 2022.

——, 'Defence force "surge" to detect asylum boats in Australia's northern waters follows visa change', *The Guardian*, 16 February 2023.

Bibliography

Keneally, Kristine, 'Australia fails the same lesson every time. The Nauru files show how secrecy hides abuse', *The Guardian*, 10 August 2016.

Kevin, Catherine and Agutter, Karen, 'The "unwanteds" and "non-compliants": "unsupported mothers" as "failures" and agents in Australia's migrant holding centres', *The History of the Family* 22, no. 4, 2017.

Khatun, Samia, *Australianama: The South Asian Odyssey in Australia*, Hurst & Company, London, 2018.

Kingston, Margo, 'Boat-people hardliner to leave Immigration', *The Canberra Times*, 9 June 1993.

Klein, Naomi, *The Shock Doctrine*, Penguin, Camberwell, 2007.

Krakouer, Jacynta, 'The stolen generations never ended – they just morphed into child protection', *The Guardian*, 17 October 2019.

Kramer, Leonie (ed.), *The Multicultural Experiment: Immigrants, Refugees and National Identity*, Macleay Press, Sydney, 2003.

Laughland, Oliver, 'Manus Island document mentions 14 alleged unaccompanied minors', *The Guardian*, 4 March 2014.

Levett, Connie, 'Traumatised in detention, Shayan now thrives on his life in Australia', *The Sydney Morning Herald*, 27 September 2008.

Liddell, Max, 'If having child-centred policy is the answer, what's the question?', *Children Australia* 35, no. 2, 2010.

Little, Graham, *The Public Emotions: From Mourning to Hope*, ABC Books, Sydney, 1999.

Lloyd, Elizabeth, 'The children of Indo-China: a study including policy recommendations of children leaving Indo-China without their parents', Department of Immigration and Ethnic Affairs, Canberra, February 1983.

Logan, William and Reeves, Keir, *Places of Pain and Shame: Dealing with 'Difficult Heritage'*, Taylor and Francis, Florence, 2008.

Malkki, Liisa H., 'Speechless emissaries: refugees, humanitarianism, and dehistoricization', *Cultural Anthropology* 11, no. 3, August 1996.

Mamdani, Mahmood, *Define and Rule: Native as Political Identity*, Harvard University Press, Cambridge, 2012.

Mares, Peter, 'Mike Pezzullo interview: the stellar political career of a thwarted historian', *The Sydney Morning Herald*, 29 July 2017.

McKenzie-Murray, Martin, 'Inside Border Force's power', *The Saturday Paper*, 5 September 2015.

Bibliography

McKinnon, Crystal, 'Expressing Indigenous sovereignty: the production of embodied texts in social protest and the arts', PhD thesis, La Trobe University, 2018.

——, 'Enduring Indigeneity and solidarity in response to Australia's carceral colonialism', *biography* 43, no. 4, 2020.

McQuire, Amy, 'Black and white witness', *Meanjin*, Winter 2019.

McSherry, Bernadette and Dastyari, Azadeh, 'Providing mental health services and psychiatric care to immigration detainees: what tort law requires', *Psychiatry, Psychology & Law* 14, no. 2, November 2007.

Medhora, Shalailah, 'Ricky Muir holds the key as Senate debates Asylum Seeker Bill', *The Guardian*, 4 December 2014.

Meiners, Erica R., *For the Children? Protecting Innocence in a Carceral State*, University of Minnesota Press, Minneapolis, 2016.

Meldrum-Hanna, Caro, 'Australia's Shame', *Four Corners*, 25 July 2016.

Menadue, John and Keating, Michael (eds), *Fairness, Opportunity and Security: Filling the Policy Vacuum*, ATF Press, Hindmarsh, 2015.

Metherell, Mark, '"I should not play God": Evans', *The Sydney Morning Herald*, 20 February 2008.

Millar, Erica, '"Too many": anxious white nationalism and the biopolitics of abortion', *Australian Feminist Studies* 30, no. 83, 2015.

Moreno-Lax, Violeta, 'Policy brief 4: the interdiction of asylum seekers at sea: law and (mal)practice in Europe and Australia', Kaldor Centre for International Refugee Law, May 2017.

Moreton-Robinson, Aileen, 'The possessive logic of patriarchal white sovereignty: The High Court and the Yorta Yorta decision', *Borderlands e-journal* 3, no. 2, 2004.

——, *The White Possessive: Property, Power, and Indigenous Sovereignty*, University of Minnesota Press, Minneapolis, 2015.

Morris, Sophie, 'Free kids, demands watchdog', *The Australian*, 14 May 2004.

Mortimer, Edward (ed.), *People, Nation and State: The Meaning of Ethnicity and Nationalism*, I.B. Tauris, London, 1999.

Morton, Rick, 'Burke has 38 minors released from detention', *The Australian*, 10 September 2013.

Murray, Duncan, 'First boat turned back under Albanese government', *News.com.au*, 24 May 2022.

Bibliography

Musgrove, Nell and Swain, Shurlee, 'The "best interests of the child": historical perspectives', *Children Australia* 35, no. 2, 2010.

Neumann, Klaus, *Across the Seas: Australia's Response to Refugees, A History*, Black Inc., Collingwood, 2015a.

———, 'The admission of European refugees from East and South Asia in 1947: antecedents of Australia's International Refugee Organization Mass Resettlement Scheme', *History Australia* 12, no. 2, 2015b.

Neumann, Klaus and Tavan, Gwenda (eds), *Does History Matter? Making and Debating Citizenship, Immigration and Refugee Policy in Australia and New Zealand*, ANU Press, Canberra, 2009.

O'Malley, Nick, 'Legendary Australian political hitman Lynton Crosby blamed for the Tory campaign', *The Sydney Morning Herald*, 10 June 2017.

Office of the United Nations High Commissioner for Refugees, *Refugee Children: Guidelines on Protection and Care*, United Nations High Commissioner for Refugees, Geneva, Switzerland, 1994.

Osborne, Zoe, 'A letter to … Australia's immigration minister from a refugee', *Al Jazeera*, 13 February 2022.

Pascoe, Michael, 'After proof Australia is racist? Just look at Morrison's latest stunt', *The New Daily*, 4 May 2021.

Pearson, Luke, 'Tony Abbott and the white man's burden', *IndigenousX*, 6 December 2018.

Perera, Suvendrini, 'The good neighbour: conspicuous compassion and the politics of proximity', *Borderlands e-journal* 3, no. 3, 2004.

———, *Australia and the Insular Imagination: Beaches, Borders, Boats, and Bodies*, Palgrave Macmillan, New York, 2009.

Perera, Suvendrini and Pugliese, Joseph, 'White law of the biopolitical', *Journal of the European Associate of Studies on Australia* 3, no. 1, 2012.

Perptich, Nicolas, 'Suicide-bid asylum boy: access denied', *The Australian*, 2 September 2013.

Persian, Jayne, '"Chifley liked them blond": DP immigrants for Australia', *History Australia* 12, no. 2, 2015.

Peterie, Michelle, 'Docility and desert: government discourses of compassion in Australia's asylum seeker debate', *Journal of Sociology* 53, no. 2, 2017.

Phillips, Janet and Spinks, Harriet, 'Immigration detention in Australia', Parliamentary Library, Parliament of Australia, 20 March 2013, www.aph.gov.au/about_parliament/parliamentary_departments/parliamentary_library/pubs/bn/2012-2013/detention#_Toc351535453.

Plant, Rod, *A New Life: An Historical Evaluation of Burnside's Khmer Unaccompanied Minors Resettlement Programme*, Burnside, Sydney, 1988.

Pobjoy, Jason M., *The Child in International Refugee Law*, Cambridge University Press, Cambridge, 2017.

Prince, Peter and Lester, Eve, 'The God of the "God powers": the gap between history and law', *Griffith Review* 76, April 2022.

Probyn, Fiona, 'The white father: denial, paternalism and community', *Cultural Studies Review* 9, no. 1, May 2003.

Pugliese, Joseph, 'Geopolitics of Aboriginal sovereignty: colonial law as a species of excess of its own authority, Aboriginal Passport Ceremonies and asylum seekers', *Law Text Culture* 19, 2015.

———, 'Migrant heritage in an Indigenous context: for a decolonising migrant historiography', *Journal of Intercultural Studies* 23, no. 1, 2002.

———, 'As above so below: drone visualities of the aftermath, testimonies of the more-than-human and the politico-aesthetics of massacre sites', *Social Identities: Journal for the Study of Race, Nation and Culture* 25, no. 4, 2019.

Reilly, Alex, 'Australian politics explainer: the MV *Tampa* and the transformation of asylum-seeker policy', *The Conversation*, 27 April 2017.

Ricatti, Francesco, 'A country once great? Asylum seekers, historical imagination, and the moral privilege of whiteness', *Journal of Australian Studies* 40, no. 4, 2016.

Robertson, Joshua, 'Baby Ferouz, born to asylum seekers in Brisbane, denied protection visa', *The Guardian*, 15 October 2014.

Rosenwein, Barbara, *Emotional Communities in the Early Middle Ages*, Cornell University Press, Ithaca, 2006.

Sandberg, Kirsten, 'The Convention on the Rights of the Child and the vulnerability of children', *Nordic Journal of International Law* 84, 2015.

Schuller, Kyla, *The Biopolitics of Feeling: Race, Sex, and Science in the Nineteenth Century*, Duke University Press, Durham, 2018.

Scott, Dorothy and Swain, Shurlee, *Confronting Cruelty: Historical Perspectives on Child Abuse*, Melbourne University Press, Melbourne, 2002.

Shaw, Ian W., *Operation Babylift*, Hachette Australia, Sydney, 2019.

Bibliography

Sheldon, Rebekah, *The Child to Come: Life after the Human Catastrophe*, University of Minnesota Press, Minneapolis, 2016.

Silverstein, Ben, '"Throwing mud" on questions of sovereignty: race and northern arguments over white, Chinese, and Aboriginal labour, 1905–12', *Australian Historical Studies* 53, no. 4, 2022.

Smith, Angela, 'Air deportation and the settler colony', *antiAtlas Journal* 5, 2022.

Snoek, Kartia, 'Marginalised subjects, meaningless naturalizations: the tiers of Australian citizenship', PhD thesis, University of Melbourne, 2019.

Stoler, Ann Laura, *Along the Archival Grain: Epistemic Anxieties and Colonial Commonsense*, Princeton, Princeton University Press, 2009.

Swain, Shurlee, 'The value of the vignette in the writing of welfare history', *Australian Historical Studies* 39, no. 2, 2008.

Talbot, Anna and Newhouse, George, 'Strategic litigation, offshore detention and the Medevac Bill', *Court of Conscience*, no. 13, 2019.

Taylor, Josh, 'What comes next for the Tamil family from Biloela?', *The Guardian*, 16 June 2021.

Taylor, Julie, 'Guardianship of child asylum-seekers', *Federal Law Review* 34, 2006.

Taylor, Lin, 'From Saigon in a shoebox: Australian "Operation Babylift" orphans reflect 40 years on', *SBS News*, 2 April 2015.

Ticktin, Miriam, 'A world without innocence', *American Ethnologist* 44, no. 4, 2017.

———, 'Thinking beyond humanitarian borders', *Social Research: An International Quarterly* 83, no. 2, Summer 2016.

Tingle, Laura, 'Great expectations: government, entitlement and an angry nation', *Quarterly Essay* 46, 2012.

Tobin, John, 'Understanding children's rights: a vision beyond vulnerability', *Nordic Journal of International Law* 84, no. 2, 1 June 2015.

Topsfield, Jewel, 'Immigration spent $1.5 million fighting boy's stress suit', *The Age*, 1 June 2006.

Tranter, Kellie, 'Dutton, Payne and Pezzullo: the truth about Australia's militarised border', *Independent Australia*, 14 June 2016.

Trask, Steven, '"Life has to go on": Captain Arne Rinnan on the day the *Tampa* changed Australia', *SBS News*, 26 August 2021.

Trioli, Virginia, 'Reith rewrites history to hide the shame of children overboard lie', *The Age*, 1 September 2012.

Bibliography

Uhlmann, Chris, 'Immigration minister aims for greater refugee intake', *7.30*, Australian Broadcasting Corporation, Sydney, 22 July 2013.

United Nations High Commissioner for Refugees, *Note on Refugee Children*, UNHCR, Geneva, 1987.

Vasefi, Saba, 'Female refugee evacuated from Nauru to Australia could be deported despite ill-health', *The Guardian*, 6 June 2021.

———, 'Refugee children want a future in Australia. So why are they excluded from universities?', *The Guardian*, 23 April 2022.

Wanna, John (ed.), *A Passion for Policy*, Essays in Public Sector Reform, ANU Press, Canberra, 2007.

Watego, Chelsea, 'The white man's burden: Bill Leak and telling "the truth" about Aboriginal lives', *The Conversation*, 5 August 2016.

———, 'A white woman took my baby', *IndigenousX*, 21 March 2018.

———, *Another Day in the Colony*, University of Queensland Press, St Lucia, 2021.

White, Benjamin Thomas, 'Talk of an "unprecedented" number of refugees is wrong – and dangerous', *The New Humanitarian*, 3 October 2019.

Whyte, Sarah, 'Government pays compensation to Save the Children workers removed from Nauru', *ABC News*, 23 February 2018.

Wolfe, Patrick, 'Settler colonialism and the elimination of the native', *Journal of Genocide Research* 8, no. 4, 2006.

Yaxley, Louise, 'ALP national conference: Labor delegates vote down ban on asylum seeker boat turn-backs', *ABC News*, 25 July 2015.

Zulfacar, Diane M., *Surviving Without Parents: Indo-Chinese Refugee Minors in NSW*, UNSW School of Social Work, Kensington, 1984.

———, 'Policies, programs and outcomes for unaccompanied Vietnamese refugee minors in Australia', PhD thesis, University of New South Wales, 1988.

———, 'A decade of (slow) progress: the evolution of policies and provisions for unaccompanied refugee minors in Australia', *Asia Pacific Journal of Social Work* 2, no. 2, 1992.

Zwi, Karen and Mares, Sarah, 'Stories from unaccompanied children in immigration detention: a composite account', *Journal of Paediatrics and Child Health* 51, no. 7, July 2015.

CPSIA information can be obtained
at www.ICGtesting.com
Printed in the USA
JSHW022303010523
41119JS00003B/164